CANDIDATE-CENTERED CAMPAIGNS

Candidate-Centered Campaigns
Political Messages, Winning Personalities, and Personal Appeals

Brian Arbour

CANDIDATE-CENTERED CAMPAIGNS
Copyright © Brian Arbour, 2014.

All rights reserved.

First published in 2014 by PALGRAVE MACMILLAN® in the United States—a division of St. Martin's Press LLC, 175 Fifth Avenue, New York, NY 10010.

Where this book is distributed in the UK, Europe and the rest of the world, this is by Palgrave Macmillan, a division of Macmillan Publishers Limited, registered in England, company number 785998, of Houndmills, Basingstoke, Hampshire RG21 6XS.

Palgrave Macmillan is the global academic imprint of the above companies and has companies and representatives throughout the world.

Palgrave® and Macmillan® are registered trademarks in the United States, the United Kingdom, Europe and other countries.

ISBN: 978-1-137-39860-4

Library of Congress Cataloging-in-Publication Data

Arbour, Brian.
   Candidate-centered campaigns : political messages, winning personalities, and personal appeals / by Brian Arbour.
       pages cm
   Includes bibliographical references and index.
   ISBN 978-1-137-39860-4 (hardback)
   1. Political campaigns—United States—Psychological aspects. 2. Political candidates—Psychology—United States. 3. Personality and politics—United States. 4. Political psychology—United States. 5. Campaign management—United States. I. Title.
   JK2281.A73 2014
   324.70973—dc23
                                                                2014002925

A catalogue record of the book is available from the British Library.

Design by Amnet.

First edition: July 2014

10 9 8 7 6 5 4 3 2 1

To Erin and Joshua,

the best things that happened to me while writing this book

Contents

List of Figures	ix
List of Tables	xi
Preface	xiii
1 The Role of the Candidate in Campaign Messages	1
2 Why Campaigns Use Candidate-Centered Messages	17
3 Candidates and Campaign Planning	37
4 The Use of Candidate-Centered Appeals	61
5 The Types of Candidate-Centered Appeals	93
6 Candidate-Centered Appeals and Personal Issues	121
7 The Effect of Candidate-Centered Appeals	141
8 Candidate-Centered Appeals and Citizens	159
Appendix	175
Notes	179
Bibliography	187
Index	199

List of Figures

4.1 Use of Candidate-Centered Appeals, 2004 House and Senate Campaigns — 70

4.2 Percentage of Candidate-Centered Phrases per Advertisement, 2004 House and Senate Campaigns — 73

4.3 Use of Candidate-Centered Appeals by Ad Target, 2004 House and Senate Campaigns — 75

4.4 Mean Candidate-Centered Phrases in Advertisements That Discuss the Sponsoring Candidate and/or the Opposing Candidate — 76

4.5 Candidate-Centered Appeals by Date, 2004 House and Senate Campaigns — 77

4.6 Candidate-Centered Appeals by Phrase Placement, 2004 House and Senate Campaigns — 79

4.7 Predicted Probabilities of Use of Candidate-Centered Appeals about All Candidates, 2004 House & Senate Campaigns — 88

4.8 Predicted Probabilities of Use of Candidate-Centered Appeals about Sponsoring Candidate, 2004 House & Senate Campaigns — 89

4.9 Predicted Probabilities of Use of Candidate-Centered Appeals about Opposing Candidate, 2004 House & Senate Campaigns — 90

5.1 The Use of Each Type of Candidate-Centered Appeal — 102

5.2 Type of Candidate-Centered Appeals by Date — 110

5.3	Candidate-Centered Appeals by Phrase Placement	112
5.4	Predicted Probabilities of Use of Different Types of Candidate-Centered Appeals, 2004 House & Senate Campaigns	117
7.1	Mock Direct Mail Piece, Version "Both Democrat"	145
7.2	Difference in Mean Thermometer Ratings from Control Group. No Party for Candidate	148
7.3	Difference of Mean Sincerity Ratings from Control Group. No Party for Candidate	149
7.4	Difference in Effectiveness Ratings from Control Group. No Party for Candidate	149
7.5	Difference in Ratings for Party Labels from No Party Group. No Party for Candidate	151
7.6	Difference in Thermometer Ratings from Control Group. All Parties for Candidate	152
7.7	Difference in Sincerity Ratings from Control Group. All Parties for Candidate	153
7.8	Difference in Sincerity Ratings from Control Group. All Parties for Candidate	154

List of Tables

1.1	Independent Variables Used in Recent Political Science Studies of Campaign Messages	13
3.1	Responses to Question: What process do you go through with each candidate/race to decide the theme of the campaign and the message of individual communications?	50
4.1	Use of Candidate-Centered Appeals in Political Advertisements, 2004 House and Senate Elections	82
5.1	Phrase by Type of Candidate-Centered Appeals	103
5.2	Combinations of Candidate-Centered Appeals, 2004 House & Senate Campaigns	106
5.3	Mean Phrases Used In Combination with Other Candidate-Centered Appeals, 2004 House & Senate Campaigns	108
5.4	Use of Candidate-Centered Appeals in Political Advertisements, 2004 House and Senate elections	114
6.1	Campaign Issue Agendas; US House & Senate Campaigns, 2000–2004	126
6.2	Ratio of Use of an Issue When Combined With a Personal Issue to All Uses of That Issue	131
A4.1	Use of Candidate-Centered Appeals, 2004 U.S. House and Senate Candidates	175
A5.1	Types of Candidate-Centered Appeals, 2004 U.S. House and Senate Candidates	176
A6.1	Use of Personal Appeals, 2004 U.S. House and Senate Candidates	178

Preface

Where did the idea to examine how candidate themselves influence campaign message strategy originate? Certainly the most direct genesis was my study in graduate school of campaigns and how political scientists thought about them. These works demonstrated great and vital insights into how campaigns think and behave. Yet from my own experience as a campaign staffer and political consultant, I felt these models were missing something. This project began as a graduate school project designed to explore how and why campaigns tried to deal with the median voter (whether aligning their candidate with the median voter's ideological position or to persuade the voter of their candidate's issue positions) and expanded from there. This expansion went far and wide but focused on the use of personal characteristics in campaign messages, a topic that is woefully underexamined in political science literature.

But there are other geneses of this project as well. I worked as a campaign staffer before I went into academia, and I have been constantly frustrated by one campaign I worked on in the 1996 cycle. I worked on the campaign of Rick Zbur, a Democratic challenger in a Democratic-leaning district represented by a popular, and well-liked moderate Republican incumbent. Rick was notable as a candidate for two reasons: (1) he was an environmental lawyer at a white-shoe law firm in Los Angeles with both smarts and passion about that issue, which would have been a real asset in Congress; (2) he was openly gay, and just by being out, Rick was a bulwark against the retrograde gay rights policies of the mid-1990s ("Don't ask, don't tell," DOMA, etc.). I am not sure the voters of Long Beach, California, knew either of these facts about Rick because, instead of focusing on the interesting elements of Rick's personality and background, we focused on Newt Gingrich. Gingrich and congressional Republicans wanted to cut Medicare, so we focused heavily on that issue, as well as Social Security. We lost. We did so for a number of reasons (the lack of a Democratic tide in 1996, our opponent's ability to maintain his personal popularity in the district), but the one that I focused on is the one that we controlled as a campaign. We did a poor job of convincing voters who Rick Zbur was and what he cared about. This loss has haunted me since, not because we came close (Zbur lost by ten points), but because I always thought our strategy was off. In many ways, this book is my attempt to figure out how we could have run that campaign better.

There is an even more distant genesis of this project. As a young boy, I was fascinated by electoral politics (big surprise, I know). When I was something like ten years old, I remember my aunt once discussing a flyer she had received from a candidate for school board extolling his service in Vietnam. "Why do you think he included that?" she asked me. Now I have a couple hundred pages of an answer.

That answer is based on the extensive research that went into this book. In it, I define the term *candidate-centered appeals*: these are pieces of campaign rhetoric that discuss the biography, background, family, political record, or private-sector accomplishments of a candidate for office. I find that this type of rhetoric is ubiquitous in political messaging. Campaigns want to tell voters "who their candidate is," and I argue that campaigns do this in an effort to develop the credibility and likeability of their candidate. Voters are skeptical of candidates because they are politicians. By discussing personal information, campaigns can erode that skepticism and get voters to listen to their candidate's issue priorities and policy proposals.

This book explores the use of candidate-centered appeals in depth and over five different empirical chapters. This exploration begins with a thorough examination of how political campaigns decide what messages to transmit to voters. I investigate this first by talking to political consultants who develop and craft these messages to assess how they work up a campaign message plan. This is a relatively unique step; political scientists have tended to focus first on the results of these message plans—television advertisements, candidate speeches, media quotes, and websites. By focusing on the planning process, I glean insights into what consultants think moves voters—stories about a candidate's background, biography, or political record, which demonstrate his or her authenticity to voters. I then go on to assess how and when campaigns use candidate-centered appeals. These patterns are consistent with the argument made by the political consultants I interviewed—candidate-centered appeals are employed to enhance a candidate's credibility and likeability (or to erode those characteristics when attacking an opponent).

A project such as this book requires the help, assistance, and companionship of a great many people. This book project began in graduate school at the University of Texas at Austin, and I have continued to work on the project as a professor at John Jay College, City University of New York. My work has been generously funded by several sources. In graduate school at UT, I received financial support from several fellowships provided by the Department of Government, including the McDonald Fellowship, the Patterson Travel Grant, and funding from the Public Policy Institute. Also, the experiment in chapter 7 was part of UT's module of the Cooperative Congressional Election Study (CCES). Funding for that survey was provided by the Annette Strauss Institute for Civic Participation, the College of Liberal Arts, and the Department of Government. At John Jay, I received support from the Professional Staff Congress of CUNY grant, administered by the Research Foundation of CUNY. I also participated in the Faculty Fellows Publications Program (FPPP) at CUNY. This program not only provided me with a course release so that I could pursue my research, but also a forum to present my work to other academics and receive feedback on my efforts. This book is stronger because of these efforts. I was ably assisted by three research assistants. All three—Yvette Armani at UT, and Cyann Zoller and Elien Migallen at John Jay—made invaluable contributions to the coding used in this book. Each has my great thanks for their help.

At the University of Texas, I was aided by an outstanding community of caring faculty. Two deserve special recognition for their efforts on my dissertation and this book, which grew out of that work. Daron Shaw, my dissertation chair, is strongly committed to graduate education. On a personal level, he has provided wise counsel and patient guidance in both my research agenda and in the job search process. I am grateful for Daron's role in helping me join the Decision Team at Fox News Channel, where we both work each election night. John Sides's research on similar subjects provided me with both inspiration and challenge—living up to his standard. In addition, the insights of my other dissertation committee members—Brian Roberts, Sharon Jarvis, and Rod Hart—have greatly strengthened my work.

My undergraduate advisor at Pomona College, David Menefee-Libey, deserves great thanks for inspiring me to want to be a political scientist and an academic. Most importantly, when I told David I wanted to go to grad school, his reaction ("You'll be great.") provided great confidence that I had chosen the right path for me.

My colleagues in the Political Science Department at John Jay College are unfailing in their commitment to developing young faculty. Harold Sullivan and Jim Cauthen have been my department chairs; they are both outstanding in this role, and both personally helped me to secure funding for research that appears this book. I also want to single out my former colleague Desmond Arias, who served as my mentor in the Political Science Department.

One of the reasons I love being a political scientist is that is has allowed me to meet a series of people who shared my interest and passion in politics. My friends provided not only emotional support, but also an encouraging environment to discuss the political world and our effort to understand it. My thanks go to graduate school colleagues Neal Allen, Brian Brox, Oya Dursun, Joe Giammo, Austin Hart, Patrick Hickey, Scott Garrison, Allison Martens, David McCoy, Ernest McGowen, Seth McKee, Mark McKenzie, Ayesha Ray, Laura Seay, Mary Slosar, Natasha Sugiyama, and Matt Vanden Broek. I especially want to thank Danny Hayes for his great friendship in graduate school and beyond, and Mike Unger, Jeremy Teigen, and Julie George, who have not only been friends in graduate school, but who I am fortunate enough to continue to live near as a professor.

At John Jay, I have been fortunate to have a diverse set of colleagues who are a genuine pleasure to work with. I thank Janice Bockmeyer, Jack Jacobs, Susan Kang, Samantha Majic, Maxwell Mak, Veronica Michel-Luviano, Dan Pinello, Peter Romaniuk, Jennifer Rutledge, Andrew Sidman, Monica Varsanyi, and Josh Wilson.

In addition, I have outstanding friends outside of political science. Damian and Laurie Abreo remain my best friends after many years, and they will continue to be so for years to come. My cousin Jeremy Ford and his wife, Brittney, are more friends than cousins, and I treasure my relationship with them. I also owe great thanks to Andi Bartlestein, Eliz Kirk, and Ellen Keith for their support of not just our family, but also my wife's career ambitions. I also owe Ellen special thanks for her help when we visited Chicago in April 2013, which allowed me to meet with my editor at Palgrave. I am not only privileged that Amy Hill is my wife's best friend, but also because she and her husband, Paul, are my friends as well.

My brother- and sister-in-law, Reuben and Christy Ackerman, and my mother-in-law, Ann Ackerman, have welcomed me into their family with open arms and generous hearts. Reuben and Christy's children, Ryan, Eli, and Maya, always bring joy and gladness to my heart. I am lucky to have joined their family.

I have been blessed with a family that has provided me comfort and guidance in equal measures. My aunt and uncle, Charlie and Sharon Ford, have always shown me love and generosity beyond what I have been able to return to them. My brother, Blake, has always been one of the warmest, most generous people in my life. His infectious and positive spirit is an always welcome part of my life. My sister, Megan, is one of my closest friends and is one of the first people I turn to for advice and support. Her husband, Wes, is also a great friend, and my two nephews, Carter and Jack, are always delightful and remind me of what is truly important in life. My brother's new wife, Lindsay, is a great partner to my brother and a joyous addition to our family. My parents, Peter and Alice Arbour, are awesome. They have taught me lessons about how to be generous, outgoing, caring, and committed to my values. They have supported me in hundreds of ways—physically, financially, socially, and emotionally. I will never be able to successfully return all that they have given to me.

Teodora Cuntapay deserves recognition. She is my son's babysitter and quite possibly his favorite person in the world. She has become a part of our family, and this book would not be possible without her help.

This book is dedicated to the two most important people in my life—my wife, Erin, and my son, Joshua. Neither were part of my life when this project started, and now I cannot imagine my life without them. Seeing Joshua's smile and hearing his laugh are the best parts of my day. Fortunately, he does both often, making my day better each time. My wife, Erin, is the best thing about my life. She is more patient and caring and loving than I deserve, and she challenges me on an intellectual level. She understands me better than anyone else and demonstrates that on a daily basis. I am the luckiest man in the world to have met her. Erin, I love you.

CHAPTER 1

THE ROLE OF THE CANDIDATE
IN CAMPAIGN MESSAGES

Entering the 1992 Democratic National Convention, the Bill Clinton campaign had a problem. "To the surprise of Mr. Clinton and his aides, voters often believe[d] that he came from a rich family—because he went to Yale Law School and won a Rhodes scholarship to Oxford University" (May 1992, A1). These voters "assume[d] he . . . went into politics because it was the line of work where his natural phoniness would prove most effective" (Klein 1992, 22). To many voters, Clinton represented the worst possible characteristics of a politician, combining slickness, inauthenticity, and an inability to understand voters' everyday problems. Bill Clinton was the son of a widowed nurse from Hot Springs, Arkansas—hardly the privileged background voters assumed. In other words, voters did not know who Bill Clinton was.

To deal with this misperception, his campaign suggested that, in accepting the Democratic nomination, Clinton "talk about his childhood broken home, working his way up by the sweat of his brow, his small-town roots and his faith in God" (Williams 1992, C1). At the convention, the Clinton campaign "made clear that his personal background would become a theme of the campaign" (Ifill 1992, A1). The centerpiece of this effort was the video *The Man from Hope*, which took its name from Clinton's birthplace, Hope, Arkansas, and focused on Clinton's humble small-town upbringing and its effect on his values (Grimes 1992).

The video proved a huge success, humanizing Clinton through stories about his biography and his accomplishments as governor of Arkansas. According to Clinton strategist James Carville, "*The Man from Hope* film . . . made all the necessary connections between who he was and where he came from; it was successful to the extent that it gave the national audience a good sense of why Bill Clinton was Bill Clinton" (Matalin and Carville 1994, 239–40).

The story of the Clinton campaign demonstrates an important component of communication strategy for political campaigns. Rather than focusing on the future, by telling voters what their candidate will do if elected, political campaigns prefer to tell voters where their candidate has been, highlighting stories about their candidate to reveal not policy preferences or priorities, but personal characteristics and values. Campaigns do this, as Carville suggests, because they succeed when voters can make the connection between who a candidate is and where he or she comes from.

It was not just Clinton's campaign that tried to give voters a sense of who their candidate was. For example, both general election campaigns in the 2008 presidential election employed similar strategies. Each candidate used his convention speech to relay information about his biography and background to the nationally televised audience watching that evening. Democratic nominee Barack Obama (2008) connected figures in his life to people affected by government policies. In the face of "young veterans," Obama saw his "grandfather who . . . marched in Patton's army and was rewarded by a grateful nation with the chance to go to college on the GI Bill." In the "face of that young student . . . I think about my mom, who raised my sister and me on her own while she worked and earned her degree." Obama also related the tale of a woman having "difficulties . . . starting her own business or making her way in the world" to his grandmother, "who worked her way up from the secretarial pool to middle management, despite years of being passed over for promotions because she was a woman." Obama used the stories of his family members in an effort to show his understanding of the problems faced by average Americans in 2008 and to show voters what Obama had in common with the average American. These stories were also designed to show that Obama's campaign promises were genuine commitments to make life better for people like his mother and his grandparents.

Obama's rhetorical connections between his own background and his campaign message could not match the power of John McCain's personal story. In his acceptance speech, the Republican nominee claimed he was "blessed by misfortune" due to his capture, imprisonment, and torture during his Vietnam War naval service. McCain (2008) argued:

I fell in love with my country when I was a prisoner in someone else's . . . I loved it for its decency, for its faith in the wisdom, justice, and goodness of its people. I loved it because it was not just a place, but an idea, a cause worth fighting for. I was never the same again; I wasn't my own man anymore; I was my country's. My country saved me, and I cannot forget it. And I will fight for her for as long as I draw breath, so help me God.

McCain's argument explicitly tied his service to the country as a naval airman to his determination to serve his country by doing what is right if elected to the presidency. In other words, McCain was trying to show voters that his desire to win office was rooted in a love of country, not a love of power or self-aggrandizement. To successfully make this argument, McCain needed to talk about himself and his background.

Arguments that focus on the candidate are not the exclusive province of presidential candidates. Campaigns for candidates throughout the ballot must explain to voters who their candidates are and where they came from. For example, advertisements for Colorado Senate candidate Ken Salazar not only emphasized his humble beginnings, but connected that experience to a populist policy platform, as shown in the following advertisement:

Salazar: When you grow up on a ranch, hard work is a way of life.

Narrator: He's been to all 64 Colorado counties many times, and he's on the road again.

Salazar: I was raised to help people—that deed, not words, are what matter.

Narrator: His values run deep: from the land, from his faith, from his family.

Salazar: My parents always said they couldn't give us riches, but they could give us some education.

Narrator: Their ranch had no power or telephone lines until 1981, but all eight Salazar children went to college. It's the classic American story. As attorney general, he's been a champion for people. He's prosecuted criminals who prey on children and seniors. Gone after those who pollute the land and water he loves. Now he's running for United States Senate.

Salazar: For too long there have been two Colorados.

Narrarator: He's talking about what Colorado can be.

Salazar: No matter who you are, no matter where where you are from, you ought to be able to live the American dream.

Narrator: Ken Salazar: from the people, for the people.

Salazar: I'm Ken Salazar. I approved this message. I hope to get to your town soon.

Such appeals are not limited to Democrats or statewide candidates such as Salazar. The campaign of Geoff Davis (R-KY) put out an advertisement in their 2004 campaign that similarly focused on their candidate's roots and background.

Geoff Davis is a leader. He graduated from West Point, became an Army Ranger, helicopter flight commander, served in the Middle East, defended America's interest. Conservative Geoff Davis. He built a business, making companies more competitive, working to keep manufacturing jobs in America. Conservative Geoff Davis: Conservative values we know. Leadership we trust. For Congress: Geoff Davis.

Davis: I'm Geoff Davis, and I approved this message.[1]

Across a wide variety of candidates in different campaigns for different offices, a similar pattern exists. Campaigns use personal stories about their candidates in an effort to show voters "who their candidates are and where they came from." The use of personal characteristics and values, as highlighted through stories told about the candidate's past in these three acceptance speeches (the one time a presidential candidate can deliver a solo, scripted messages to a national audience during the campaign) and in these broadcast advertisements (the most unfiltered, and expensive, form of mass communication available to campaigns for the US Senate and House), helps demonstrate their importance to political campaigns. Campaigns seek to tell voters about their candidates in an effort to give voters a better sense of who their candidates are and what they will do in office. Campaigns tell stories about their candidates in an effort to make their candidate more credible and likeable. Campaigns believe that enhancing these aspects of their candidate is an essential first step to winning votes on Election Day.

What is missing in the speech excerpts and advertisements above is just as interesting as what is included. These appeals do not focus on candidates' five-point plans for the economy or their intention to vote for tax cuts or health-care reform. Instead, they focus on who the candidates are, where they come from, and the values and principles these past experiences taught them. To some, the focus away from issue-based campaigning and toward personality-based campaigning might seem strange. Campaigns should be forward-looking operations, telling voters about where a candidate wants to take the country or state, instead of focusing on the personal values of candidates through stories about their past. The focus on candidate-centered characteristics, such as biography and political record, shows that voters are not primarily looking at candidates as mechanisms to achieve specific policy goals. Instead, voters first assess a candidate as they would a new neighbor or coworker, determining how much they like and trust this person. Establishing trust is a prerequisite for candidates; only after having done so will voters consider the candidate's plans if elected.

Most political scientists' studies of campaign advertising have focused on the issue agendas of political campaigns (see Goldstein and Ridout 2004 for a summary), sharing the assumption that campaigns are about what candidates will do. As a result, political science has not sufficiently examined the role of candidate-centered characteristics in campaigns' message-development processes. Instead, studies on campaign messages and issue agendas have focused on exogenous factors (district characteristics, party-issue ownership, national-issue salience).

In this book, I try to turn attention back to the candidates and the vital role they play in the messages that campaigns transmit to voters. I argue that candidates themselves, most particularly their personal characteristics, stand at the center of their campaigns' message-development process. Campaign strategists begin their work by assessing the strengths and weaknesses of their candidate, focusing on how the candidate's personality and background fit into a narrative and theme, as well as an issue agenda. I attempt to account for how this process works in political campaigns, to develop expectations about how campaigns will use candidate-centered information in political messages, and to then measure when these appeals are used.

The Argument of the Book

Campaigns must sell voters on who their candidate is before they sell them on what their candidate will do. In order to do this, campaigns must establish the credibility of their candidate with voters. The most common method that campaigns use to establish their candidate's credibility with voters is to focus on their candidate's past experiences and accomplishments. Campaigns relate stories about their candidate's past in an effort to show voters their candidate's basic values and commitments. These stories highlight the personal characteristics of the candidates and attempt to introduce the candidates to voters as one might meet friends or neighbors.

Campaigns can use this candidate-centered information to establish their candidate's credibility in one of three ways. First, campaigns can share details from a candidate's biography or family life to show their candidate's character, often using these appeals to show what their candidate has in common with voters. Second, campaigns can use their candidate's past actions (either in public office or in the private sector) to demonstrate their candidate's commitment to a particular issue and increase the confidence that voters have in their understanding of the candidate's issue positions and priorities. Finally, campaigns can discuss a candidate's past accomplishments to show their candidate's particular knowledge on an important subject or competence working inside the government.

Why do political campaigns need to emphasize candidate-centered appeals? I argue the key reason is credibility. When individuals find the source of a communication to be credible, they are more likely to be persuaded by the message of that source (Hovland and Weiss 1951; Zaller 1992). Credibility has particular importance for political candidates, but developing it is a tall order. It is difficult for candidates seeking office to develop such a level of trust and credibility because candidates are, by definition, politicians. And the inherent level of trust voters have in politicians is close to nonexistent. Jokes about two-faced politicians who will do or say anything to stay in office, except for addressing the problems of their constituents, are commonplace.[2] Voters think most rhetoric by candidates is nothing but hot air, cheap talk, and empty promises (Hibbing and Theiss-Morse 2002).

Developing credibility is also difficult because of the future-oriented nature of political campaigns. Candidates state their positions during the campaign but can only implement these policies in the future. Developing the credibility of a candidate allows voters to believe that the candidate's promises are firm commitments to action, not empty promises that expire on Election Day. As a result, candidates who talk about their issue positions and policy proposals will be greeted with immense skepticism from most voters. "Why should we believe you?" say these skeptical (and hypothetical) voters. "You sound just like every other politician we've heard."

If voters are inherently skeptical of those who run for office, it is worthwhile to ask what they want from those who serve in public office. The most detailed examination of voter preferences about their elected officials shows that Americans want decisions made by publicly minded experts. Americans' frustrations with the political system are caused by the perception that special interests dominate the political process, serving their own interests and not the nation's. Voters want the government to be run by virtuous experts: "virtuous" because they put the interests of their community and nation above themselves and "experts," who demonstrate the knowledge and competence necessary to understand civic problems and identify solutions (Hibbing and Theiss-Morse 2002).

If voters want officeholders who are both selfless and competent, the priority for campaigns is how to persuade voters that their candidate meets both of these criteria. Campaigns persuade voters that their candidate possesses both of these traits through candidate-centered appeals. Messages about a candidate's work on an issue in a previous political office, stories from the candidate's childhood, or testimonials from a spouse or friend: all can attest to who a candidate is and imply that voters can trust the candidate if elected, and can demonstrate the candidate's qualifications for that office.

Candidate-centered information is the most effective means of developing the credibility of the candidate because it presents candidates in a similar way to how individuals would encounter a new person in their daily lives. The average voter does not encounter policy-based information on an everyday basis, and policy information seems different than other forms of communication—often containing a great amount of numerical data and jargon. Instead, voters want to assess candidates like they do friends and neighbors. Voters want to determine how much they like and trust people when they meet them, and candidates are no different. Thus, voters see candidates first from a personal standpoint.

Campaigns respond by presenting personal information about the candidate, telling stories about the candidate's accomplishments in previous elective office the candidate's experience and expertise in a particular field, or the candidate's dedication and service to causes greater than his or her own personal satisfaction. Candidate-centered information also provides an advantage for campaigns that have both a competitive primary *and* general election. With a partisan and ideological electorate in the primary and a centrist electorate in the general, campaigns must walk a fine line in positioning their candidate to succeed in both electorates: wavering toward the extremes during the primary and the center during the general raises questions about the candidate's credibility. By focusing on the candidate's background and accomplishments, campaigns can fix their message to something that will not change throughout the course of the campaign. Focusing on the candidate not only creates credibility via a specific message, but it also can build credibility over the course of a campaign.

In this book, I present evidence of the importance placed on the candidate throughout the campaign's message-development process. In deciding the message for their campaign, political consultants and campaign managers weigh the strengths and weaknesses of their candidate, assessing a candidate's background and résumé, record in political office, speaking style, and issue expertise. Consultants and managers then examine factors outside of their control—the political preferences of the district, the national mood and issue agenda, their party's reputation and standing—and calibrate these factors against their assessment of their candidate. These internal and external data points are then used to determine what message to transmit to voters, calibrating not only which issues to emphasize, but also the broader themes of the campaign and the specific wording and imagery they want to use in their messages.

I find evidence for the use of candidate-centered messages in all elements of a campaign's message-development process. Consultants almost unanimously report that they seek to learn personal elements about their candidate at the beginning of their work for a candidate, in an effort to identify candidate-centered messages they can transmit to voters. I then find substantial evidence for the ubiquity of candidate-centered appeals in campaign advertisements and evidence of the improved perceptions of a candidate when campaigns use such candidate-centered appeals.

The Importance of Candidate-Centered Appeals

Examining what campaigns say to voters and understanding the origins of campaign strategies have great importance in assessing the democratic health of the American system of campaigns and elections. There is a simple and important reason for evaluating candidates' claims—what they say during a campaign is the best guide to understanding what they will do once elected to office. Studies of campaign promises have reached the same conclusion—officeholders work to fulfill the pledges they make during their campaign (Sulkin 2009; Fishel 1985; Krukones 1984).

Campaigns are selling candidates as individuals. Campaign rhetoric focuses on the personal qualities of the candidate and how these qualities contribute to a set of broad-minded values. Campaign rhetoric presents candidates as individuals with the knowledge and experience to make good decisions and the character and concern to make sure those decisions will serve the community and the nation. In other words, campaigns are about creating a bond of trust between the candidate and the voters, and thus, that the bond of trust produces good results on Election Day.

Campaigns also sell their candidates as individuals because they gain advantage by remaining ambiguous in their policy stances. Identifying a clear set of issue positions has the drawbacks of alienating members of the public who disagree with that position (Shepsle 1972, 565) and providing a juicy target for attacks by the opponent (Meirowitz 2005). Further, avoiding specifics during a campaign allows a candidate greater flexibility upon entering office (Alesina and Cukierman 1990; Aragones and Neeman 2000). As a result, campaigns try to calibrate their rhetoric to be all things to all people, and the rhetoric of campaign advertising is especially notable for the vague claims—"tough on crime," "reform health care," "fight for our country"—that are not connected to a clear issue position (Sides 2006). Candidate-centered information can take the place of specific policy stances by a candidate, allowing voters to infer the good intentions of a candidate via the enhanced credibility developed by the candidate-centered focus of the appeals.

Thus, campaigns are about an implicit promise from the candidate to the voter: "Trust me; this will work." Focusing on candidate-centered appeals and this implicit promise helps explain the relationship between elected officials and voters. For example, what happens when it does not "work out"? Officeholders are punished electorally, and the chances of incumbent victory are reduced in harsh economic times and during unsuccessful wars. Often, these results are dismissed by noting that the fickle public does not have true preferences on its policy goals for the government. A focus on candidate-centered appeals shows that what voters are being promised are not specific policies to achieve a set of ideological and policy goals. Instead, voters are being promised positive results because the people elected have the values to know what is best for a community and the competence to implement those decisions successfully. So when voters see negative results from government, they come to the conclusion that they were sold a bill of goods as to the positive qualities of the candidate they elected to office. Their trust in the candidate was in vain.

A focus on candidate-centered appeals demonstrates that American elections are individualized, with a focus primarily on the personalities of candidates and voters' perceptions of the trust and competence of the individuals who run for office. This observation is not original. The U.S. Constitution has no role for political parties, and the founders assumed individual candidates would stand or fall in elections in small geographic units based on their own merits. Modern-day candidates are self-motivated, making their own decision to run for office (Ehrenhalt 1991) and creating their own campaign organization (Herrnson 2011). Not only is the decision to run and the campaign organization personalized, but so too is the message of that campaign. This means that a nationally important issue can be important in a particular U.S. House election, but only if that issue can be personalized to the candidate. Campaigns create a message that fits their candidate and is tailored to voters in their district. As such, they are not necessarily repeating the same issues and themes of their party's presidential candidate or national leaders. The identity of the person who runs for office matters more than national conditions in determining what a campaign says. Who runs is important because it determines what is said to voters. And what is said to voters determines what the candidate does if elected and how voters understand their representatives.

As a result, campaigns focus on perceptions of the honesty and trustworthiness of the men and women who run for office. Of course, it is vital to have individuals of good character and public-spirited values controlling government policies on spending and criminal justice. But my read is that campaigns have tilted too far in the direction of relating the character and goodwill of our elected officials and too far away from explaining their policy views. The job of our elected officials is not to care about citizens more than the average person or to reflect our values. Their job is to craft policies that will improve the social welfare of the citizenry. The focus on the candidates means that the focus is placed on the past and away from future plans. Such an emphasis poorly serves citizens because it is not descriptive of the primary job of elected officials, which is to create and implement policies in their subsequent term in office.

CANDIDATE-CENTERED APPEALS AND POLITICAL SCIENCE

A study of candidate-centered appeals also has great value among political scientists who study campaigns and elections. I believe a focus on the role of candidates themselves in campaign messages serves as a necessary corrective to a political science literature that has focused too heavily on what issues campaigns talk about. Campaigns and elections research has focused heavily on the effect campaigns have on the decisions made by voters. While political scientists know a great deal about how voters process campaign information (cf. Campbell et al. 1960; Fiorina 1981; Popkin 1994; Zaller 1992), we know little about what political campaigns say and, more importantly, why they choose to say what they do. Studies of campaign behavior have tended to focus on how campaigns do things: showing that spending more money, (Ansolabehere and Gerber 1994; Jacobson 1978; 1990; 2007), airing more advertisements (Freedman and Goldstein 2000), or visiting a state more often (Shaw 1999; 2006) produces marginal increases in vote share. These works are silent, though, on the question of the effectiveness of a particular message in a television advertisement, a rally in a battleground state, or an acceptance speech.

There is indeed a significant literature on what political campaigns say, but that literature focuses too heavily on the issue agendas of political campaigns. Inspired by the Anthony Downs's median voter theorem—which holds that campaigns will "formulate policies" (28) and position their candidate on an ideological spectrum to win the votes of the median voter—a number of works have examined whether political campaigns converge to create a dialogue on the same issues (Kaplan, Park, and Ridout 2006; Sigelman and Buell 2004; Simon 2002; Spiliotes and Vavreck 2002). Other works have focused on the ability of campaigns to frame the issue agenda on favorable grounds. These studies find that local issue priorities (Sulkin and Evans 2006) and the national issue agenda (Brasher 2003) affect what issues campaigns highlight. The most contentious debate in this area is over John Petrocik's theory of issue ownership (1996), with some finding that campaigns are more likely to highlight the issues owned by their party (Brasher 2003; Budge and Farlie 1983; Kahn and Kenney 1999; Spiliotes and Vavreck 2002; Sulkin and Evans 2006; Druckman, Kifer, and Parkin 2009), while others find the two parties equally willing to talk about the same issues (Damore 2004, 2005; Kaplan, Park, and Ridout 2006; Sides 2006; Sigelman and Buell 2004).

What is notable about this group of studies though is that they do not include a role for candidates themselves as an explanatory factor in campaign message strategy. Table 1.1 shows this in graphic form. It includes information from 11 published papers in the last decade that have modeled some aspect of the issue agenda for political campaigns. These articles, and the specific tables where the models are presented, are listed in each row. The columns represent the different independent variables used in these models. The results show the importance of exogenous factors, as party, competitiveness, and candidate status (incumbent, open seat, or challenger), in political science thinking on campaign messages. These exogenous factors play important agenda-setting roles. But the ability of candidates to convey messages on national issues is not equally distributed across all members of a party. Taken to their logical conclusion, these models assume that it does not matter who the candidate is; their campaigns will say the same thing. It is improbable that the authors listed in the table believe that, but only a handful of studies have tried to see what role candidates play in this process.

As a result, political scientists lack a sufficient understanding of what campaigns know (or think they know) about how voters make decisions. We also have a limited understanding of the decision-making process of political campaigns. What do campaigns think motivates voters to get to the polls and choose their candidate? How do campaigns plan the broad themes and narratives of their campaign, and how do they try to fold those broad themes and narratives into particular advertisements, speeches, and messages? As political scientists, we have done little to address these questions.

I take up these questions in this book, starting with an examination of the campaign planning process. In particular, I interview campaign consultants who develop campaign messages, assessing what they think of voters and how they try to map out a message strategy for their campaign. In these interviews, consultants emphasize the importance of the candidate and demonstrating who the candidate is to voters. Consultants are not trying to sell their candidates as a package of issue stances or a representative of their party, but as an individual who voters can trust to do a good job in office.

PLAN OF THE BOOK

As noted, the argument of this book is that campaigns use candidate-centered appeals with great frequency in an effort to develop the credibility of their candidate. To make this argument, I assess campaigns' message-development processes from the beginning, as campaigns map out their message strategy for a campaign that includes both a primary and general election; to the middle, examining the content of campaign messages; to the end, as voters evaluate the candidate-centered messages that campaigns employ. This book proceeds in a manner that allows this assessment of all aspects of the role of candidate-centered appeals in campaign messages.

Each chapter begins with a case study that examines one particular campaign and how that campaign successfully used candidate-centered appeals to overcome doubts and political obstacles to emerge victorious

Table 1.1 Independent Variables Used in Recent Political Science Studies of Campaign Messages

	Candidate Reputation	Incumbent, Challenger and/or Open Seat	Competitiveness	Year	Senate/House	Party	Gender	Money Raised/Spent	District Partisanship	Front-Runner	Interest in the Issue	District Demographics	National Salience	Owned Issue	Minority Candidate	Opponent Mentions Issue	District Issue Salience
Trumbore and Dulio 2013 Tables 1, 2 and 3		X	X			X		X									
Pietryka 2012 Table 2		X	X						X	X				X	X		X
Strach and Sapiro 2011 Tables 3, 4, and 5		X	X			X	X		X								
Sapiro et al. 2011 Table 2			X			X											
Druckman et al. 2010 Table 7		X	X	X		X						X					
Druckman, Kifer, and Parkin 2010. Tables 3 and D; Figures 2, 3, 4, 5		X	X	X	X	X	X	X	X	X	X						
Sulkin 2009 Table 3, Stage 1;	X		X										X	X			
Kaplan, Park, & Ridout 2006 Table 6		X	X					X						X	X		
Sigelman & Buell 2004 Table 1					X												
Spiliotes & Vavreck 2002 Table 1.		X				X	X		X								
Brasher 2003 Table 2						X								X	X		
Sides 2006 Table 4	X	X	X		X	X	X	X		X		X					
Dulio and Trumbore 2009 Tables 2 and 3		X				X						X				X	
Sulkin, Moriarity & Herner 2007 Table 1					X									X			
Sulkin & Evans 2006 Table 4	X	X	X														
Damore 2004 Tables 2 and 3			X		X								X			X	

Note: Data collected and compiled by author.

on Election Day. The data used in the book focus on U.S. House and Senate campaigns, primarily for 2004, but the argument goes beyond the U.S. Congress and beyond one particular election cycle. The case studies allow me to demonstrate the importance of candidate-centered appeals for campaigns for different offices (whether for president, Congress, state governor, or municipal mayor) and in different election cycles. Further, the case studies bring a flavor and a real-world context to the quantitative findings of the book.

In chapter 2, I develop the theoretical argument of the book, focusing on the importance of credibility for political candidates and the particular difficulty of developing credibility for political candidates. I argue that candidate-centered information provides the most effective means for a campaign to enhance their candidate's credibility with voters. From this argument, I develop a series of expectations for how campaigns will use candidate-centered appeals—expectations that I test in the subsequent chapters.

That testing begins in chapter 3, where I interview political consultants who create and develop campaign messages. The interviews focus on the campaign planning process and how campaigns decide what message to transmit to voters. The consultants report their desire to show voters who their candidate is through stories about their candidate's past actions and experiences that demonstrate the core beliefs of their candidate. I then test whether plans coolly made in the early planning stages of a campaign hold up in the heat of a contested political campaign. For the most part, they do. In chapter 4, I analyze the frequency and timing of candidate-centered appeals in campaign advertisements. I find that campaigns use candidate-centered appeals in a majority of the advertisements they air, but that candidate-centered appeals are connected to other types of appeals in most of these advertisements. Chapter 5 identifies three types of candidate-centered appeals—position-based, character-based, and competence-based—and examines what type of campaigns use each type of appeal in which type of circumstance.

I argue that political science literature has not placed enough emphasis on candidate-centered appeals, despite their importance to the development of campaign messages. In chapter 6, I examine *personal issues*, which are usually ignored in the political science literature on issue agendas in favor of *policy issues*. I find that while all campaigns use personal issues to enhance their candidate's likeability and credibility with voters, there are a specific set of issues (terrorism, the environment, corporate corruption, and taxes) that campaigns are more likely to combine with personal issues. On these issues, the personal credibility of a candidate is especially important. Chapter 7 addresses the effect of candidate-centered appeals on voters. Using an experimental design, I find that the use of candidate-centered appeals produces a modest but real increase in voter perceptions of favorability for that candidate.

Chapter 8 serves as a conclusion to the book, but it also serves as an opportunity to assess the implications of the widespread use of candidate-centered appeals. It emphasizes the importance of candidate entry to the content of the messages that campaigns transmit to voters and argues for the need to include candidates themselves in political science models of campaign messages. More importantly, the final chapter serves as my argument for why candidate-centered appeals poorly serve voters by shifting the emphasis to candidates as individuals and away from candidates as governors and policy innovators.

While I think that voters are ill-served by the emphasis on candidate-centered appeals, what is clear is that campaigns use them, and use them with great frequency because they believe these appeals will improve their candidate's standing with voters. That is, voters want to know who they are electing and to assess candidates primarily as individuals. The story at the beginning of this chapter shows that the Bill Clinton campaign learned a lesson on the importance of showing voters "who he was and where he came from." That lesson has been learned by campaigns again and again, and they have adapted by emphasizing their candidates' backgrounds and accomplishments. These are necessary steps to build candidate credibility, which is needed to win.

CHAPTER 2

WHY CAMPAIGNS USE
CANDIDATE-CENTERED MESSAGES

As the 2013 New York City mayoral election began, public advocate Bill de Blasio seemed to be a candidate without a constituency. City council speaker Christine Quinn led not only in establishment endorsements and donations, but also among voters, in early polls. Former city controller Bill Thompson, who proved his political bona fides by beating expectations in a seemingly hopeless 2009 mayoral run against Michael Bloomberg, had significant support among African American voters. Current controller John Liu, though beset by criminal charges against his fund-raising team, as the city's first Asian American elected official possessed the affections of the Asian community. Finally, former congressman Anthony Weiner entered the race and created a media firestorm, sucking up coverage and shooting to first place in polls taken immediately after his entry into the race (Smith 2013). With but a month left in the campaign, de Blasio stood in fourth place in the Democratic primary and seemed to be an "afterthought," according to the *New York Times* (Barbaro 2013).

How did de Blasio turn the election around to win a smashing victory in the Democratic primary and in the general election? Two elements were key. First, de Blasio charted a liberal set of policy positions and messages. Most notably, he described "a tale of two cities" to highlight the issue of inequality. In addition, de Blasio was a harsh critic of the 12-year term of incumbent mayor Michael Bloomberg. These tactics did not necessarily make sense in trying to identify the views of the median voters, who were more moderate than de Blasio and who approved of the job Bloomberg had done as mayor and thought the city was headed in the right direction. But these strategic decisions made sense in enhancing de Blasio's credibility. De Blasio had a record as a liberal activist and as a critic of the mayor, and he explained to an advisor that "it would be phony of me to be anything but a critic [of Bloomberg]" (Barbaro 2013). De Blasio understood the importance of authenticity and needed to craft a campaign message that enhanced, rather than detracted from, his liberal biography and record.

The second element of de Blasio's meteoric ascent in the polls was the use of his family as a credibility-developing device in the campaign. In particular, de Blasio shot to the top of the polls thanks to an advertisement that featured his 15-year-old biracial son, Dante.

The advertisement begins by introducing "Dante, 15 years old, Brooklyn":

> I want to tell you a little about Bill de Blasio. He's the only Democrat with the guts to really break from the Bloomberg years—the only one who will raise taxes on the rich to fund early-childhood and after-school programs. He's got the boldest plan to build affordable housing, and he's the only one who will end a stop-and-frisk era that unfairly targets people of color. Bill de Blasio will be a mayor for every New Yorker, no matter where they live or what they look like. And I'd say that even if he weren't my dad.

After showing Dante sitting in a kitchen with his impressive afro,[1] the visuals then turn to standard campaign fare—de Blasio addressing a multiracial group in a diner and a tracking shot of children in a crosswalk on their way to school. But after Dante refers to the stop-and-frisk program—the Bloomberg program that allowed police officers to stop pedestrians and frisk them for guns and other contraband—the visuals turn to the de Blasio family eating breakfast in a kitchen and then show Bill walking Dante to school.

The ad was a sensation, as it personalized one of the key issues in the campaign—the stop-and-frisk program—for de Blasio. The presence of his 15-year-old African American son demonstrated "that the aggressive policing of the Bloomberg era was not an abstraction to Mr. de Blasio, it was an urgent personal worry within his biracial household" (Barbaro 2013). According to an anonymous Christine Quinn aide, "That ad killed us" (Freedlander 2013).

De Blasio strategist John del Cecato argued that the advertisement worked because of credibility. "What people vote on at the end of the day is 'Do I like this person? Do I understand this person? And most importantly, do they understand my life'" (Freedlander 2013).

Dante's advertisement personalized de Blasio's on an abstract issue. The text of the advertisement, interestingly enough, contains almost no candidate-centered information—it is a statement of de Blasio's policy proposals—but the presence of de Blasio's son personalizes the content of the message. The ad helped de Blasio overcome the tribal voting allegiances of ethnic politics. The ad implicitly offers de Blasio's multiracial family as an analogy for a positive, multiracial city (Smith 2013). One New York City journalist argued the ad was "politically powerful because de Blasio didn't target it at any particular audience, aiming in tone for it to be broadcast" (Smith 2013) According to del Cecato, "The power of the ad to me was in the messenger and the message and that is what made the ad. I made the ad, but Dante *made* the ad" (Freedlander 2013).

As demonstrated in the first chapter, political campaigns must show voters who their candidate is and where their candidate comes from. By doing this, campaigns try to develop the sincerity and enhance the credibility of their candidate among voters. One common way that campaigns try to do this is by producing ads that feature children extolling their father or mother (i.e., the candidate). These ads are not unusual and are used by candidates across the political spectrum. In fact, the 2004 Wisconsin Senate races featured advertisements narrated by the teenage son of Republican challenger Tim Michels and the college-age daughter of incumbent Democrat Russ Feingold. Often, these types of ads feature hokey jokes about the parent's values (e.g., the child talks about not getting a higher allowance as a sign of pop's budget views). But the powerful de Blasio ads, like ads from other candidates that feature their children in serious roles, provide a textbook demonstration of how a well-crafted advertisement can take abstract issue positions and make them more real to voters through the role of someone who is affected by policy positions of their parent. In other words, candidates are at the center of these messages, even if it is their child who delivers that message.

Ads featuring children help to show that the candidate has the same concerns as any other parent and to help voters get to know the candidate. When voters know little about a candidate, they may assume that candidate is running for reasons of self-interest. Political candidates discuss their background—and relate it to their political convictions and determination to serve goals greater than their own gratification—to overcome voters' natural skepticism. Only by enhancing perceptions of their sincerity can candidates overcome voter skepticism and get voters to assess the candidate's policy aims.

As a result, candidates themselves stand at the center of each campaign's message-development process. Those who create messages for political campaigns first assess the strengths and weaknesses of their candidate's personality and background. This analysis of focuses on how their candidate's personality and background fit into the various components of a campaign message—the theme, the narrative, and even the issue agenda. Campaigns need to show voters that their candidate is not a typical politician and is worthy of a voter's trust.

In this chapter, I argue that campaigns must develop the credibility of their candidate in an effort to overcome the natural skepticism people have about those who run for office. I then develop a series of hypotheses that will allow me to test if candidate background and personality stand at the center of the campaign message development process. The importance of the candidate starts with planning the strategy and message of a campaign. Then the planning is put into practice, as messages specifically about the candidate pervade campaign advertising. I identify three explanations for how and why campaigns can talk about the candidate—to demonstrate character, to reduce uncertainty about policy positions, and to demonstrate a candidate's competence. Also, the candidate's own reputation and past work shapes what issues a campaign wants to talk about. Finally, I move from campaigns to voters, determining that candidate-centered information is regarded more favorably than policy-based information.

In detailing each of these key steps in the campaign process, I show that candidate-centered information stands at the heart of campaign messages and that scholarly discussion of campaigning must focus more on the role candidates play in campaign strategy decisions.

SOURCE CREDIBILITY

I have argue that the current political science model of issue agenda is incomplete, because it includes only exogenous factors—party reputation, incumbency, district composition, and so forth. This model lacks an understanding of the variation in the ability of particular candidates to deliver particular messages. Some candidates can talk about particular issues better than others, and some can use particular rhetorical devices with more credibility than others.

In the first chapter, I discussed how John McCain's acceptance speech at the 2008 Republican Convention resonated around themes from his capture and imprisonment in Vietnam. McCain argued, "I fell in love with my country when I was a prisoner in someone else's . . . And I will fight for her as long as I draw breath, so help me God."

His campaign continued that theme with their slogan—"country first"—which attempted to connect McCain's service as a naval airman to his determination to serve his country by doing what would be right if elected to the presidency. In other words, McCain was using personal information to show that his desire to win office was rooted in a love of country, not a love of power or self-aggrandizement. Barack Obama could not use the same slogan or arguments. Obama had never served in the military; he had not had a searing and testing personal episode that caused him to rethink his values. In short, Obama did not have the credibility to say what McCain said. As a result, the McCain campaign had advantages on themes of patriotism and sacrifice and the issue of national security, and they worked to shift the conversation to these favorable messages. The Obama campaign was compelled to identify other themes and issues to sell their candidate.

In order to understand what political candidates say to woo voters, it is important to know where these candidates come from. Just as McCain's experience as a naval pilot and a prisoner of war gave him credibility to make a different argument than Barack Obama, each campaign will calibrate its rhetoric to the background, experience, and political record of their candidate.

Campaigns use candidate-centered information because it serves as a *source-credibility mechanism* for voters. What is *source credibility*? It is the notion that the source of a communication has an important effect on a respondent's willingness to accept a message. That is, one messenger is more effective than another not because of the persuasiveness of the rhetoric, but because of background, experience, or knowledge (see Pornpitakpan 2004 for a review of source-credibility literature in psychology and marketing). When respondents find the source of a communication to be credible, they are more likely to use the message the source gives to change their opinion (Hovland and Weiss 1951; Hovland, Janis, and Kelley 1953; McGuire 1968; Zaller 1992).

Source credibility contends that the form in which a message is delivered has a substantial (if not determinative) impact on the persuasiveness of the message. For a political campaign, the question becomes what form is most likely to persuade voters of the message their candidate is trying to deliver. I argue that candidate-centered appeals serve as the most effective means for campaigns to do so. Information about a candidate—told through stories about a candidate's past actions—can allow voters to confer trust and expertise upon the candidate. If a candidate has worked on an issue in the past or voted a particular way in office, voters can trust that candidate to do the same in the future. A second way that source credibility works is that information about a candidate's accomplishments and experience can positively affect perceptions of the candidate's potential effectiveness, if elected to office. Both of these possibilities lead to the same expectation—candidate-centered appeals produce more favorable impressions of a candidate.

Scholars of political communication have identified a number of ways in which the source of a communication can positively alter the effectiveness of a message. One set—which includes party reputation (Iyengar and Valentino 2000), ideology (Zaller 1992), and candidate status (Page, Shapiro, and Dempsey 1987)—is exogenous to campaigns, and cannot be altered. But the second series of source effects—a source's trustworthiness (Popkin 1994), public approval of a source (Mondak 1993, Mondak et al. 2003), and the perceived commonality between source and recipient (Lupia and McCubbins 1998, Druckman 2001)—are endogenous to a candidate. Thus, campaigns can affect these perceptions and thereby positively affect their candidate's persuasiveness.

CREDIBILITY AND POLITICIANS

Source-credibility literature holds that individuals are more persuasive when respondents view them as more trustworthy. Thus, political campaigns must find ways to demonstrate the trustworthiness of their candidate to voters. Developing trust and credibility is the vital first step to getting voters to listen to a candidate's policy stands.

Of course, it is not easy for campaigns to develop perceptions of their candidates' trustworthiness. The future-oriented nature of campaign promises means that voters assess their own confidence in the issue positions and promises made by each campaign. Downs (1957, 109) argues that voters "must be able to predict [candidates'] actions reasonably well from what [candidates] say." The best way for candidates to demonstrate their reliability is through integrity—their campaign pledges must match their actions in office—because "integrity is by far the most efficient form of reliability" (Downs 1957, 108). In other words, voters must believe that the promises of political candidates are firm commitments to action and not empty promises that expire on Election Day.

Campaigns must also overcome the skepticism voters have about politicians and their belief that most campaign rhetoric is nothing but hot air, cheap talk, and empty promises (Hibbing and Theiss-Morse 2002). As a result, a candidate who talks about issue positions and policy proposals will be greeted with immense skepticism from most voters. "Why should we believe you?" say these skeptical (and hypothetical) voters. "You sound just like every other politician we've heard."

What do voters want from those who serve in public office? The most detailed examination of this question is provided by John Hibbing and Elizabeth Theiss-Morse (2002, 85–86). They argue that voters want *stealth democracy*: "People want to turn political matters over to somebody else because they do not want to be involved themselves, but they do not want to turn decision making over to someone who is likely to act in a selfish, rather than other-regarding, manner . . . The people are surprisingly smitten with the notion of elite experts making choices—provided those experts have nothing to gain from selecting one option over another."

The goal for most voters, according to Hibbing and Theise-Morse, is not to take power themselves but to find representatives that will serve the public rather than special interests. These ideal representatives would combine virtue—worrying about the interests of the nation rather than seeking power and money for themselves—and knowledge by demonstrating the intelligence to understand civic problems as well as the competence and skills to identify solutions. Campaigns want to enhance perceptions of their candidates' sincerity and competence. The question for campaigns is how they can accomplish both of these goals in their messages to voters.

Background, Credibility, and Voters

Voters have reasons to distrust those who run for office. I argue that campaigns must overcome this distrust and develop the credibility of their candidate. The premise behind this argument is that it is less what you say than whether people trust what you say in a campaign. Voters assess whether they trust what a candidate says. Or to put it in a more formal way, voters use information shortcuts to "read" politicians and their positions (Popkin 1994, 7). Popkin further argues that "in using information about candidates, voters extrapolate from personal characteristics to policy preferences."

How do voters extrapolate from the personal to policy? And how do voters assess the credibility of candidates and their messages? The most detailed explanation of this process is provided by Samuel Popkin in *The Reasoning Voter*. Popkin argues that voters use "low information rationality," or "gut level reasoning," to make their decisions. In doing so, voters gain a great deal of insight from small bits of information. Most of the information that voters gather about politics and candidates comes not from detailed study of political events or campaign platforms, but from small bits of data gathered primarily as a "by-product" of an individual's daily life. Individuals learn about politics from fleeting glances at television advertisements or news reports and from brief conversations with friends, family, and coworkers. According to Popkin, "Most of the information voters use is a by-product of activities they pursue in their daily lives. In that sense, political uses of information are free" (23).

Individuals assess political information in a similar way to how they gather new information in all situations. They try to determine how much faith they place in this new information. When new information conforms to an individual's previous knowledge or experience, that individual is more likely to accept this information. And when new information comes from a believable source, an individual is more likely to accept that new information. People encounter new information from new sources with great frequency and are well practiced at determining the credibility of a new information source. Individuals will size up how much they like the source of information, their level of trust in the source, and their opinion of the competence or expertise of the source.

Popkin explains this process through examples such as selecting a babysitter or an emergency nurse (65). I prefer the example of listening to a new mechanic. One with a car problem must decide whether to believe the diagnosis of this mechanic and whether to be willing to pay him or her. If you don't trust the mechanic, you take your car to a different shop. In making this decision, you will consider how much you think the mechanic has the knowledge to accurately diagnose the problem and whether you trust the mechanic to be truthful in his or her diagnosis. And we all prefer to deal with people we like. Selecting a candidate is analogous. In assessing a candidate, voters will examine not just what the candidate says, but also whether the candidate has their best interests at heart, is sincere in his or her pledges, and is competent to achieve certain goals if elected to office. Since most political information that voters receive comes as a by-product of their everyday lives, it is not surprising that voters evaluate this information in a similar way to the information they receive in their everyday lives. According to Popkin, "Voter evaluations depend on whether their reasoning connects their situations to the actions of their leaders" (31).

Further, analyzing personal data about a candidate is much easier for nearly every voter than analyzing policy data. Policy data can be immensely complex and technical, and with experts on every side of the issue, voters are likely to feel more overwhelmed than confident in assessing what policies a candidate should follow. More importantly, voters do not encounter policy information on a regular basis in their daily lives. Evaluating such information is uncommon and foreign to most voters. Popkin argues that in the absence of knowledge or experience with policy information, voters will assess the personal information about the candidate and then extrapolate their perceptions of the candidate's policy views from the personal information. Voters develop "a personal narrative and then assess political character from personality and character" (Popkin 1994, 78).

So if voters are going to size up candidates like they do babysitters, auto mechanics, neighbors, and friends, it should follow that campaigns will present their candidates to voters like a neighbor or friend. Campaigns are advantaged in doing so because the audience for political messages is focused more on the personal characteristics of candidates than on policy platforms, and such messages are easier for voters to understand; then it only stands to reason that campaigns should present voters messages focused on the personal characteristics of the candidates. Campaigns should present messages that enhance the positive personal characteristics of their candidates and present the information in a way that seems similar to how voters evaluate people in their everyday lives. How do campaigns do this? They present personal information about the candidate. Campaigns tell stories to show voters who the candidate is. Most of these stories involve past actions by the candidate—stories about the candidate's accomplishments in previous elective office, experience and expertise in a particular field, or dedication and service to causes greater than his or her own personal satisfaction.

What unites these various personal appeals is not just their focus on candidates themselves, but their focus on the candidate's past. Candidate-centered appeals do not just talk about the candidate, but try to tell stories about who the candidate really is. Telling such stories implies relying heavily on the candidates' past, whether discussing their biography, their record in political office, or their experience in the private sector. Telling stories about a candidate's past relates not only the issue positions and priorities of a candidate, but also attempts to develop a sense of trust and likeability. A well-crafted campaign message will prompt voters not only to support the issue stands of the candidate, but also to trust that the candidate is sincere in his or her dedication to the issue and will work to implement those policies if elected.

As noted in chapter 1, few political science studies of campaign messages have examined the role that personal characteristics play in political campaigns. Yet those studies that do show that political campaigns make frequent use of the candidate's personal information. Presidential campaigns make "experience images"—which focus on past jobs, political positions, or accomplishments—the most commonly used personal trait in television advertisements (Shyles 1984). And nearly half of the campaign literature examined in one study included the candidate's occupation (McDermott 1999). Other studies show the effectiveness of personal information about a candidate's background, record, or biography. William Benoit (2006) finds that presidential candidates who make more retrospective utterances are more likely to win. Even the appearance of a candidate's occupational title on a ballot helps to win votes (McDermott 2005).

Patrick Sellers (1998) provides the most detailed analysis of the role that political record plays in campaigns. He finds that when a candidate has built a favorable political record on an issue, the campaign is more likely to highlight that issue. Further, Sellers finds that "candidates win more favorable evaluations if they focus on their records" (170). Thus, what research has been done on background appeals finds that campaigns use background appeals frequently, and they benefit when they do so.

The Use of Personal Messages

So far in this chapter, I have detailed the importance of source credibility in political rhetoric as a response to voter skepticism and how voters use personal information in their decision-making process. I now try to put these disparate threads together to explain how campaigns use candidate-centered appeals in real-life campaigns, develop hypotheses about the use of these appeals by campaigns, and develop measures to provide evidence to test these hypotheses.

I have argued that political campaigns use candidate-centered appeals as a means of developing the credibility of their candidates in the eyes of voters. Political consultants and campaign managers weigh the strengths and weaknesses of their candidates and craft a message that highlights the best features of their candidate's experience, background, and accomplishments. In short, campaigns are selling candidates as candidates. The question is how do they do so. My argument says that campaigns benefit when they include candidate-centered messages in their appeals to voters. Voters must find a candidate credible and likeable, and the way for campaigns to do this is by emphasizing the personal qualities of their candidate by relating stories about the candidate's broad background. Thus we would expect campaigns to talk about their candidate with great frequency.

Part of the reason that campaigns talk about their candidate (or the opponent) with great frequency is that there are a variety of ways to talk about a candidate, and campaigns can use these different ways to achieve different goals. I identify three separate goals that campaigns might have in using candidate-centered appeals.

1. Highlighting Character: Campaigns use personal messages to overcome the skepticism voters have about the intentions of those who seek office. Messages that highlight character try to communicate the values of the candidate running for office.
2. Reinforcing Issue Positions: Voters are skeptical of the issue stands and policy proposals made by candidates. In an effort to make these stands more credible, campaigns will highlight the political record of their candidate, focusing on their candidate's past actions on particular issues to imply that their candidate will do the same in the future.
3. Demonstrating Competence: These messages emphasize the particular knowledge, skill, or insight that candidates have previously demonstrated, whether in the private sector or in elective office.

These types of appeals are not exclusive to background, experience, or values. Campaigns can combine an appeal about their candidate's character or priorities with a discussion of issues. In fact, such a combination should be more persuasive, as the personal focus of the issue message should increase the credibility of the candidate.

I now sketch out why campaigns use each of these types of candidate-centered messages. I also discuss which types of campaigns would be most likely to use each of these types of appeals, developing hypotheses about the use of candidate-centered appeals.

Highlighting Character

As I argued above, voters are skeptical of the claims made by those who seek political office. One need only think of the stereotypical image of the two-faced politician, or jokes where the punch line features a politician out only to preserve his or her position in order to line his of her own pockets. The corrupt, greedy politician is a well-known cultural trope. Research also shows that voters assume that the solutions to political problems are relatively easy, and only the selfish motives of elected officials keep our government from solving problems (Hibbing and Theiss-Morse 2002).

Campaigns must figure out how to overcome this skepticism held by voters. If voters think all politicians are two-faced, corrupt, selfish, and the cause of problems, the solution for a campaign is to make voters think their candidate is not a typical politician. Campaigns have two methods to do this. First, they can show that their candidate represents a set of exceptional qualities. John McCain is the archetypical example for this, as his campaigns have emphasized his heroism as a POW in Vietnam, as well as issues that easily connected to his service, such as national security. The McCain story is powerful because it demonstrates his personal sacrifice for the cause of his country, and voters can assume that he will once again put the country first (in fact, his 2008 slogan said so). Other candidates tell stories of their achievements in business, in charitable endeavors, in other forms of public service, or, as McCain did, in their military career, to show they have lived a life of service in the interest of others, not the interests of themselves.

Most campaigns do not have a candidate with such a heroic biography as John McCain. These campaigns can instead argue that their candidate holds values in common with the people of the district. These appeals, which can feature the candidate's upbringing and dedication to family, imply that by understanding communal values and because of their important in the candidate's life, he or she will remember and treasure these values if elected. Voters assume that candidate who can remember communal values are (1) rare and (2) valuable.

What unites these two methods of overcoming voter skepticism is their focus on the character of the candidate. The working definition of character for these purposes is "who the candidate is." Campaigns hope to show voters the most favorable side of who their candidate is. Campaign strategists collect stories about their candidates as part of their initial research and use these to present a narrative of selflessness by their candidate, which demonstrates his or her nonpolitician qualities to voters.

Because voters are skeptical of politicians, all campaigns must address the character of their candidate. This issue should be sharpest for campaigns whose candidate is unfamiliar to voters. Incumbents and other high-profile politicians have had ample opportunity to make themselves known to candidates before the campaign. Incumbents likely established their character to voters in their initial run for office. Incumbents have also had the opportunity to use their time in office, and requisite publicity that comes with it, to make further character appeals to voters. Challenging candidates, especially those who are newcomers to politics and who are not well known to voters, must introduce themselves to voters. Voters, knowing only that they are running for office, will begin by assuming the candidate is a typical politician.

Campaigns cannot rely on voters to know what their candidates have done in their past. At the beginning of every campaign, each candidate is somewhat unfamiliar to even very knowledgeable voters. Even campaigns for long-serving and well-known incumbents, though advantaged by voter familiarity with their candidate, must introduce their candidates and their recent accomplishments to voters. Further, campaigns must develop their candidate's credibility first before then having the credibility to discuss various issue stands in detail.

Reinforcing Issue Positions

Voters are uncertain of what candidates will do if elected to office. Formal models have found that uncertainty can have a substantial effect on whether an individual votes for his or her preferred candidate (Alvarez 1997, ch. 3; Enelow and Hinich 1981; Hinich and Munger 1997, ch. 6).[2] These models find voters discount the benefits they believe they will receive from a candidate in proportion to their uncertainty about that candidate (Alvarez 1997, ch. 3; Hinich and Munger 1997, ch. 6). Empirical evidence provides strong confirmation for the findings of these formal models. When voters are uncertain about the issue positions or the traits of a particular candidate, they will regard that candidate less favorably (McGraw, Hasecke, and Conger 2003; Glasgow and Alvarez 2000). Regardless of whether a voter is uncertain about a candidate's issue positions, trait characteristics, or both, uncertain voters are less likely to vote for that candidate (Alvarez 1997). In fact, uncertainty can have a similar effect to issue distance in determining an individual's vote choice (Bartels 1986; Gill 2005).

As a result, campaigns have a strong incentive to emphasize the issue positions of their candidate in an effort to increase voter certainty. Franklin (1991) finds that campaigns can increase voters' perceptions of the clarity of their candidate's issue positions by emphasizing those issues. But the incentive for campaigns to reduce voter uncertainty conflicts with another incentive—to remain ambiguous in their issue stands (Shesple 1972; Page 1976; 1978; Enelow and Hinich 1981).

There are several explanations for why ambiguity provides strategic and tactical advantages to candidates and campaigns. First, campaigns do not want to offend voters by advocating an issue position that takes a clear position and risks alienating a significant number of potential voters who hold a different position (Shepsle 1972, 565). Thus their "best strategy is to avoid issues of a divisive sort," and they should instead "devote all [their] time, money, and energy to matters of consensus" (Page 1976, 749). Second, ambiguity provides strategic advantages over their opponent; a campaign that takes definitive issue positions early provides a clear target for their opponent to attack over the course of the campaign (Meirowitz 2005).[3] Third, campaigns that remain ambiguous maintain flexibility in policy choices once their candidate takes office (Alesina and Cukierman 1990; Aragones and Neeman 2000).

For all of these reasons, campaigns are loath to be specific in their issue positions during a campaign. In his 1978 book *Choices and Echoes in Presidential Elections*, Benjamin Page describes the frequency of ambiguity in presidential campaign rhetoric (152): "Indeed, the most striking feature of candidates' rhetoric about policy is its extreme vagueness. The typical campaign speech says virtually nothing specific about policy alternatives; discussions of the issue are hidden away in little-publicized statements and position papers. Even the most extended discussions leave many questions unanswered. In short, policy stands are infrequent, inconspicuous, and unspecific. Presidential candidates are skilled at appearing to say much while actually saying little."

Page (1978, 152–91) then describes the skill with which presidential candidates of the late 1960s and 1970s avoided taking specific stands while making statements of seemingly great import. When these candidates did discuss their stands on the issues of the day, candidates were rarely fully specific. Page writes, "In these respects—intention, timing, direction, and magnitude—candidates' proposals almost always fall far short of clarity" (163–64). Today's campaigns for the U.S. House and Senate are just as skilled in avoiding specifics in their television advertisements as the presidential campaigns of the 1960s and 1970s (Sides 2006; Arbour n.d.).

Using candidate-centered messages provides campaigns a way to give the perception of certainty to voters while remaining ambiguous. In particular, talking about a candidate's past actions that achieved policy goals provides "certain" information about the candidate's past while maintaining future ambiguity. Rather than saying, "Smith supports tax cuts," a campaign can say, "Smith fought for tax cuts in

Washington." An appeal that discusses the past political action of the candidate shows not only that the candidate advocates the particular position, but that they back up their position by action on an issue. In demonstrating past action, in showing what the candidate has done, such a message is more credible and trustworthy to voters.

Demonstrating Competence

Voters want to elect candidates who are not only sincere, trustworthy, and credible, but also ones that will actually be able to implement policy positions. They also want officeholders to know how to do the job. In other words, voters prize competence in their elected officials. Popkin argues that "voters care about the competence of the candidate, not just the candidate's issue positions, because they do not follow most government activity and because they care about what the candidate can deliver from government" (61).

Voters tend to care about the competence of their candidates for three reasons. First, officeholders make policy, which can deliver benefits to particular constituencies. Voters want a candidate who they think will successfully deliver benefits to them. Second, voters want candidates who are competent at managing the country, who understand its problems and use their knowledge and judgment to make good decisions about how to solve these problems. The third reason candidates want competent candidates who can deal with problems that cannot be anticipated at election time. For each of these reasons, voters want a candidate who has experience, knowledge, and expertise that fit with the job being sought and the issues of concern.

Campaigns whose candidate has an advantage in experience, knowledge, or expertise over an opponent have a valence advantage. Stokes (1963, 373) sees valence issues as those that link a party or candidate "with some condition that is positively or negatively valued by the electorate." Competence, the ability to successfully achieve the goals one has set out and to manage the affairs of the office being sought, is clearly a condition positively valued by the electorate. When a campaign has such an advantage, they should of course exploit that advantage by highlighting the valence issue. How would a campaign do so with a competence advantage? Popkin argues that "voters could assess the competence of a candidate by assessing how well he or she has dealt with past administrative and legal problems and then extrapolate from that performance to how the candidate would manage the affairs of the state" (62). So a campaign for an experienced incumbent might highlight their candidate's substantial accomplishments in office and emphasize how their candidate's power produces benefits for their district. The campaigns for a candidate with substantial private-sector experience might emphasize the special knowledge the candidate has gained on, say, education, as a teacher, or in balancing budgets and creating jobs, if a business owner. So campaigns that have a valence advantage on a particular issue or trait would be sure to use it.

Candidate-Centered Issue Agendas

I have discussed the different goals that campaigns might have in using candidate-centered appeals, identifying the multiple ways that campaigns can use these appeals. But candidate-centered appeals can also not only affect the framing campaigns use to talk about issues, but also the issue themselves. As Sellers (1998, 170) argues, "Candidates win more favorable evaluations if they focus on their records." And as suggested above, a focus on the record of a candidate helps a campaign by highlighting character, developing certainty, or demonstrating competence.

But the goal for voters is not just to put into office competent people of high character, but to put into office competent people of high character who can improve their lives in some way. A good story is not enough (ask John McCain). Instead, the architects of campaign messages want to connect candidate-centered information to a particular issue and policy agenda. When candidate-centered messages match well with a campaign's issue agenda, consultants find their messages most effective. When the match between background and issues is tenuous, the messages are less successful.

The issue agenda of a political campaign is not fixed. Instead, campaigns tend to highlight favorable issues and make them the basis for voters' decisions. Political scientists have noted the effectiveness of this strategy from the earliest studies of political behavior. In *Voting*, Berelson, Lazarsfeld, and McPhee argue that "it is difficult to change people's preferences; it is easier to affect the priorities and weights they give to subpreferences bearing on the central decision" (206). John Petrocik (1996, 826) argues that the "critical difference among elections . . . is the problem concerns of the voters not their policy attitudes" (826), and thus campaigns have an "effect when a candidate successfully frames the vote choice as a decision to be made in terms of problems facing the country that he is better able to 'handle' than his opponent" (826). In Petrocik's model, campaigns should highlight issues on which their candidate has a handling advantage over their opponent. How do these handling advantages originate? Petrocik posits that they come from two sources: "ownership of problems is conferred by the record of the incumbent and the constituencies of the parties" (827).

Many scholars have utilized Petrocik's views on issue handling to assess how individual campaigns use their party's handling advantages to shape their issue agenda. In doing so, they have not taken seriously that ownership can also be "conferred by the record" of candidates for office. Here, I take up that challenge. As shown above, focusing on candidate-centered messages provides a series of benefits to campaigns, benefits they want to exploit to the fullest. Suppose a candidate has a reputation on health care. Maybe he or she sponsored a health-care expansion bill in the state legislature or is a doctor who is running for public office. It seems like political malpractice for their consultants not to emphasize health care as a key issue.

Highlighting issues that candidates own based on their personal reputation provides a credible and effective method to demonstrate their candidate's sincerity and credibility to voters. When a candidate has a favorable reputation on an issue, their campaign will seek to highlight that issue to voters.

Candidate-Centered Appeals and Voters

This chapter has spelled out a logic for why background appeals should hold particular benefits for campaigns and has explained why such appeals should be so common in political communication. At the heart of this logic is that candidate-centered appeals increase favorable perceptions of candidates among voters and, as a result, campaigns benefit by employing such appeals. Candidate-centered appeals are effective because they develop the candidate's credibility in the minds of voters. The credibility of the source matters a great deal in determining the persuasiveness of a message, and campaigns use candidate-centered appeals in an effort to make their candidate's messages credible.

Researchers who have examined source credibility in communications, marketing, and psychology find that the dimensions of "expertise and trustworthiness" can be affected (Pornpitakpan 2004, 244). Candidate-centered information can influence perceptions of both of these elements. Candidate-centered appeals can affect perceptions of trust by focusing on the character of the candidate and by reinforcing a candidate's issue position. Information about candidates themselves helps assure voters that a candidate has their best interests at heart and that their commitment to solving an issue is rooted in genuine concern, not electoral expediency. In addition, candidate-centered appeals can increase favorable perceptions of a candidate's competence, by highlighting past accomplishments. Regardless of the goal of a message, voters should regard candidates more favorably when they receive a message with a candidate-centered appeal.

Hypotheses

I have outlined why campaigns would want to use candidate-centered appeals. The question is, do they? Now I will detail the specific hypotheses I have developed based on the theoretical expectations developed above. The discussion of these hypotheses includes a discussion of the data I collected to test them.

First, the basic argument is that campaigns will use candidate-centered appeals with great frequency in an effort to develop the credibility of their candidate. To test whether this is true, I start at the beginning—the beginning of a campaign that is. Hypothesis 1 holds that the candidate stands at the center of message development. As discussed, campaigns evaluate the background, experiences, accomplishments, and political record (where applicable) of their candidate as an important (if not the most important) factor in developing their campaign message. Testing this hypothesis is not a straightforward calculation of specific factors and the weights to attach to them. The process is based much more on the feel of each consultant, based on their experience, their judgment of each particular candidate, and their understanding of the ever-changing political conditions. To examine the details of the message-development process, I conducted interviews with a sample of political consultants who are involved with planning and executing campaign messages.

I have outlined why campaigns might want to use candidate-centered appeals, and campaigns may intend to do so at the beginning stages of a campaign, but the question remains whether they actually do so. So hypothesis 2 holds that political campaigns should use candidate-centered appeals in real-world messages frequently. By "frequently," I mean that candidate-centered appeals will occur in a majority of a campaign's appeals to voters. And for real-world message, I examine the texts of campaign advertisements from U.S. House and Senate candidates, assessing how often they use candidate-centered appeals. Examining House and Senate candidates provides for broad variation in candidate status, electoral competitiveness, and the background and experience of candidates to allow for generalizable conclusions. Thus a finding that campaigns focus on their candidate across a multitude of districts, states, political consultants, and candidates would only strengthen my conclusions.

In addition to assessing whether campaigns use candidate-centered appeals, I also want to examine for what purpose they use them. I previously identified three reasons for campaigns to use candidate-centered appeals: to highlight the character of the candidates, to reinforce the issue positions of the candidates, and to demonstrate the competence of their candidates. The most important of these should be highlighting character. All candidates are, by definition, politicians. As a result, all campaigns have to deal with trying to demonstrate their candidate's character to the voting public. Thus, hypothesis 3 holds that character-based appeals will be the most common form of candidate-centered appeals.

I also discuss the effect of candidate-centered appeals on the issue agendas of political campaigns. I do this first by investigating the use of *personal issues*, such as biography, political record, and personal values. Campaigns have different imperatives based on the status of their candidate. Thus, hypothesis 4 holds that challenging and open-seat campaigns are more likely to employ advertisements that focus on biography and personal values, while incumbent campaigns will focus more on their candidate's political record. Again, I use campaign advertising data to test this hypothesis, assessing what issues are discussed in each advertisement.

Finally, I turn to voters and assess the impact of candidate-centered appeals on their target. As discussed, I argue that campaigns benefit from candidate-centered appeals by improving perceptions of their candidate's sincerity and effectiveness. To test this, I conducted an experiment. In the experiment, respondents viewed a mock direct-mail flyer advertising a hypothetical congressional candidate. While the candidate and the issue position were held constant, I varied the framing of the appeal to voters. Hypothesis 5 holds that respondents who learned candidate-centered information about a hypothetical candidate will regard that candidate more favorably than those respondents in the control group, who received only policy-based information about the candidate.

Conclusion

This chapter has put forth the argument that political campaigns benefit when they use candidate-centered appeals. I have sketched out the logic for this argument, explaining not only why campaigns want to make candidate-centered appeals, but how they do so. I also developed a testable definition of candidate-centered appeals and sketched out a series of hypotheses and tests of my argument.

The next five chapters will examine this argument empirically. These chapters will examine how important candidate-centered messages really are to political campaigns and what type of campaigns make what type of candidate-centered appeals. The evidence presented in these chapters will demonstrate the strength, or weakness, of the argument presented here.

CHAPTER 3

CANDIDATES AND CAMPAIGN
PLANNING

Political candidates bring their own particular set of experiences with them, and their campaigns will often discuss the same characteristics repeatedly. The classic example of this is John McCain. The key event of John McCain's life was his capture, imprisonment, and torture by the North Vietnamese while serving as a naval fighter pilot. The event demonstrated McCain's heroism and service to his country, and no other candidate he ever encountered could top his biography.

Not surprisingly, McCain campaigns highlighted his biography with great frequency; it was an irresistible asset for them. In McCain's first political campaign, one of his advertisements showed McCain delighting in breathing the clean Arizona air, in contrast to the air of the Hanoi Hilton. In that campaign, McCain responded to criticism that he had not lived in the district long enough by saying, "I wish I could have had the luxury, like you, of growing up and living and spending my entire life in a nice place like the First District of Arizona, but I was doing other things. As a matter of fact, when I think about it now, the place I lived longest in my life was Hanoi" (Nowicki and Muller 2007).

I noted in the first chapter how McCain used his 2008 acceptance speech to highlight his service in Vietnam and to explain how his capture and imprisonment made him belong to his country, rather than himself. McCain's Vietnam service provided a theme that ran throughout his 2000 and 2008 primary campaigns and the 2008 general election. McCain was able to root his stands in favor of campaign finance reform (2000) and in favor of the surge in Iraq (2008) in love of country (as opposed to political expediency) through the use of his biography. Even McCain's campaign slogans—"no surrender," "country first"—and the star on his campaign signs recalled military themes for voters.

McCain's campaign strategy shows the enduring importance of biography as a central element of candidate-centered appeals. Whenever McCain had a difficult campaign, he relied heavily on his heroic biography as a key campaign asset. It demonstrated McCain's love of country to all voters, regardless of campaign context. The consistency with which McCain campaigns used his biography as a campaign asset shows that candidate-centered themes can be important to establishing constancy and reliability for a candidate across elections. Further, the conduct of the 2008 McCain presidential campaign shows how candidate-centered themes can bridge the distinct but not separate message strategies used in primary and general election campaigns.

In March and April of 2008, the McCain campaign took a "biography" tour across the United States. The timing here is important. At this moment, McCain had recently clinched the Republican nomination, while the Democratic fight between Barack Obama and Hillary Clinton would go until the end of primary season in 2008. McCain had a two-month opportunity to exclusively address general-election voters while Obama and Clinton still had to focus on the Democratic electorate in specific states. McCain's campaign thus had a head start for the general election. And what did the McCain campaign do with this head start? They discussed their candidate.

The biography tour took McCain to places across the country that had particular resonance in McCain's life story. On Monday, March 31, McCain went to Meridian, Mississippi—his family's ancestral home and not far from McCain Field, the airstrip at the local naval air station named for his grandfather—and highlighted his family's long history of military service. "My grandfather was an aviator; my father a submariner," McCain said. "They were my first heroes . . . They gave their lives to their country, and taught me lessons about honor, courage, duty, perseverance and leadership" (Shear 2008). At his high school, in Arlington, Virginia, on April 1, McCain lauded his high school teacher William Ravenel, saying, "I have never forgotten the confidence Mr. Ravenel's praise and trust in me gave me. Nor have I forgotten the man who praised me." According to McCain, "I will always believe that there is a Mr. Ravenel somewhere for every child who needs him" (O'Keefe 2008). At the U.S. Naval Academy (his college alma mater) on April 2, McCain focused on the obligations of citizenship, arguing that "for too many Americans, the idea of good citizenship does not extend beyond walking into a voting booth every two or four years and pulling a lever" (Jackson 2008).

McCain gave his most detailed speech during his biography tour in Jacksonville, Florida, on April 3. McCain had been stationed there at Cecil Field Naval Air Station before and after his service, capture, and imprisonment in Vietnam. His speech focused on the lessons he had learned in his service in the Vietnam War and the sacrifices made by those who fight for their county. "If glory can be found in war, it is a different concept altogether," McCain said. "It is a hard-pressed, bloody and soiled glory, steely and forbearing. It is decency and love persisting amid awful degradation, in unsurpassed suffering, misery and cruelty. It is the discovery that we belong to something bigger than ourselves." In discussing how he "hates" war but finds it necessary, McCain hoped to use the credibility he had developed as a war hero to show voters he would be a wise commander-in-chief, willing to use force only reluctantly, because he knew well the ravages of war (Kormanik 2008).

According to campaign manager Rick Davis, the objective of the biography tour was "to tell how Senator McCain's life experience has shaped his values—values we firmly believe will resonate," said Rick Davis, his campaign manager (quoted in the Institute of Politics 2009).

In this chapter, I interview political consultants who craft campaign messages on a regular basis and examine how they go about this work. Much like Rick Davis of the McCain campaign, the consultants I talked with focus heavily on selling who the candidate is to voters. Campaigns want to show voters the core values of their candidate, and they usually demonstrate this by discussing the life experience of their candidate. They argue that they must do so in order to develop the credibility of their candidate. The McCain campaign hoped to show that McCain's policy commitments were rooted deeply in his values and that he would be a wise and prudent decision maker in the Oval Office. As the interviews with a wide variety of consultants in this chapter show, the strategy of the McCain campaign was not a particular adaptation to McCain's heroic biography, but a consistent strategy used across a wide variety of political campaigns.

This chapter thus tests the theoretical arguments made in the first two chapters. I have discussed why we should expect political campaigns to use candidate-centered appeals with great frequency and that the focus on candidate-centered appeals has significant meaning for how political campaigns are conducted and the relationship between candidates (i.e., future officeholders) and voters. Here, I

Interviewing Political Consultants

I examined how political consultants determine the messages they want to transmit to voters by directly asking consultants how they determine their messages. I conducted a series of interviews with those who develop the messages that campaigns transmit to voters. Interview research allows for an open-ended process of learning the various factors that go into these decisions, provides for a sense of the relative importance of these different factors, and allows one to maximize one's understanding of context and nuance (Fenno 1986; Aberbach and Rockman 2002). Studying campaign messages requires a great deal of understanding of context and nuance.

I conducted 26 semistructured interviews between February and November 2006 with consultants primarily involved in developing campaign messages.[1] The interview sample is evenly split between Democrats and Republicans.[2]

I designed the questionnaire in an effort to learn in general about campaign message development and did not ask questions that would tip off interview subjects to my interest in candidate-centered appeals. I also tried to ask similar questions to each interview subject. These questions focused on broad questions about the campaigns' message-development processes. I also asked each respondent the same question at the beginning of each interview—"What process do you go through with each candidate to decide the theme of the campaign and the message of individual communications?"—in order to avoid biasing the interview by focusing on candidate-centered appeals. I recorded all but eight of the interviews, with the permission of the subjects. I asked no questions about specific campaigns, but only general questions about campaign messages.[3] Each interview subject agreed that I could quote anything from the interview. Due to legal and privacy concerns, I do not use their names in this book.[4]

Credibility and a Skeptical Public

Voters are skeptical of politicians. "[The average voter] thinks politics is strange, bizarre, corrupt, and wrong. They're not into it," says a Republican media consultant. "They think [politicians are] just selling me—that he's going to cut taxes, when they don't. That he's going to stop crime, when he won't." A Texas Democratic consultant believes that voters start by thinking the worst of candidates: "To put yourself out in the public, most people just don't do. So if you're going to [run for office], they think that you are egotistical or power hungry or there's a financial motive." In general, "people have a downgraded view of politicians," according to a Republican consultant.

So when voters hear a political message, they discount it. Some voters think one political message is just like any other and tune it out. "Once [voters] hear something, it's real easy to go, 'Oh yeah, same old, same old; they're just like the rest of them,'" says a Texas-based Democrat. A California Democrat concurs: "Voters are not inspired by a mail piece just on health care; it looks like all the others." A local Democratic consultant finds the same thing among voters: "Nowadays, everything is poll driven. So you're almost sounding like your opponent or like every other person from your party. I think the voter just discounts that as campaign rhetoric." A Democratic campaign manager says voters see all politicians as the same: "I think they will lump them all together, if they are yelling at each other. Voters will say, 'God, they're just like politicians.' And they're disgusted by that."

Campaigns do not want voters to ignore their message, but ignorance is better than the alternative—distrust. Voters can regard political promises as nothing but cheap talk, meaningless after Election Day. "In general, people don't like politicians. The lack of trust of elected politicians, all the way across the board, is big," says a Democratic consultant. An Oklahoma-based Republican puts it more succinctly. "Voters can spot a phony from miles away. If a candidate is not authentic, voters can figure it out pretty quickly."

A former director of a state Republican Party gives a simple explanation for voter skepticism: "People have been lied to so many times by politicians who will tell them anything to get into office; they've seen it so many times." A national Republican media consultant says that the expectations placed upon incumbents make them particularly vulnerable to voter distrust: "If you're an incumbent and say, 'I'm for tax cuts,' but you have no record of it, then you're a hypocrite . . . That's a dangerous position to put yourself in."

In general, voters believe they are impervious to campaign messages. "They're skeptical," a Democratic consultant says. "They want to think that they don't believe anything that politicians and campaigns say. No one wants to believe that they are persuaded." The most important assumption that consultants make is that voters do not a priori believe the messages of political campaigns. As consultants introduce new candidates, or reintroduce candidates who have run before, the challenge is to identify a message strategy that can overcome the cynicism and distrust of voters. They must make voters believe in the sincerity of their candidate.

Credibility, Authenticity, and Likability

Essential to overcoming voter skepticism is demonstrating the trustworthiness of their candidate. "Credibility is just everything; you can only comment and be convincing on what you've got credibility at," says a Texas-based operative. Voters are quite skillful in their ability to assess the credibility of a campaign message. "The remarkable thing about voters everywhere is that we have this gut instinct or this screening process of what's credible and what's not credible . . . It's something that's clearly ingrained in everybody," says a Republican direct-mail consultant. Campaigns must first demonstrate that credibility before voters will listen to their candidate's message. "The most important value that's reflected is authenticity to the public. The public will get a sense of it," says a consultant who worked on multiple presidential campaigns.

Voters want authenticity from their politicians because, despite their skepticism, they want to believe in politicians. "While we're really cynical in our crust, deep down we're looking for someone to inspire and motivate us," says a Democratic consultant. Political consultants have an image as hard-bitten, cynical political lifers who will say anything to win. But important to them is identifying candidates who can inspire and motivate voters. Not surprisingly, the consultants see electoral advantages in their desire for inspiration and motivation—candidates who can accomplish these two goals can overcome voter skepticism. Campaigns must demonstrate to voters "who [the candidate is] in their gut. It's important to understand that gut value they convey and who they are," says a national Republican consultant. "I want somebody whose ambition is not just to have the title and the office. I want somebody who's got something they want to do, something that's driving them beyond the ambition of office," says a Texas-based Democrat. "Are they passionate?" another Democratic consultant asks. "Are they really going to go and be able to give people confidence in what they are saying?" A Republican says that consultants "want to understand why [their candidate] want[s] this position," so they find the most effective way to convey that rationale to voters.

How do campaigns demonstrate their candidate's authenticity and passion to voters? The first step is to make voters like their candidate.

Campaigns want to make a candidate look more normal, more like the people he or she wants to represent, and less like a caricature of a "typical politician." "The only real magic to any campaign is how you make a candidate look human and sincere," says a Democratic consultant. Consultants need to make voters see the similarities between themselves and the candidate. "You have to have something that connects with the people . . . have something that somebody can say, 'God, that's a great guy. He's like me,'" says a local Republican consultant. By making a candidate look human, sincere, and like the voter, campaigns hope to get voters to pay attention to their candidate. "Before anybody cares about your position, they have to trust you and like you. There is a likability and credibility threshold that a candidate must cross before people will listen to their issue positions," says a Republican media consultant.

What is the key way for campaigns to demonstrate their candidate's likability? A Democratic consultant argues that candidates do this through demonstrating their concern to voters.

> There's got to be a certain empathy that people see in you. It's not just that you want to solve their problem. But you've got to know what [their problems] are. It is that level of empathy that gives them assurance that you might get it done because you seem to understand. I think their first take on you had better be how much you know about what they need. And I think that's how you earn their trust to start with.

Another Democrat believes that campaigns need to make voters believe that candidates are similar to themselves: "You've got to say, 'I'm not a politician; my name [is this]. This is my life. These are my kids.' You've got to communicate that this is a personal thing. You have to be a friend, rather than a sleazy politician." A New York–based Democrat sums up this rational succinctly: "Likability is as important as capability."

Consultants argue that demonstrating concern is more important than taking a specific issue position because voters lack detailed information about specific issues. "A typical voter doesn't really care about the ins and outs and the nitty-gritty of that issue. Because you've got a family and a job and other concerns in your life. What you care about is that the candidate can communicate a concern for that same issue. That's all you care about. And then, you give him or her your vote and ask him or her to go off and solve that problem," says a Texas-based Democrat. The average voter "just wants the candidate to say something brief that communicates that they get it and that they share your values."

In many ways, this quote imitates the political science understanding of how voters come to acquire data, as expressed in *The Reasoning Voter*. Voters learn about political information as a "by-product of activities they pursue as part of their daily lives" (Popkin 1994, 23). Campaigns seek to connect an "issue to a candidate" and the "issue and the benefits [voters] care about" (Popkin 1994, 100). Campaigns can only do this by making their candidate authentic and likeable. The need for these characteristics means that campaigns cannot "pull any wool over the eyes of the public," says a Republican consultant. "They are so sophisticatedly smart. If I don't sell a candidate the right way, they're going to be on me. So you can't get away with much." A Republican media consultant agrees: "Voters are really smart. It's really hard to fool the public . . . You have to know what your candidate is about. You don't want to have to reinvent someone." A national Republican concurs with the idea that "you can't fool the public" because "people know [if your candidate is authentic]." The public's sophistication in spotting insincerity and phoniness compels campaigns to hew close to the candidate's true self. "You can't be somebody you're not," says that consultant. "Your message has to be real." A local Democratic consultant also agrees that campaigns cannot fool the voters: "You can only shade people really here or there. You can't really tell the voters they're someone they don't believe who they are."

The key first assumption of political consultants is that they must demonstrate the sincerity and likability of their candidate to voters. Plus, consultants do not believe that they can fake these elements. Consultants join political scientists (see Popkin 1994) in believing that, while voters may not have a detailed understanding of complex policy proposals and positions, they do a better job reading people. Thus, campaigns need to sell people, not policy. They must first convince voters that their candidate is as trustworthy and likeable as their neighbors. The important question for campaigns is how to do this.

STORYTELLING

While political consultants have a seemingly daunting challenge in trying to make their candidate seem authentic and likeable enough to overcome a skeptical electorate, they are unified in their belief of the best way to meet this challenge—by telling voters stories that demonstrate the core beliefs of their candidate.

"Messages are about telling a story," says a Republican media consultant. "You need to try to demonstrate to voters who your candidate is. And to do this, you need to tell a story." Consultants used that same phrase—"who your candidate is," or variants of it—frequently.[5] And the paramount importance of storytelling as a means to connect candidates and voters. "What we like to do is to get them to talk about their own personal story because, ultimately, that's we have to tell—their story," says a Republican consultant. "You start with the narrative," says a Democratic campaign manager. "You need to tell their story. [Candidates] all need a narrative in some form, and [voters] want to know who you are."

For consultants, the goal of telling stories about their candidate is to demonstrate their candidate's sincerity. Consultants would like these stories to provide evidence from past actions taken by the candidate that explain the candidate's motivation and values. A Republican consultant says, "Where it really connects is that we do it based on some incident. We like a tipping point in their life; we like to find a rationale . . . So, [finding a story] connected to somebody's real life experience is the best way to show that somebody's values are legitimate."

Campaign messages must complement the story of their candidate, or they will fall flat. A national Republican consultant says, "You can't plan [your message] divorced from the realities of your own candidate. You can't come up with some things, and then it's like, 'Why is this candidate talking about whatever, when he's never dealt with it?' You must have that context—who the candidate is, what strength or weaknesses they have—and see how that fits with the theme of the campaign." A Democratic consultant says that if campaigns cannot tell a good story about their candidate, they cannot overcome voter skepticism. "You can think of candidates that don't match their life experience. You see it quickly, and it doesn't make sense. It doesn't ring true to folks."

Consultants argue that stories work for two reasons. The first is that they enhance their candidate's authenticity to voters. "The history of a candidate says, 'This is what I've done. These are facts that show who I am.' Many voters, particularly swing voters, vote for the person—not the candidate or the politician, but the person. When you personify the candidate with their story, it is very, very beneficial," says a Texas-based Democrat. "People will see through them. They've got to be who they are," says a Democratic consultant.

These stories also work because they make the candidate seem more like a friend or neighbor, and less like a politician. "The way that you connect with an average voter is through a story. You really connect in an effort to say, 'You're what you care about,'" says a Republican consultant. According to a local Democratic consultant, voters in focus groups he conducted "wanted to know about candidates and the story that they bring. And then, they also wanted [the story] presented to them in an interesting way." A national Republican says that he wants to "allow a candidate to tell a firsthand story . . . That helps tremendously, especially when that story is around an issue that voters care about." A Democratic consultant finds that stories about his candidates humanize them. "When you are able to tell stories of struggles and triumph, everybody relates to it. Everybody says, 'I have a cousin who did the same thing. I can relate to everything that you're telling me.' Now I've got a bond with person: this person and I have something that's in common. It's that initial bond that gets you to listen."

Why Candidate-Centered Appeals

To summarize the consultants, campaigns benefit by making candidate-centered appeals. Campaigns want to tell voters who their candidate is, and they use stories about the candidate as a way of demonstrating their candidate's sincerity and likability. "For voters, trust is everything. Trust is built on knowing who that candidate is. They're going to look back at all the different things that the candidate has done over the course of his life," said a Republican direct-mail consultant. A Democratic consultant finds that discussing candidates themselves is the most effective way to build a relationship with voters. "The personal background gives you more of a dimension and shows a candidate's values, like trust, honesty—those sorts of things. [Voters] are looking for somebody they can trust."

Consultants want to show voters who their candidate is by showing what he or she has done. A national Republican consultant finds that discussing his candidate's past actions is crucial to developing voter trust: "The background is only a place to give you credibility to fight the campaign over the theme and the things that voters are connected to. You're background should give you the credibility to talk about the issues." A California-based Democrat says, "If your [candidate's] history illustrates current priorities and values, then you want to jump into that" with your campaign messages. A candidate's background is so important to one Democratic consultant that he says, "When I start a campaign, the very first thing I do is write the campaign bio. That's how important it is to me. Because it is in the bio that I find the themes that will inform the messages in a campaign. And from the bio comes the theme of the campaign, the slogans, the messages, eventually the ads, and the basic stump speech. Everything comes from the bio."

Consultants identify three reasons why they want to make candidate-centered appeals to voters: to demonstrate what the candidate has in common with voter, to provide evidence of their candidate's political beliefs, and to show expertise and knowledge.

Showing Commonality

Consultants want to emphasize their candidate in their messages to voters in an effort to demonstrate their candidate's commitment to the issue. Voters assume that political candidates behave like stereotypical (read: two-faced, says only what people want to hear) politicians. Thus, campaigns must first build up perceptions of their candidate's sincerity. According to one local Democratic consultant, "People want someone they feel that they know and can trust. They want to trust them to make the right decisions. And the only way to cut through that is to make it seem as if that voter does know you and can trust you, rather than a straight-up litany of issues." A Republican direct-mail consultant agrees: "Voters feel like they need to trust a candidate, and trust is built on knowing who that candidate is." A national Republican believes that focusing on a candidate's past can demonstrate that candidate's priorities: "It's not only bio, but it's also who they are in their gut . . . It's much more important to understand the gut value they convey and who they are as reflected in some policy things. That's more important than anything else. All of those things add up to something, but all of those things should be a direction to a gut value that you're figuring out."

The key to developing trust is demonstrating the credibility of a candidate's concern for an issue, which is done by telling voters about a candidate's actions or accomplishments. One Democratic consultant is looking for a "story we can tell about the candidate that says, 'I understand this. I can deal with this issue in a serious way.'" Part of that understanding is demonstrating what the candidate and the voter have in common. Another Democrat says, "You've got some [voters] who ask, 'Why am I even listening to this person?' What's the hook that's going to get you to pay attention? [Candidate-centered information] allows them to say, 'I've got a lot in common with this person.'" By demonstrating what their candidate has in common with voters, consultants can develop trust between the two. "It's going to be how you grew up. It's going to be what professions you did and what experiences you've had . . . And if [voters] have a simple cue that they can use to say there's a trust factor, they'll take that cue," says a local Democratic consultant. A New York–based Democrat summarizes the importance of commonality: "From their legislative leaders, people want empathy. And they will ask, 'How does he fit in with us?'"

One method that consultants highlighted as a particularly useful means of developing common bonds was through understanding the demography of the district. "There's a variety of measures that [voters] use to decide who's most like me. In small towns and rural areas, it's a huge credibility factor that you're at least from a small town, from a rural area, as well," says a Democratic consultant. A local Democratic consultant is looking for "something that will give [voters] a cue that that's our guy. For example, did the candidate go to high school or work on a particular project in the district? What [makes people in] that area [say], 'Hey, that's my guy.' That makes it real."

Evidence of Political Beliefs

Consultants argue that a record in previous elective office provides credible evidence of a candidate's political beliefs. Candidate-centered appeals that focus on a candidate's accomplishments in public office leads voters to feel more certain that a candidate will meet campaign promises once in office. "Record is a validation of your beliefs," says a former state party executive. "And that's a pretty good validation. It's so much easier [for a campaign] to say, 'He deals with theory . . . but I've shown you. You know what you've got with me.' . . . The contrast isn't on the issue; the contrast is on the results." A Republican direct-mail consultant argues that an appeal that focuses on political record "says to the voter that I've done this before. Not only am I smart and I know what I'm talking about, but I've actually done it before."

The need for evidence of political belief is, not surprisingly, very important for incumbent candidates. "Every campaign you ever work in with an incumbent, you go back and say, 'We told them we were going to do this. Did we do it?' And then we come back and we do and we make sure we talk about it. So, yes, incumbents who say, 'I'm for tax cuts; I'm for cheaper health care,' have to have the record to prove it," says a Republican media consultant. A Democratic consultant says voters use a candidate's record not only to look back, but also to look forward. "With an incumbent, you're talking about some voting record, but you're also projecting it to the future. 'I've done this. Therefore, I will do this.' Rather than just, 'Reelect me because I did this.' If you leave that second part out, you're in danger."

Demonstrating Expertise

Consultants also use candidate-centered appeals to demonstrate their candidate's knowledge, ability, and competence. "What you look for in somebody's background is something that you can say, 'This is why I'm better prepared than this person. This is why I can get things done better than him,'" says one Democrat. Another Democrat finds that incumbents can use their accomplishments to connect to voters. "People can point to a state legislator or a city councilperson and say, 'They're the environmental guy. She's the parks lady. He's public safety person.' In that case, they kind of know what their issues are and where they're coming from." A third Democrat also sees qualifications as important components of background appeals: "A key factor is have you lived a life, have you had an experience that makes you more qualified than I am to go [to the Capitol] and vote for me and all my neighbors."

What consultants look for is the ability to connect a candidate's experience with an issue of concern in the election. "That's how you develop your message, or who you are. You relate your life experience before you ran for office to how you can make a difference and how you can apply that to being a good congressman or governor," says a Republican media consultant. Another Republican agrees: "Once the threshold of knowledge has been crossed, you can take their expertise and roll it into their messages."

Consultants thus argue that candidate-centered information is the most effective way to demonstrate "who your candidate is" and to overcome the skepticism and cynicism of voters. Campaigns need a credible candidate and seek to focus on the stories of that candidate. Focusing on the candidate also demonstrates a commitment to problem solving. "I'm looking for somebody who's realized that life's about more than themselves. And that they've been a participant in the community, in the state, in their local neighborhood. Is their biography available to the electorate?" says a Democratic consultant. In the end, candidate-centered appeals provide the best information about the core values of a candidate. "Everyone has choices to make. A person tells who they are in the choices they make," says a local Democratic consultant.

The Focus on Candidates

So far, consultants have argued that they face a skeptical electorate, that they must demonstrate the credibility of their candidate, and that stories about their candidate are the best mechanism to demonstrate that credibility. Consultants thus place candidates at the center of their efforts to develop a message for their clients.

Table 3.1 provides evidence for this. The initial question in the interview asked, "What process do you go through with each candidate/race to decide the theme of the campaign and the message of individual communications?" Of the consultants interviewed for this project, nineteen out of twenty-six mentioned their *candidate's biography* in their answer. This is more than twice as many as the eight who mentioned district factors, such as demographics, and three times the six who discussed the environment. In other words, the most important factor in developing a message for these consultants is the candidates themselves.

Some consultants gave multiple answers to the question, and consultants often think about particular elements of their message strategy in combination with the background of their candidate. Five consultants mentioned district factors *and* candidate biography, four combined *biography* and the environment, and two discussed not only their candidate's biography, but also the opponent's biography. So while there is diversity in what consultants consider the second most important factor, or the factor that goes along with

Table 3.1 Responses to Question: What process do you go through with each candidate/race to decide the theme of the campaign and the message of individual communications?

Response	N
Candidate Background	19
Combined with District Factors	5
Combined with Issue Environment	4
Combined with Opponent's Background	2
Combined with District *and* Issues	2
District Factors	8
Combined with Issues	2
Issue Environment	5
Combined with Campaign Mechanics	1
Opponent's Background	2
Campaign Mechanics (Money, Name Identification, etc.)	3

Note: N = 26; Multiple responses to the question were coded, so results do not add up to 26.

biography, there is consensus on the importance of candidates to message development.

As a result, consultants who craft campaign messages spend a great deal of effort, and use a variety of techniques, to learn about their candidate and to shape that information into a campaign message. According to a California-based Democrat, "The first step [to developing a campaign message] is finding out about your candidate and their background." An Oklahoma-based Republican says, "We need to spend time with the candidate. . . . You need to have a deep and thorough understanding of who that person is." Another Republican wants to know his candidate's life stories in great detail: "When we are first talking with the candidate, meeting with the candidate, we really shut up a lot and let them talk. And what we want them to do is, we'll say, 'Tell us about your family. How did you get started in this? What's your motivation for running?' You ask some very fundamental questions about their heart first, to know who they are as a human being."

A local Democratic consultant also participates in a long message meeting with his candidates. "When we're doing direct candidate work, we'll start with a two-and-a-half- to four-hour session, where you forget about what's politically smart and what you're going to say in front of people and just build an inventory of what [the candidate] can draw from." A Democratic consultant wants to hear the candidate tell his or her own story. "The first thing I'll do is ask the candidate to tell me their life story, in the most detailed lengthy way they can. If you don't have a half-an-hour life story, then you ought not be running for office."

Other consultants have a more formal process they go through with their candidates. A Republican media consultant goes through a questionnaire with his clients. "I ask them to tell me their life story," asking questions like, "Why do you want this job? What can you do for people? What are your strengths? . . . Most of the time, I ask them pretty standard stuff." A New York–based Democrat likes to "sit down and talk unscripted" with candidates to find out "where they're from, what they've accomplished, what their values are . . . I find that very useful. And then I pull out what's compelling."

Other consultants believe that it takes more time to truly understand their candidates and to identify background items to include in their message. A Republican direct-mail consultant says he likes to "spend an enormous amount of time trying to get inside the candidate's biography and look at the things that that candidate tells me are most important to him about his background, his personality, his character, and really delving into that. And then what shaped his political philosophy, and really delving into that." A Republican media consultant learns about his candidates by "spending a day or two with them. That way, I can learn what they're like—how they talk, how they give a speech . . . I want to just hang around and see them do a variety of activities so that I can get a sense of what they are like and how I can best present that to voters." For one local Democrat, message development "is a slow process. I don't think you can get it in an interview. That's why I like to start early with a campaign, even if I'm not actually going to produce anything for months on end. Because I want to start to learn more and more about that candidate."

A local Republican consultant evens goes so far as to "make my candidates write me an essay . . . Tell me your life story in five pages. I literally say write me a little book about you. Let me know who you are. I don't want to know where you stand on immigration. I want to know what affected you as a teenager to make you do what you did when you were twenty-five years old. What's the charity you were a part of? When did you have your first child? What was that experience like? When did you marry your wife? When did you meet her? What is your relationship with your parents? What did your dad teach you? Did you play sports in school? Were you in student government? Did you learn anything through that? Did it affect you? Those kinds of things. It's the only way you're going to learn about somebody, in my opinion, and to have an effective way of telling people . . . Find something that connects, that feels good in people."

By asking candidates detailed questions about their biographies, consultants hope to identify the elements of their candidate's background and life story that will quickly but comprehensively demonstrate to voters who their candidate is. One Democrat tries to identify, "number one, the strengths of your candidate. That's one of the first things that I do when talking to people: trying to find out what they do and why they're running." That consultant also wants to find "what their personal story is, that they can have other people relate to them." A Republican direct-mail consultant notes, "You have to remember that there is no message at the beginning of a race. It's more about your candidate and your candidate's philosophies. The first thing you want to do is define your candidates. You'll pick your adjectives. And say our goal is define him by these adjectives."

Combining Biography and Issues

Political consultants' focus on candidates and their backgrounds and stories stands in contrast to the focus of political scientists, which has traditionally been the issue content of campaign messages. Issue positions are indeed important to political campaigns, but consultants argue that their importance is in the context of the background of a candidate. Consultants use the background of their candidate to shape the messages that they transmit on the issue stands of their candidates.

Consultants argue that background information must come first in a campaign because, as noted previously, candidates must pass voters' thresholds for likeability and credibility. A national Republican also finds that "it becomes more credible if you filled in the candidate's [background] in a way that connects to your broad theme first." Only then "can you go on to the issues."

That national Republican consultant wants to include those candidate-centered elements as part of a campaign's broader message. "You may say that a gut value in this election is strength of leadership or compassion. Then you can go back and look at their background and see what they've done that would convey that ... You say what do we think this election is going to be about, and is it realistic or credible that our candidate fits that value that what we think it's about? And then what proof do we have that what he's done in his life or accomplished as a legislator makes people say, 'Yeah, I feel that in my heart, now I gotta get that into my head'?"

A local Democratic consultant says that he looks for elements of a candidate's background that fit together into a broader message: "The more important part is how you put yourself into your message. It's being able to share. It's having an inventory of anecdotes that you can draw from and make connections to. Because typically, if you spend a couple hours going through family stuff, going through role models, going through community and religious stuff, going through what they think is wrong or why they're running, you'll find that there are the same thematic values or principles."

A Republican consultant says that a campaign must first establish their candidate's credibility and likability before you can discuss the issues with voters. "The best way is to sell straight by going straight to their heart, by saying I'm going to tell a story about our guy. And then if you like our guy, you're going to listen to him. If you listen to him, you're going to pay attention to the next phase of our campaign, which is the issue phase ... You really want to start with that [background] phase to connect to those values that [voters] have in their heart and soul . . . Then after they like you, they're going to listen to you and vote for you."

Political consultants believe that information about the background and record of their candidate is essential to win the trust and confidence of voters. But background information itself is insufficient to win an election. "You cannot win a campaign just by virtue of 'I'm the better person because I graduated valedictorian,'" says a national Republican. "You have to take that and connect it to what you want to do in office." One local Democratic consultant concurs, "I don't think you can just run a campaign on one, two, three issues, without attaching it to a face and a story." Only through attaching their candidate's issue positions to voters' perceptions about the candidate can a campaign succeed. Retrospective information is not sufficient to win hearts, minds, and votes. Campaigns must connect the candidate's background to other campaign elements to use it in the most effective manner.

A California-based Democrat neatly summarizes the relationship between background and issues for political campaigns: "If you do pure issues without the candidate's story, you come across as flat. When you do a pure story without issues, it comes across as fluffy." Obviously, campaigns want to avoid both and combine background and issues to achieve a presentation that is both emotionally and intellectually compelling.

OTHER FACTORS

The consultants say they must combine the biography and record of their candidate with two other factors—district demography and issue salience—to develop the most effective message strategy. Consultants are seeking "a marriage between the background of the candidate, the people of a district, and the issues of a concern," according to one local Democratic consultant. Another Democrat concurs, finding that the ideal message includes "political environment times geography times the candidate bio. That would be sort of a simplistic formulation that would sort of instinctively go through." A Republican consultant says that knowing these three factors "will lead you to what your message is," as well as helping a campaign realize "what [their candidate's] strong points are or what areas they need to become stronger in."

A campaign must start by combining biography with demography. Candidates should focus relentlessly on local concerns, according to a Democratic consultant. "I find that it's better in convincing people to stay completely out of big issues, anything broader than neighborhood issues, practically. Keep it all down to where people know whether you know what you're talking about . . . If you can convince them that [of your knowledge on the topic], then you will expand your credibility with them." Another Democrat says it's vital for campaigns to not only "know the community," but also "knowing how to weave [your knowledge of the community] into your broader message." A Democratic campaign manager "You have to connect at some point with what [the local community] believe[s] . . . You have to bring it home to the district, and you have to bring it home to the candidate."

A Democratic consultant explains how this process works: "What you really want to do is match the community or the voters with your messenger. And how is it that [voters in a district] see themselves in that person, or they see their hopes and aspirations in that person . . . And you're using the record to expose character traits about somebody, either positive or negative. You're looking for things again that provide common experiences. It's the oldest cliché in politics to say, 'One of us: Joe Smith is one of us.' But without using the cliché, that's what you're trying to communicate." A Texas-based Democrat says, "You recruit a candidate who fits that general profile. You have to kind of keep the geography, the local issues, all of these things in mind." Another Democrat puts it in more succinct terms: "You've got to have the right candidate for the right district."

Another connection that campaigns must make is between their candidate's background and the issues of concern to voters. "I think that the best combination are those issues that people care about in this election and those on which your candidate can show authenticity and can speak about with passion," says a national Republican. Others share the perspective that campaigns must connect dry issues-based discussions to a more emotional pitch. "If you don't have authenticity" developed by discussions of who the candidate is, "you don't have credibility to talk about the issues," says an Oklahoma-based Republican. "There's a human story on every issue, so it's finding where you can connect on it and talk about it credibly," says a local Democratic consultant. "There's something in [the candidate's] history; there's something about who [the candidate] is as a man that we're going to translate into all of these issues in this campaign," says a Democratic campaign manager. A Republican media consultant says there is even a human side to discussion of an incumbent's political record. "You spend most of your time talking about your record or votes you made. You sometimes turn those into human issues and make them real." According to a Democratic consultant, the important goal is to find in a candidate "a biography that matches what he's saying" on the campaign trail.

That biography is insufficient should not be surprising; a candidate's biographical information or previous efforts will not, in and of themselves, produce any results for voters in the upcoming term of office. Appeals focused on a candidate's background and record do provide voters with an assurance of a candidate's concern, commitment, and capability. But as consultants argue, such qualities are only worthwhile if voters think they will lead to positive action once the candidate enters office.

Who Your Opponent Is

Political consultants point out one other important area where candidate-centered information is important—in attack messages. Just as they try to present positive information about "who their candidate is," campaigns are looking to attack opponents on evidence that shows "who your opponent is," in a negative light. "You would prefer to run a race that is a choice versus a referendum. So having an opponent who has a record is preferable because it allows you to say, 'This is who I am, and these are what I consider priorities. This is who my opponent is, and this is what his priorities clearly are because his record shows this,'" says a Republican direct-mail consultant. Central to showing who your opponent is, is thoroughly examining the political record of incumbents and candidates who have previously held political office. "You put them on the defensive. You go after their record and say, 'This guy voted for this and this and this.' He's got to defend himself," says a former state party executive.

If campaigns want to show who their opponent is, they cannot take obscure elements of their opponent's background and try to make a case out of that. "A sure loser is where somebody sets out to attack an opponent on less-than-credible research—or thin research. It's because voters see through it in the end," says a Republican consultant. A local Democratic consultant agrees: "I mean, if they vote on something that's meaningless, that doesn't get you anywhere. It's got to be some serious issue, where they just have taken the wrong tack."

What is important in your research, says one Democratic consultant, is to identify contradictions between your opponent's messages and actions. "If you can find something that is contrary to [your opponent's] message . . . And that way, voters say, 'Wait a minute'— for example, a candidate who runs on a very strong tort reform plank but has sued three or four people." The best attacks highlight actions by the opponent that are difficult to dismiss. "What you really want to find are the nuggets that really represent the man in full—that there are many areas where there is a similar flaw. What you want to do is you want to have the same story by hav[ing] multiple [pieces of evidence] . . . So the strongest punch is when you can say, 'He didn't do it once. He's a multiple offender,'" says a Republican consultant.

In order to make a case against an opponent, consultants need strong evidence from their opponent's past to make their attacks credible. In fact, negative messages need more evidence than positive messages. "Your evidentiary proof line is higher for a negative or a comparative ad than it is for a positive ad. It's higher, which is why more negative or comparative ads are more factual than positive ads. Because people are initially skeptical," says a national Republican. According to a local Democratic consultant, evidence gives "a depth of assurance that this is true. It just gives it that much more credibility. So we just would not do something that we couldn't put good, clear public documentation to."

Good, clear public documentation is important not just as evidence, but because it comes from a neutral party. Neutral sources allow voters to see evidence as unbiased, and thus, they give such evidence more credibility. "It typically does help to have documentation to show that what you are saying is true or that people can go find that out themselves. You need to have, at least, third-party affirmation about the charge. Whether that's just a headline—that the charge has been made makes it more legitimate. It can just be a citation of a House record vote number," says a Texas-based Democrat. A Republican consultant also sees the value of neutral sources. "You have to use third-party sources for your credibility. It's credible as long as someone else says it. Those third-party sources are critical to get."

Conclusion

The consultants interviewed in this chapter make one point clear—for candidates to talk to voters about the future, they must start with the past. The John McCain campaign did this, highlighting their candidate's past as a means to demonstrate his commitment to his country. As hypothesized in chapter 2, information about candidates themselves is indeed a priority for political campaigns in developing their message; in fact, it is the highest priority.

Just like the John McCain campaign did, other political campaigns use candidate-centered appeals as a means of developing their candidate's credibility. Consultants agree that voters are skeptical of campaign messages. Even when voters are not skeptical, campaign messages have difficulty breaking through the clutter of everyday life. To break through voters' filters, campaigns must tell the story of their candidate in a way that makes him or her seem authentic and likeable. Information from a candidate's background and record provides the evidentiary basis for these stories, showing a candidate's concerns, political beliefs, and competence to voters. But information about a candidate's values and past concerns on an issue are not sufficient to win an election; campaigns must connect stories about their candidate to the people of a district and their issues of concern.

In chapter 2, I argued that the theory of source credibility holds that the more an individual believes in the trustworthiness and expertise of the source of a communication, the more positive their evaluation of that sources' opinion will be (Hovland and Weiss 1951; Sternthal, Phillips, and Dholakia 1978). The parallels between the findings of political science research on source credibility and the message-development strategies of political consultants are clear and stark.

First, credibility is obviously central to both. If candidates cannot demonstrate their credibility to voters, consultants believe they have no chance of emerging victorious on Election Day. And in both, credibility is given by the recipient. Candidates must demonstrate to voters that they are worthy of receiving the voters' trust. Second, credibility is enhanced in both when recipients perceive themselves as having something in common with a source. Political consultants use candidate-centered appeals to show what candidates have in common with the voters they hope to represent. Third, if a source can demonstrate expertise, a recipient will regard him or her more favorably. Again, consultants use candidate-centered appeals to demonstrate their candidate's competence and fitness to serve in office.

Because credibility is so central to the messages that political campaigns transmit to voters, campaigns highlight the background of their candidates. The need to connect to their candidate's biography or political record affects what issues a campaign can credibly discuss and, more importantly, how campaigns can talk about issues. Candidates whose experience and expertise does not lend itself to discussing an issue with expertise are at a disadvantage against opponents with more relevant experience. Political scientists have found that the national issue agenda, partisan-owned issues, and district demographics are key factors in determining the "issue agendas" of campaigns (Sides 2006; Sulkin and Evans 2006; Kaplan, Park, and Ridout 2006). The findings in this chapter show that campaigns consider these factors in determining what issues to emphasize, but they consider them primarily through the prism of their candidate's background. Without doing so, they cannot credibly connect to voters.

To put it another way, the background and record of their candidate constrains the messages that political campaigns can transmit to voters. Political consultants can change their candidates only around the margins, identifying the best stories and best evidence that demonstrate who the candidate is, using the techniques of modern media to highlight their message. But in the end, "who your candidate is" determines the message of a campaign.

CHAPTER 4

THE USE OF
CANDIDATE-CENTERED APPEALS

In the 2012 Massachusetts Senate race, Democrats cleared the field for Harvard law professor and consumer advocate Elizabeth Warren as their nominee to take back the seat won by Republican Scott Brown in a 2010 special election. While Warren had the advantage of running in a Democratic state, many political observers were impressed by the political skills Brown demonstrated in his 2010 victory and in his time as a U.S. Senator. Brown emphasized his independent streak in his campaign rhetoric and voting record. As he drove around the state in his pickup truck, he called his seat "the people's seat," a not-so-subtle contrast to those who called it "the Kennedy seat"[1] (Romano 2010). Brown talked up his independence from the national Republican Party and, in Washington, had a moderate voting record, highlighted by his support for the Dodd-Frank Wall Street Reform bill (Khimm 2012).

Brown's campaign opened up a potentially effective line of attack on Warren—calling her an elitist whose Harvard connections made her unable to understand the average Massachusetts resident. Brown's campaign responded to Warren attacks by calling her an "elitist hypocrite" (Johnson 2012) and having "an elitist attitude" (O'Brien 2012). The Massachusetts Republican Party made a parody video titled *The Elitist* (Miller 2012), and Republican flacks in Massachusetts said she was a "typical Harvard elitist" (Kroll 2011). The Brown campaign and Republicans always referred to Warren as "Professor Warren" in an effort to tie Warren more closely to the Harvard faculty club and further way from middle-class Massachusetts voters (Bierman 2012).

How did the Warren campaign respond? By highlighting her biography. Her campaign's first advertisement of the campaign was titled

"Who I Am," and it highlighted her working-class background and her family's struggles, as a shield against the attacks of the Brown campaign. The ad features Warren saying:

> I'm Elizabeth Warren. I'm running for the United States Senate, and before you hear a bunch of ridiculous attack ads, I want to tell you who I am. Like a lot of you, I came up the hard way, my dad sold carpet and when he had a heart attack, my mom went to work so we could keep our house, we all worked. My three brothers joined the military. I got married at 19, had two kids, worked my way through college, taught elementary school, then I went to law school. For years I worked to expose how Wall Street and the big banks are crushing middle-class families, it just isn't right. I stood up to the big banks and their army of Washington Lobbyists, I worked to hold them accountable. I led the fight for a new agency to protect consumers and we got it. But Washington is still rigged for the big guys and that's gotta change. I'm Elizabeth Warren and I approve this message because I want Massachusetts families to have a level playing field.[2]

A subsequent Warren ad pivoted from her background to her populist anticorporate message:

> I grew up in a family hanging on by our fingertips to a place in the middle class. But back then, America invested in kids like me. We had a lot of opportunities. Today, Washington lets big corporations like GE pay nothing—zero—in taxes, while kids are left drowning in debt to get an education. This isn't about economics; it's about our values. I'm Elizabeth Warren. I approve this message because Washington has to get its priorities straight.[3]

Washington Post blogger Greg Sargent (2012) identified these ads as a key component of the strategic imperative for the Warren campaign. These ads are "about more than reminding voters that her upbringing was anything but 'elitist.' It's also about pivoting off her life story to reframe the race's central argument over government and taxation as one about fiscal values and priorities."

In other words, the Warren campaign wanted her to show voters "who I am" in an effort to demonstrate what she really cared about. And while Warren's populist stands on issues like taxes and financial regulation were demonstrations of her focus on middle-class issues, they were not by themselves believable, especially in a context where Brown's campaign was attacking Warren as elitist. The Warren campaign needed to do what political consultants talked about in the previous chapter—show voters who their candidate was through candidate-centered appeals in an effort to develop the credibility and likability of their candidate in the eyes of voters.

Sargent (2012) sketched out the logic of using candidate-centered appeals for the Warren campaign: "The race will turn heavily on whether Warren can clear a basic likability threshold—which is why Brown's allies have spent months attacking her as an elitist in order to drive up her negatives . . . Warren wants voters to get to know a maintenance man's daughter who made good through education and hard work, and as a result knows how urgently we need to take action to shore up and sustain the middle class. The question of which Warren undecideds accept could decide the race."

Voters apparently did find that they could accept Warren as an effective advocate of middle-class values. Pulled along by the national Democratic trend and the clear blue leanings of Massachusetts, Warren beat Brown by 7 points. Key to Warren's victory was her campaign's ability to maintain positive favorability ratings (they were at or slightly above 50 percent on Election Day), which demonstrated her basic likability among voters. The Warren campaign achieved this through their use of candidate-centered appeals, which developed the credibility of their candidate. By discussing their candidate's biography and focusing on the most homespun ("My three brothers joined the military. I . . . had two kids, worked my way through college, taught elementary school") and humble ("My dad . . . had a heart attack, my mom went to work so we can keep our house") aspects of that biography, the Warren ads focused on what she had in common with Massachusetts voters. Her discussion of her resume and accomplishments ("stood up to the big banks," "led the fight for a new agency to protect consumers") demonstrates how the lessons she learned from her biography and background have made consumer protection a commitment—and not just an issue position—for Warren. Warren then calls that commitment not "about economics; it's about our values." Only by establishing her credibility through biography and record could Warren make such a bold claim effectively.

In this book, I argue that the strategy employed here by the Warren campaign is common. Campaigns use candidate-centered appeals as a means of developing the credibility and likability of their candidates. In chapter 3, I showed that campaign consultants who develop messages for their campaigns want to sell voters on their candidates by telling stories that demonstrate "who the candidate is." In this chapter, I examine how widespread the use of candidate-centered appeals is, by defining these appeals and coding for them in campaign messages. My expectation, as outlined in chapter 2, is that political campaigns should use candidate-centered appeals with great regularity. I examine how often campaigns use candidate-centered appeals in television advertisements, testing what percentage of advertisements include a candidate-centered appeal, and find that campaigns use candidate-centered appeals in a majority of their advertisements. At the same time, candidate-centered appeals make up a minority of all phrases in each advertisement, which indicates that campaigns combine candidate-centered appeals with other types of appeals.

Developing the credibility and likeability of the candidate is not just a matter of how often candidate-centered appeals are used. Campaigns want to establish their candidate's credibility at the beginning of their messages to voters. I measure the date that campaigns employ candidate-centered appeals and the placement of these appeals inside advertisements themselves to test whether campaigns do indeed use candidate-centered appeals early in their messages. I also examine what types of campaigns use more or fewer candidate-centered appeals and examine the context for these appeals.

Data and Methods

I have talked about the use of candidate-centered appeals through anecdotes from the 2008 presidential campaign and from my interviews with political consultants. In chapter 3, I used the interviews to show that political consultants put the candidate at the center of the message-development process and intend to use candidate-centered appeals. In this chapter, I examine whether they do so, turning from qualitative methods to quantitative measure to assess whether campaigns use candidate-centered appeals as a means to develop their candidate's credibility. To make this argument, I need to examine the message strategy of a broad range of political campaigns. This examination needs to be systematic, which means that it needs to develop a clear definition of what is and what is not a candidate-centered appeal that can be applied across different campaigns.

In order to conduct this examination, I need three things—a system to code candidate-centered messages, a data set of campaign messages, and a method to analyze how much of a message uses candidate-centered appeals. In this section, I sketch out how I meet all three of these conditions.

Coding for Candidate-Centered Appeals

In order to assess the impact of candidate-centered messages on political campaigns, I need to be able to explain what is—and (more importantly) what is not—a *candidate-centered message*. Creating such a definition is difficult because any piece of campaign rhetoric can be defined as candidate-centered. Any image or part of speech can be connected to the candidate. And if that is the case, then all campaign information is candidate-centered, and there is no variation in campaign messaging to study. Boundaries are needed.

To achieve these boundaries, I limit *candidate-centered messages* to those that focus on the background of the candidate. What do I mean by "the background of the candidate"? *Background* in this definition is any discussion of past actions or experience of a candidate. When discussing the background of a candidate, the common understanding is that this refers to biographical information about the candidate's parentage and ancestry or upbringing and education. For example, the Wisconsin Advertising Project has an issue code for "Background" that seems to focus on this definition. My conception of *background* is much more expansive. My definition of *background* refers again to *any* past action. Past actions or experiences by candidates often come from their prepolitical biography. But my definition also accounts or discussions of a candidate's experience in the private sector or record in public service.

Limiting candidate-centered appeals to a candidate's background has two advantages. First, information about a candidate's background must be candidate centered—no one else could use that particular experience to make the same argument. Second, my definition of *candidate-centered messages* is flexible enough to include the various methods by which campaigns make candidate-centered appeals. My definition not only meets the traditional definition of *background* as foundational biographic information about a candidate, but also includes more contemporary information about a candidate's past actions and accomplishments in public office or in the private sector, as well as evidence of a particular skill or expertise a candidate can bring to the job sought. Definitions of *background* that focus exclusively on a candidate's prepolitical biography unnecessarily limit one's understanding of a candidate's background. I use a definition broad enough to account not only for the different methods in which campaigns discuss the background of the candidates, but also for the wide variety of contexts in which they do so.

As noted, this definition allows me to say what is and what is not a candidate-centered appeal. So what is *not* a candidate-centered appeal based on this definition? My analysis shows two types of appeals make up the bulk of this group. The first are statements of a candidate's issue positions and priorities (e.g., "I support tax cuts to give incentive to parents to send their kids to college." "We owe [our troops] respect, gratitude, and support. And the resources and the will to get the job done so they can come home quickly and safely."[4]). The second are thematic statements that set up the context of an advertisement (e.g., "Mark Kennedy has done a great job representing our Minnesota values in Washington." "I want to take those Oklahoma values to Congress and work for you."[5]). By clarifying what is and what is not a candidate-centered appeal, I can then assess their use in political campaigns and leverage the variation in the use of these appeals to determine how and why campaigns use them.

Advertising Texts as Data

I next need a data set of campaign messages. For this, I use the text of television advertisements. Television advertisements provide the best method to understand campaign messages for two reasons. First, the primary form of political communication for most voters is television, and campaigns for Congress spend more money on television advertising than any other form of communication (Ansolabehere and Gerber 1994; Hernnson 2011, Ch. 7). Second, television advertising is an unfiltered and completely purposeful message directly from the campaign to voters.[6] As shown in chapter 3, campaigns take great care to develop a message for voters. Consultants painstakingly think through each word and image used in a television advertisement, hoping to maximize the ad's effect for voters. No other form of campaign communication receives as much thought, discussion, and editing as do television advertisements. As such, they represent the deliberate message of a campaign better than any other potential data set.

The television advertisements that I examine are from the 2004 general election House and Senate campaigns. I choose congressional elections rather than state and local campaigns because television advertising is the most important communications form for these campaigns, which cannot necessarily be said for campaigns for lower offices. I also chose congressional elections over presidential elections because of the immense variation in the candidates who seek office. Congressional candidates not only vary in terms of traditional variables such as incumbency, party, and gender (Kahn and Kenney

1999), but also in their experiences, political records, resumes, and backgrounds.[7] While a particular candidate or campaign strategist may compel an individual campaign to discuss the background of their candidate, the use of an entire class of congressional candidates provides the large N needed to make firmer conclusions.[8]

I examine these advertisements using data sets acquired from the Wisconsin Advertising Project (Goldstein and Rivlin 2005). The Wisconsin Advertising Project provides the most comprehensive data set available on campaign communications. It includes not only the widest sample of campaign advertisements currently available, but also the most detailed information available about both the content and the distribution of campaign messages. The Wisconsin Advertising Project takes data made available by the Campaign Media Analysis Group (CMAG), a private company that tracks the satellite transmissions used by broadcast channels for most of the country. The system's software recognizes the electronic seams between programming and advertising. As a result, the Wisconsin database includes information on every airing of every political advertisement broadcast in over 80 percent of the country.[9] Most importantly for my purposes, the system's software captures and downloads the text from all the advertisements. Thus, the Wisconsin Advertising Project provides as comprehensive a data set of television advertisements as possible based on contemporary technology.

The Wisconsin Advertising Project collects data not only about each advertisement that a campaign produces, but also each time the advertisement airs. For these analyses, I examine the number of ads a campaign aired, rather than the number of ads produced. I do this for three reasons. First, using each broadcast as a case yields the most complete data set available. Second, Prior (2001) finds that campaigns air advertisements in varying proportions. Campaigns decide not only what to say, but also how often to say it. Some advertisements run over a longer stretch of time and across more markets within a state. Thus, campaigns place more emphasis on the messages in these advertisements than they do in advertisements that run for a short period of time or that are focused on particular markets. In particular, campaigns are more likely to run negative advertisements for a smaller number of airings than positive advertisements (Prior 2001). Failing to take into account how often each advertisement airs can lead to distorted analysis (see also Jamieson et al. 2000). The third reason I examined all aired advertisements is because of the difference in aired advertisements between House and Senate campaigns. Senate campaigns are statewide endeavors, which, in most states, compels campaigns to air advertisements in multiple media markets. House campaigns are more likely to be located in a single media market. As a result, the average Senate advertisement airs with greater frequency than the average advertisement from a House campaign. The data bear this out, as the mean Senate advertisement airs 417 times, while the mean advertisement from a House campaign aired 167 times. But since there are more House campaigns that air advertisements than Senate campaigns, using each produced advertisement would skew the results toward House advertisements (the data set has 145,429 advertisements aired by House campaigns and 172,815 aired by Senate campaigns). By using ads aired, the analysis reflects the mix of advertisements that voters see: 55 percent advertisements about Senate candidates and 45 percent advertisements from House candidates.

The Wisconsin Advertising Project provides a great advance for scholars interested in the study of campaign messages. Previous databases of campaign advertising are limited because they lack a full data set of advertisements from U.S. House and Senate elections, as well as the capability to determine how often and where each advertisement aired (see Geer 2006; Goldstein and Ridout 2004, 216–17). The Wisconsin data set addresses each of these weaknesses of previous data sets. By tracking the satellite broadcasts of political advertisements, the CMAG system provides for a method to receive all advertisements from all campaigns without relying on intermediaries to provide that data. Our scholarly knowledge of the content of congressional campaigns has been severely constrained by the (understandable) limitations of previous databases of campaign advertisements. The Wisconsin Advertising Project now provides data that allows scholars to study campaign messages and strategy in much greater depth than ever before (cf. Abrejano 2010; Freedman, Franz and Goldstein 2004; Goldstein and Freedman 2002; Sides 2006; 2007; Sides and Karch 2008; Sulkin 2009; Sulkin and Swigger 2008).

Aggregating Candidate-Centered Appeals

How often do campaigns employ candidate-centered appeals? There are two ways to answer this question. The first is by determining whether an advertisement uses a candidate-centered appeal at any point in the text and then coding the advertisement "1" if yes and "0" if no. Throughout the book, this will be referred to as the "in an ad" analysis. Such a measure has great value in telling us whether campaigns are employing candidate-centered messages, but it does not tell the whole story about the frequency of these appeals. If a campaign uses just a small portion of a 30-second advertisement for a candidate-centered appeal, how much are they really using candidate-centered appeals? I need a second measure to examine how much an advertisement focuses on candidate-centered appeals.

To do this, I divide each advertisement by its phrases. Phrases are a sequence of words that have a particular meaning, which can be the constituent part of a sentence. Dividing a text into its phrases breaks it down into more basic parts, allowing separate analysis of each argument in an advertisement. Sentences, of course, can contain multiple arguments or discuss multiple issues, so it is necessary to break down the text into even smaller units. Analyses that examine whether a candidate-centered appeal is in a phrase are called the "in a phrase" analysis.

Each phrase can be aggregated with other phrases on measures of interest. For example, dividing each advertisement by its phrases allows me to know how many phrases there are in an advertisement and how many discuss the background of either candidate. I can sum the number of phrases in the advertisement that deal with the candidate's background and then aggregate these numbers across all the advertisements from a particular campaign to learn the importance of background to the campaign's message strategy, weighted for the importance of each issue inside each advertisement itself. I also code the placement of each phrase in an advertisement, which allows me to assess when in an advertisement campaigns discuss candidate-centered messages.

Other scholars have divided up advertising texts into component parts in order to deduce greater meaning from their component parts. Geer (2006), for example, codes all appeals (see pp. 29–39) from presidential election advertisements. Benoit (1999, among many works) separates ads into "themes, or parts of the ad that addressed a coherent idea," which can range from a phrase to several sentences.

THE USE OF CANDIDATE-CENTERED APPEALS

The previous section laid out my data set and the methods I used to analyze that data set. Having established that, I can return to the main thrust of this chapter—how campaigns use candidate-centered appeals to woo voters. This section examines this question, and answers a number of more specific questions about the use of candidate-centered appeals: How often do campaigns employ them? How are they used in positive and negative messages? When are they used? And what type of campaigns use candidate-centered appeals with greater or lesser frequency?

How Often Do Campaigns Use Candidate-Centered Appeals?

To review, I expect to find that campaigns use candidate-centered appeals with great frequency, in a majority of the advertisements under study. The results in Figure 4.1 show that this expectation is met—political campaigns do indeed use candidate-centered appeals with great frequency. Of the 331,399 airings of the 1,397 advertisements under study, campaigns discussed candidate-centered

a. In an Ad Analysis

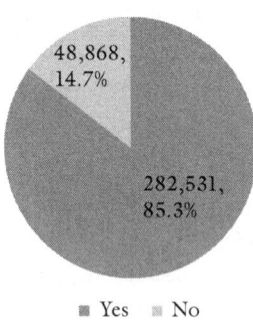

b. In a Phrase Analysis

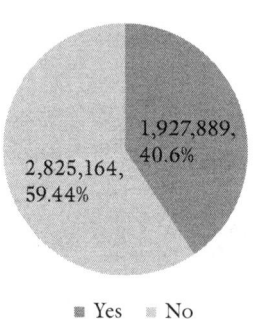

Figure 4.1 Use of Candidate-Centered Appeals, 2004 House and Senate Campaigns.
Mean Phrases: 15.2
Mean Candidate-Centered Phrases: 5.9
Mean Candidate-Centered Phrases if Candidate Centered Phrases Employed: 7.3

Note: Data and coding calculated by author using data from the Wisconsin Advertising Project. Dataset includes each airing of each advertisement.

information of one of the two candidates in 282,531 of them—that's 85.3 percent. But in those advertisements, candidate-centered information is not necessarily the main component of each advertisement. The ads included 16,644 different phrases; among all airings, there were 4,753,053 phrases. Of these, 1,927,889 (40.6 percent) included a candidate-centered appeal. Or to put it in simpler terms, of the 15.0 mean phrases in each advertisement under study, 6.1 of the phrases included a candidate-centered appeal. Of course nearly one-sixth of the advertisements did not discuss either candidate's background at all. In the advertisements that did mention a candidate's background, a mean 7.3 phrases discussed the candidate's background.[10]

Campaigns use candidate-centered information in the vast majority of the advertisements they show to voters. Campaigns do not use candidate-centered appeals in a majority of the phrases they use. Thus, campaigns use candidate-centered appeals with great frequency, while connecting these appeals to other types of appeals. Campaigns can use a variety of strategies to do this.

Some campaigns focus nearly entirely on candidate-centered appeals in an advertisement. For example, an advertisement from the Steve Pearce (R-NM) campaign has the candidate relating the values taught him by his father. As a result, it used candidate-centered information in every phrase but the legally mandated disclaimer:

> I'm Steve Pearce, and I approved this message. My father led by example. He put us to work picking cotton, moving irrigation pipe, and cleaning pens. That was hard to appreciate when I was ten, but today, I honor him for teaching me to work hard. My father never went to college, but he made sure each of his six children could. When I left for Vietnam, my father promised to pray for me every day. And he did. He helped make me into the person I am today, and for that I am eternally thankful.[11]

Other campaigns use candidate-centered information only sparingly in an effort to create credibility for the other parts of an advertisement. In one advertisement, Chuck Schumer (D-NY) says, "A Senator has to deliver for New York, but another job is to think ahead." The first phrase is the only candidate-centered phrase in the advertisement in which Schumer lays out his policy proposals for energy independence. In a negative advertisement, a campaign can use a single phrase of candidate-centered information to enhance a key point. The Doug

Walcher (R-CO) campaign noted that their opponent John Salazar "voted for high taxes" in an advertisement that compared Salazar unfavorably to Democratic nominee John Kerry.[12]

The bulk of advertisements, though, connect candidate-centered appeals to other types of appeals. For example, an advertisement from the Ben Chandler (D-KY) campaign weaves candidate-centered information into statements about the candidate's values and issue priorities.

> Key values and a belief that protecting families and educating our children is more important than special interests or party politics. *It's why as attorney general he took on his own party leaders to stop the early release of criminals* and why he'll work to restore values in our schools. The press has called him "independent" and "effective." *But for Ben Chandler the best thing he's called is "Dad."*
>
> Chandler: *How was school today?*
>
> Child: *It was good.*
>
> Chandler: I'm Ben Chandler, and I approved this message.

I have italicized the 6 candidate-centered phrases in the advertisement. In this ad of 13 phrases, these 6 represent 46 percent of the phrases in the advertisement—which is equal to the median (46.7 percent) usage of candidate-centered appeals and very close to the mean (48.5 percent) among all advertisements.

Figure 4.2 is a histogram showing the percentage of phrases in advertisements that include candidate-centered appeals. It shows that there is wide variation in the percentage of campaigns-centered appeals that campaigns employ in television advertisements. Only a handful of advertisements use candidate-centered appeals in nearly every single phrase, like the Steve Pearce ad above. A similarly small handful use such appeals in just a phrase or two, as do the Doug Walcher and Chuck Schumer ads. Instead, the distribution is relatively normally distributed, with the bulge showing that the modal campaign uses candidate-centered appeals in about half of the phrases in an advertisement.

Thus, there is no one preferred strategy for the number of candidate-centered appeals that campaigns use. Some advertisements feature them with great frequency, others much less so, and others a moderate amount. What is clear is that, with rare exceptions, campaigns connect their candidate-centered appeals with other types of appeals.

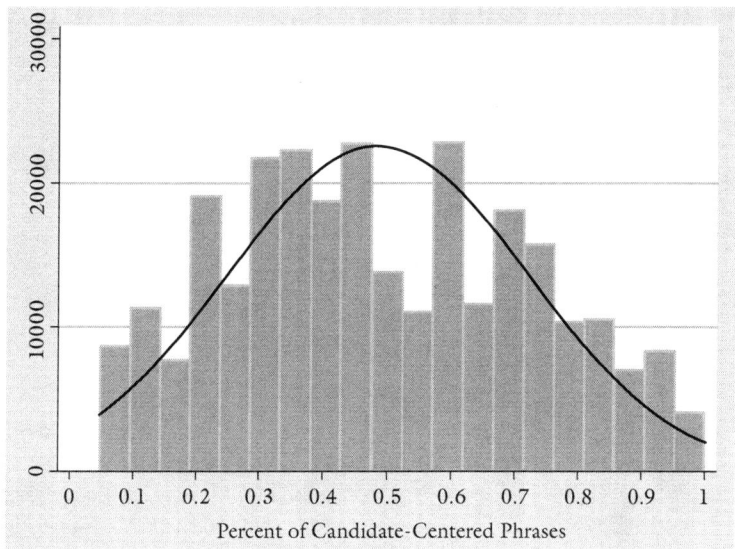

Figure 4.2 Percentage of Candidate-Centered Phrases per Advertisement, 2004 House and Senate Campaigns.

N = 278,252

Median: 46.7%

Mean: 48.5%

Note: Data and coding calculated by author using data from the Wisconsin Advertising Project. Dataset includes each airing of each advertisement.

Candidate-Centered Appeals in Positive and Negative Ads

It is also worthwhile to note that campaigns can, and do, use candidate-centered appeals about both their own candidate and their opponent. Just as campaigns need to establish the credibility of their own candidate, negative discussions of the opponent must ring true to voters. In fact, John Geer (2006) argues people are less likely to believe negative information. As a result, the evidentiary and credibility barriers increase when campaigns go negative. Providing candidate-centered information about the opponent helps campaigns meet the credibility threshold.

Campaigns thus want to present candidate-centered information not just about their own candidate, but also about their opponent. For example, the campaign of John Porter (R-NV) used the contrasting résumés of their candidate and their opponent to frame the choice for voters.

> Let's compare the candidates for Congress: a failed gaming executive who laid off thousands while he made millions, who moved here from California and rented a house in Henderson just to run for Congress. John Porter ran a small family business here, served as our mayor, state senator, and is fighting for us in Congress.
> Two very different candidates; one very simple choice.
> Porter: I'm John Porter, and these are my kids, and I approved this message.

The subtext of this advertisement is that the opponent (Tom Gallagher, the "failed gaming executive") is out for himself, while John Porter, the sponsoring candidate, has the best interests of the Nevada 3rd District at heart. Just as the advertisement uses candidate-centered information to present Porter as caring about his community ("small family business," "served as our mayor [and] state senator," "fighting for us"), it also uses specific information about the past of the opponent—Tom Gallagher ("failed gaming executive," "laid off thousands," "just moved here [to run for Congress]). Rather than stating that Gallagher is out for himself, the Porter campaign uses evidence from his past to demonstrate this contention to voters. Similarly, past information is used to show that Porter has always had the best interests of the community at heart and that voters can expect him to do the same in a subsequent term in office.

How often do campaigns use candidate-centered appeals when talking about their opponent? I coded whether a phrase discussed the sponsoring candidate, the opponent, or neither candidate, and Figure 4.3 presents the results. The most common form of candidate-centered appeal focuses on the sponsoring candidate. They appear in over half of all the advertisements aired in the 2008 campaign (51.8 percent to be exact, which represents 175,027 aired advertisements). Over a sixth of all advertisements include candidate-centered information about the opponent (61,608 airings, which is 18.2 percent of all aired ads), while 13.5 percent discuss candidate-centered information about both candidates (45,541). The second panel measures the percentage of all phrases that are candidate-centered appeals that focus on the sponsor or the opponent.[13] The second panel measures whose background was discussed in each candidate-centered phrase. While this measurement shows that the majority of phrases in an advertisement are not candidate

a. In an Ad Analysis

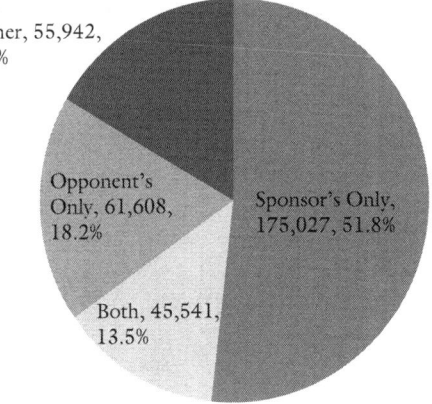

b. In a Phrase Analysis

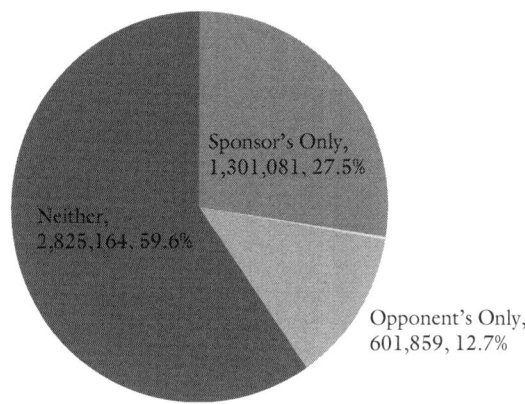

Figure 4.3 Use of Candidate-Centered Appeals by Ad Target, 2004 House and Senate Campaigns.

Note: Data and coding calculated by author using data from the Wisconsin Advertising Project. Dataset includes each airing of each advertisement.

centered, it also shows that most candidate-centered phrases focus on the sponsoring candidate: 27.5 percent of all phrases. Only 12.7 percent of all phrases are candidate-centered appeals focusing on the opposing candidate.

There are certainly more candidate-centered appeals that focus on the sponsoring candidate than the opponent. The nearly three-to-one difference in use of these phrases about the sponsor is created because the majority of advertisements are positive (Geer 2006). Campaigns use candidate-centered phrases at a similar rate when talking about the sponsoring candidate and the opponent. Figure 4.4 shows the mean number of phrases in advertisements that discuss the sponsor and the opponent, respectively. Campaigns use nearly the same percentage of candidate-centered appeals when discussing their candidate as when discussing the opponent. (For the sponsor, campaigns use a mean 6.4 candidate-centered phrases out of 15.7 phrases, which is 40.9 percent; for opponents, campaigns use a mean 6.1 phrases out of 14.6 total phrases, which is 41.6 percent.) Campaigns connect candidate-centered information with other types of appeals, regardless of which candidate they are discussing.

When Do Campaigns Discuss Candidate-Centered Appeals?

As noted, I expect that campaigns will employ candidate-centered appeals *early* in their messages to voters. I expect campaigns to do this because campaigns use candidate-centered appeals as a means to developing the credibility of their candidates. The question is how to determine what is *early*. Here, I examine *early* in two ways—early by date and early by placement in a message.

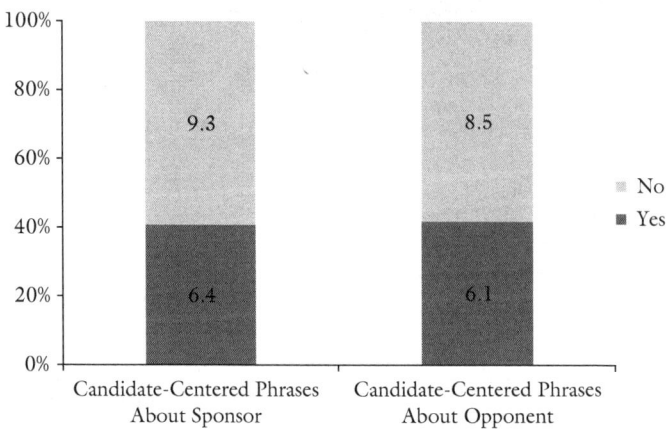

Figure 4.4 Mean Candidate-Centered Phrases in Advertisements That Discuss the Sponsoring Candidate and/or the Opposing Candidate.

Note: Data and coding calculated by author using data from the Wisconsin Advertising Project. Dataset includes each airing of each advertisement.

The first is by date. The Wisconsin Advertising Project provides data on the date each advertisement aired, allowing me to assess when campaigns use candidate-centered appeals and to assess changes over the course of the campaign. I calculated the percentage of all advertisements aired that included a candidate-centered appeal for each day

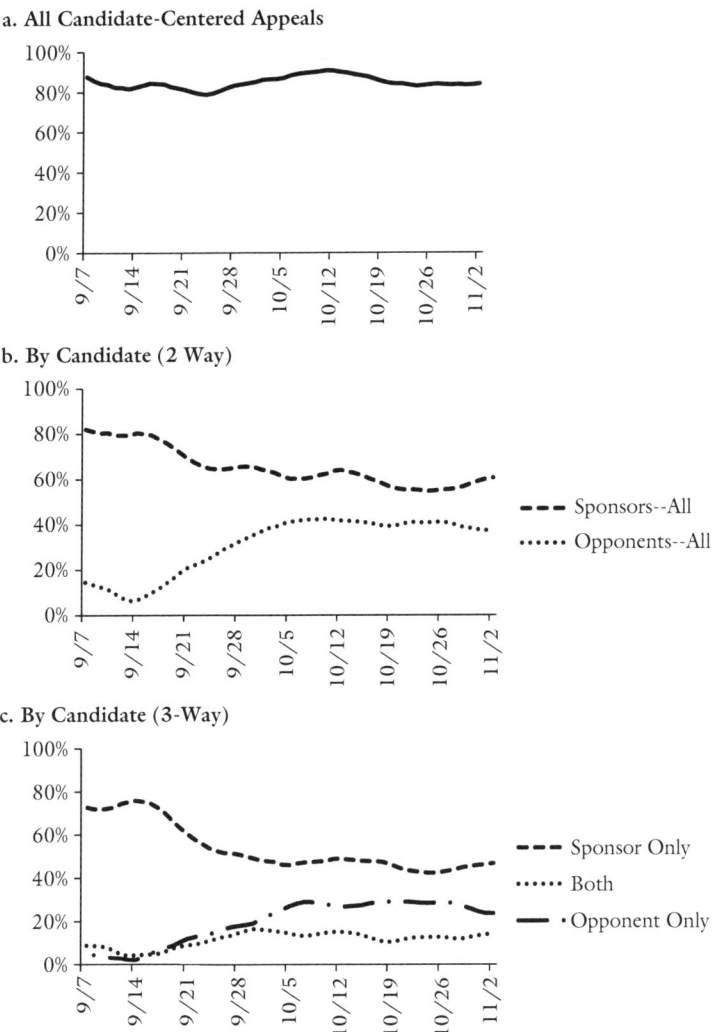

Figure 4.5 Candidate-Centered Appeals by Date, 2004 House and Senate Campaigns.
Note: Data and coding calculated by author using data from the Wisconsin Advertising Project. Dataset includes each airing of each advertisement.

from Labor Day to Election Day.[14] Figure 4.5a displays the seven day moving average[15] for all candidate-centered appeals. The results change little over time. Campaigns use candidate-centered appeals in nearly 80 percent of all advertisements aired each day of the campaign. But Figure 4.5b shows that the type of candidate-centered appeal changes greatly over the course of the campaign. At the beginning, campaigns rely heavily on candidate-centered appeals about their own candidate. As the election continues, they rely less and less on these types of appeals. Instead, the proportion of candidate-centered appeals focused on the opponent increases. After an initial dip, the proportion of advertisements featuring negative candidate-centered information increases rapidly through the second half of the month of September, before plateauing at around 40 percent through the month of October. In the last few days of the campaign, the percentage of positive candidate-centered appeals increases at the expense of negative appeals.

Breaking down the results one step further, Figure 4.5c shows the results for advertisements that use candidate-centered information exclusively about the sponsoring candidate, exclusively about the opponent, and for both candidates. The patterns essentially remain the same. Campaigns discuss their candidate in the vast majority of advertisements during the first two weeks. The difference between the sponsor's lines in the two figures is in the sharpness of the decline. The use of candidate-centered appeals exclusively about the sponsor declines rapidly through the second half of September, while the use of advertisements about both candidates rises during the period. The use of candidate-centered appeals about the opponent rises steadily for about a month from mid-September to mid-October.

For the most part, these results follow what campaign professional Ron Fauchaux (2002) calls the "classic" sequence of campaign messages, in which a campaign will "start positive" and then "respond to opposition attacks" and go "negative/comparative against opposition" (53). The results also show that campaigns have a slight tendency to "end on a positive," leaving voters with a final positive impression after a month that features a relatively high number of negative appeals. Again, this pattern follows classic campaign strategy.

More importantly, the results for the use of candidate-centered appeals about the sponsoring candidate fits with the hypothesis that campaigns use candidate-centered appeals to develop the credibility of their candidate. Campaigns use sponsor-centered appeals with enormous frequency at the beginning of their advertising campaigns, when voters know the least about their candidate. This fits with the discussion in the previous chapter regarding political consultants, who emphasized that they needed to first introduce their candidate to voters before they could move on to either discussing their candidate's issue agenda or attacking their opponent. The results here provide support for that credibility hypothesis.

There is a second way to determine when campaigns use candidate-centered appeals—assessing when candidate-centered appeals are used during an advertisement. Again, if campaigns use candidate-centered appeals to establish the credibility of their candidate, they should use these appeals *early* in an advertisement.

As noted, I coded each phrase in each advertisement. I also coded whether each phrase was the first, second, third, fourth, and so phrase in the advertisement. This coding allowed me to assess when campaigns employ candidate-centered appeals during an advertisement. I present the results in the bar graph in Figure 4.6. The y-axis represents phrase placement (i.e., the first phrase, the second phrase, the third phrase, etc.), and the x-axis represents the percentage of first, second, third, and so on phrases that discuss candidate-centered information.[16] For example, campaigns discuss candidate-centered information 20.8 percent of the time in the first phrase of an advertisement. The use of candidate-centered appeals rises quickly; by the

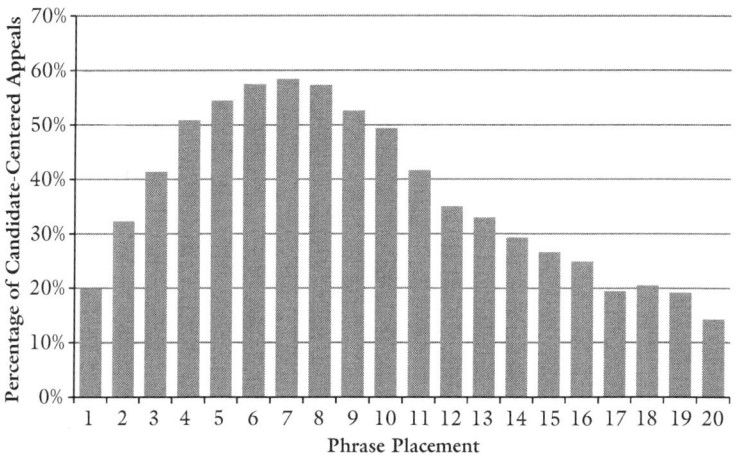

Figure 4.6 Candidate-Centered Appeals by Phrase Placement, 2004 House and Senate Campaigns.

Note: Data and coding calculated by author using data from the Wisconsin Advertising Project. Dataset includes each airing of each advertisement.

fifth phrase of an advertisement, campaign use them a majority of the time (51.4 percent of all phrases). Candidate-centered appeals are used a majority of the time in sixth, seventh, and eighth phrases. Toward the end of advertisements, candidate-centered use drops off. Among eighteenth phrases, candidate-centered information is present only 19.5 percent of the time.[17]

Figure 4.5 shows that campaigns tend to focus on candidate-centered information in the first half of advertisements and then tend to use other types of appeals in the latter half of their messages. For an example of a campaign using candidate-centered appeals early in an advertisement to build credibility for their appeals, consider this advertisement from Sen. Russ Feingold (D-WI):

> I'm Senator Russ Feingold, and I support this message. Over the last few years, I've fought hard to return over $200 million in Medicare dollars to Wisconsin, to supply our communities with hundreds of life-saving defibrillators, and to provide dental care to children in our state. But still too many Wisconsin businesses can't afford health coverage. I won't stop fighting until the burden of rising health-care costs has been lifted from businesses and families, and every American has health coverage that's at least as good as what I have as a member of Congress.

In this advertisement, Feingold uses his actions in Congress to demonstrate his bona fides on the issue of health care. He has "fought hard" to achieve some gains on the issue through his work in the Senate. Having established his credibility through past actions, he pivots to his plans for health care in the future—fighting to lift the burden of health-care costs and to cover every American. While Feingold is undoubtedly sincere in his beliefs about providing universal health care,[18] in order to convince voters of this, he must talk about what he has done in the past. By discussing what he has accomplished on health care in his previous terms in office, Feingold establishes that his commitment to reducing health-care costs and increasing coverage is not just a stance adopted for the campaign; it represents a genuine commitment.

These results in this section provide, for the most part, confirmation of my expectations. Campaigns do indeed use the background of the candidates with great frequency, in the vast majority of the advertisements under study. But candidate-centered phrases are not a majority of the phrases in an advertisement, and campaigns work to connect information about the background of their candidate with other types of appeals. The results also show that campaigns tend to discuss their candidate's background earlier in an advertisement. These results are consistent with the suggestion that campaigns use candidate-centered information (especially background information) in an effort to develop the credibility of their candidate. Thus, they discuss the candidate's past early and then focus on other appeals, such as the candidate's issue stands (which are inherently prospective). We see evidence that campaigns use retrospective evidence about candidates to make prospective arguments for his or her election.

THE CONTEXT OF CANDIDATE-CENTERED APPEALS

As noted, I have given a broad definition of candidate-centered appeals and justified this by arguing that campaigns can make these appeals in a broad variety of contexts. In coding the advertisements, I took note of the context in which campaigns used each candidate-centered appeal. For the sponsoring candidate, I coded whether the ad mentioned the candidate's political record as an incumbent, in another political office, or in the private sector. I also coded if the ad mentioned the candidate's prepolitical biography or family, or made a general appeal about the candidate's experience. For the opponent, I coded whether the ad mentioned the opponent's record as incumbent, in other political office, or in the private sector. This list should provide a complete a list of the methods of background usage that campaigns employ.[19]

Table 4.1 shows how often campaigns use each type of candidate-centered appeal. The "In an Ad" column measures whether a candidate-centered appeal has a candidate-centered appeal using that context. For example, 32.0 percent of all advertisements include a candidate-centered appeal about the sponsor as an incumbent. The "In a Phrase" column measures which context is used in each phrase; 10.4 percent of all phrases use a candidate-centered appeal about the opponent. I added one additional column to these measures, the "Candidate-Centered Phrases" column uses only candidate-centered phrases in the denominator and allows one to see the balance of contexts for candidate-centered appeals. All three columns show the same thing—most candidate-centered appeals focus on actions taken in political office.

In particular, incumbent campaigns want to talk about the accomplishments of their candidate in his or her previous terms in office. This is the single most common context for the discussion

Table 4.1 Use of Candidate-Centered Appeals in Political Advertisements, 2004 House and Senate Elections

	All Phrases (%)	Candidate-Centered Phrases (%)	All Ads Produced (%)
Any Background Mentioned	40.5		84.1
Sponsor's Background Mentioned	27.6	68.1	63.5
As Incumbent:	16.3	40.1	32.0
In Other Political Office:	4.4	10.8	21.4
In the Private Sector	2.6	6.3	9.9
General Appeals to Experience	0.6	1.4	6.7
Biography	3.8	9.5	16.2
Opponent's Background Mentioned	12.9	31.9	29.5
As Incumbent:	3.6	9.0	9.9
In Other Political Office:	5.3	13.1	17.2
In the Private Sector	4.0	7.6	3.7
Observations	2,365,932	958,741	338,112

Individual advertisements can employ candidate-centered appeals in different contexts, so percentages do not add up to 100% Data and coding calculated by author using data from the Wisconsin Advertising Project. Dataset count each airing of each advertisement.

of candidate-centered appeals. For example, take this advertisement from the campaign of Rep. David Price (D-NC):

> Girl: Dear Congressman Price,
> How can I ever thank you for helping my big brother go to college? Thanks to the bill you sponsored, my parents can deduct the interest on student loans, and they can use the money from their IRA to pay for college with no penalty. Now my parents can get a break, my brother can get a college education, and I can get something I've always wanted—his room.
> Price: I'm David Price, and I'm proud to have approved this message."[20]

This advertisement focuses on Price's accomplishment in passing the tax deduction for interest on student loans, a topic of great concern to his district.

Challenging and open-seat campaigns do the same when touting their candidate. Here is an advertisement from Randy Kuhl (R-NY), a 24-year veteran of the New York state legislature running in an open seat:

> Randy Kuhl has a well-deserved reputation as an independent legislator who puts people before politics, sponsoring landmark legislation like the Women's Health Care Act, protecting children from the threats of Internet pornographers and violence in schools, and helping create the nation's first agri-terrorism law to protect our food supply.
> Randy Kuhl: real experience for Congress. He puts people first.
> Kuhl: I'm Randy Kuhl, and I approved this message.[21]

Similar to the Price advertisement above, the Kuhl advertisement emphasizes specific actions taken by the candidate in office. The only difference is that the Kuhl campaign cannot talk about what he has done in Congress; he has not won election to it yet.

Less common but still important are references to the private-sector experience of the candidates. These appeals appear in 9.9 percent of all advertisements and 2.2 percent of all phrases. Campaigns cannot talk about their candidate's political experience, so they fashion messages about the candidate's private-sector experience in a way that connects to how the candidate might serve in Congress. For example, take this advertisement from the campaign of Geoff Davis (R-KY):

> Davis: I'm Geoff Davis, and I approved this message.
> Woman: You may have seen Nick Clooney attacking Geoff Davis. What Nick Clooney isn't telling you is that, so that his employees could keep their health-care coverage, Geoff Davis reincorporated his business into Tennessee. You see, my husband was working for Geoff Davis when I was told by my doctor that I had breast cancer. Without Geoff's commitment, I wouldn't have been able to get the health care that I needed. Geoff's decision made a difference in my life.[22]

Candidate-centered appeals focusing on the sponsoring candidate in the private sector are used less often, primarily because candidates for the U.S. House and Senate are usually experienced politicians. The Davis ad above shows that just as in advertisements based on the public record of elected politicians, stories focusing on the private-sector experience of a candidate can just as readily demonstrate the credibility and likeability of a candidate.

Using biographically based appeals is a frequent strategy for political campaigns, especially for the campaigns of unknown challengers or open-seat candidates. Biographically based appeals appear in 16.2 percent of all advertisements and 3.8 percent of all phrases. For example, here is an advertisement from the Jeanne Patterson (R-MO) campaign:

> Mr. Patterson: This is one of my little girls, Jeanie—now Jeanie Patterson. I've always admired Jeanie's work ethic. Growing up, she mowed grass, worked in a restaurant, a shoe store, and a hospital. But I couldn't afford to send her to college. Jeanie earned scholarships, worked her way through school, and helped build the Cerner Corporation from scratch. Jeanie will work twice as hard in Congress to create jobs and reform health care. I know because fathers know best.
>
> Patterson: I'm Jean Patterson, and I approve this message.[23]

The Patterson campaign gets their candidate's father to talk about her upbringing and her willingness to work hard to achieve her goals. He serves as the most credible witness of his daughter's work ethic and transfers this credibility to her when he argues that she "will work twice as hard" to achieve her policy goals. In making biographical appeals, campaigns hope to convince voters that the values and beliefs of their candidate are lifelong commitments, and thus, voters can trust that the candidate will maintain these values if elected to office.

As noted above, campaigns use candidate-centered information not only to build up their own candidate, but to attack their opponent. As Table 4.1 shows, 29.5 percent of ads and 10.4 percent of phrases use candidate-centered appeals about the opponent. The table also shows, with some surprise, that the opponent as incumbent is not the most common context for negative candidate-centered appeals. That being said, attacks on the opponent's service as an incumbent are an important part of campaign message strategy. An example is this advertisement from the Patty Wetterling (D-MN) campaign:

> Kennedy—falsely attacking Patty Wetterling so we won't focus on his record. Mark Kennedy voted against letting us buy cheaper prescription drugs from Canada and voted against guaranteed coverage for mammograms. He voted to cut overtime pay. And Kennedy even voted against more funds to prevent terrorists from getting nuclear weapons. The *Star-Tribune* and *Pioneer Press* agree: we need Patty Wetterling working for us in Congress.
>
> Wetterling. I'm Patty Wetterling, and I approved this message.[24]

The Wetterling campaign wants to discredit Kennedy and his views on issues. While voters might be skeptical that Kennedy opposes guaranteed coverage for mammograms or overtime pay, demonstrating that he has cast votes against these ideas (and citing these votes in the ad's visual) makes these claims potentially credible for voters.

Campaigns will use similar arguments when facing a challenger or open-seat candidate with political experience. When the opponent has experience in the private sector, campaigns will use information from their opponent's experience in the private sector to try to discredit the opponent. Candidate-centered appeals about the opponent in the private sector appear in 3.7 percent of all produced advertisements and 4.0 percent of all aired phrases. This is the only context that is present in a higher percentage of phrases than advertisements. This indicates that when campaigns discuss the opponent's experience in the private sector, it takes up a large number of phrases in the ads where they appear. For example, here is an advertisement from the campaign of Rick Renzi (R-AZ).

> Renzi: I'm Congressman Rick Renzi, and I approved this ad.
>
> Announcer: This is Paul Babbitt's mine. It polluted the water and air. The Singer family owned this land for 16 years. Then Babbitt started mining the mountain, and people got very sick.
>
> Singer: I've been diagnosed with having breast cancer. I had to go to chemotherapy, radiation. I am not going to vote for Paul Babbitt.[25]

Here, the Renzi campaign uses the story of the Singer family to demonstrate that their opponent, Paul Babbitt, is a typical politician, even in his actions when he was not a politician. Babbitt, according to the Renzi campaign, is just out for himself and cares little about other people.

Overall, the results of Table 4.1 show that when campaigns use candidate-centered appeals, they focus these efforts on a candidate's actions in political office. This finding is robust regardless of the measure. The comparison of the "In an Ad" and the "In a Phrase" columns provides further evidence that political campaigns use candidate-centered appeals with great frequency, but do so by connecting candidate-centered appeals to other types of appeals. Again, candidate-centered appeals are made in a majority of ads produced by campaigns, but candidate-centered appeals are not a majority of phrases used in advertisements.

Who Uses Candidate-Centered Appeals?

To this point, I have shown that campaigns use candidate-centered appeals with great frequency, that campaigns use candidate-centered appeals early in their messages to voters, and that campaigns use candidate-centered appeals in a wide variety of contexts, though there is a focus on previous political work. Now I address what types of campaigns are more likely to utilize candidate-centered appeals.

A candidate's experience is one factor that should have a strong influence on the likelihood of transmitting a candidate-centered appeal. Campaigns for experienced candidates can more easily connect the previous actions of their candidate to the concerns of a voter than the campaigns of inexperienced candidates. This is especially true since most candidate-centered appeals are given in the context of the candidate's previous political experience. Thus, the use of background appeals in campaign advertisements should increase as a candidate's experience is more proximate to the office sought. In particular, incumbent campaigns should employ background appeals most frequently. An incumbent's experience in their previous term in office is quite obviously exactly proximate to the job sought. Background usage should fall as a candidate's experience is less proximate to the job of member of Congress and should be least among candidates who have not previously held elective office.

To examine what type of campaigns use candidate-centered appeals, I use a multivariate logistic regression. Multivariate analysis allows for the measurement of a specific variable while controlling for the other variables in the model. The key variable to test is candidate status—"Incumbent," "Open Seat," and "Challenger"—and multivariate analysis allows me to test whether any difference in the use of candidate-centered advertisements between incumbent, challenging, and open-seat campaigns are based on candidate status or the result of a correlation between these variables and another variable in the model.

I run models for both the "in an ad" and the "in a phrase" analysis and do so for all candidate-centered appeals. I also run a model for candidate-centered appeals about the sponsoring candidate and one for candidate-centered appeals for the opponent.[26] Each model uses logistic regression because the dependent variable is dichotomous. The independent variables of course include candidate status— "Incumbent," "Open Seat," and "Challenger." Because competitive elections increase the negativity and produce more specific campaign rhetoric (Kahn and Kinney 1999), I include a "Competitiveness" measure based on race ratings from *Congressional Quarterly*.[27] Two other variables measure the experience level of a candidate. "Freshman" notes if an incumbent is running for reelection for the first time and thus has less experience than the average incumbent. I also include a variable for "Experienced Challengers," those who have held elective office previously. Because experienced challengers have experience in elected office, their experience is more proximate to the office sought than inexperienced challengers (Jacobson 2007). Both may affect the rhetorical strategies of their campaigns. I also include variables to control for other factors that may influence campaign rhetoric—office sought ("Senate" with House candidates as the excluded category), party ("Republican" with Democratic campaigns as the excluded category), and the conservatism of the district or state.[28]

Rather than report the coefficients produced by the models, I calculated predicted probabilities (see Appendix Table A4.1 for full regression results). The "Freshman" and "Experienced Challenger" variables are not significant in any of the models. Instead, the candidate status variables ("Incumbent" and "Open Seat") provide the largest influence on the rhetorical strategies of congressional campaigns. Figure 4.7a shows the predicted probabilities broken up for incumbent, challenging, and open-seat campaigns for the "in an ad" measurement. Figure 4.7b shows the same probabilities in the "in a phrase" measurement. There is relatively little difference in the likelihood to use candidate-centered appeals between the three types of candidates in both measures.

The figures for sponsor-based appeals (Figure 4.8a-b) and opponent-based appeals (Figure 4.9a-b) tell a different story. The sponsor-based appeals figure shows significant differences in the use of these appeals based on candidate status. Challenging campaigns talk about their candidate's background in fewer than half of their advertisements and in fewer than a sixth of their phrases. Open-seat campaigns use these appeals much more frequently (.624 for "in an ad" and .214 for "in a phrase"). But it is incumbent campaigns who talk about their candidate's record and experiences most frequently, in over three-quarters of all aired advertisements (.744) and over one-third of all phrases (.348). The pattern for candidate-centered appeals about the opponent is exactly the opposite. Incumbent campaigns are the least likely to talk about their opponent's actions and experiences. Open-seat campaigns are more likely to talk about the opponent than are incumbent campaigns, but less likely to do so than challenging campaigns. Challenging campaigns are more likely to talk about the incumbent they are squaring off against than they are their own candidate, discussing their opponent in over five-eighths of all advertisements (.640) and one-quarter of all phrases (.271).

These results are very consistent with the notion that many campaigns are referenda on the incumbent—with the incumbent's campaign touting his or her achievements and opposing campaigns

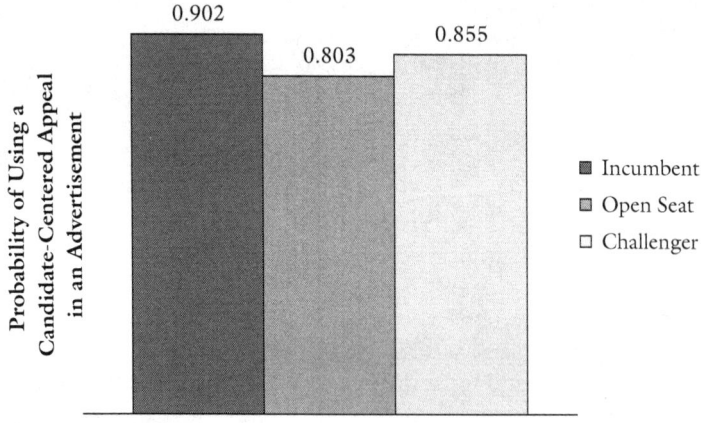

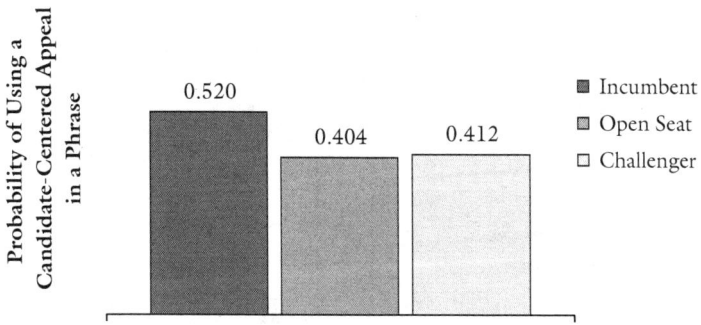

Figure 4.7 Predicted Probabilities of Use of Candidate-Centered Appeals about All Candidates, 2004 House & Senate Campaigns.

Note: Data and coding calculated by author using data from the Wisconsin Advertising Project. Dataset includes each airing of each advertisement. The candidate here is a Republican non-freshman House incumbent whose race has a "Likely" competitiveness rating. All other values are set at their mean.

a. In an Ad Analysis

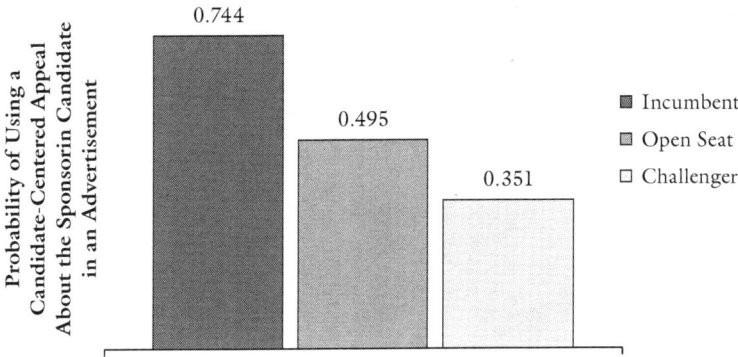

b. In a Phrase Analysis

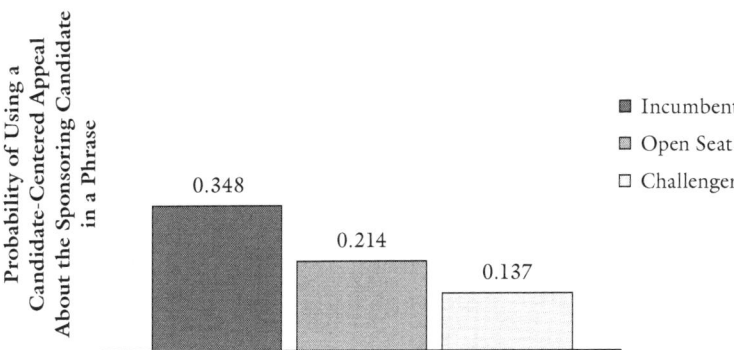

Figure 4.8 Predicted Probabilities of Use of Candidate-Centered Appeals about Sponsoring Candidate, 2004 House & Senate Campaigns.

Note: Data and coding calculated by author using data from the Wisconsin Advertising Project. Dataset count each airing of each advertisement. The candidate here is a Republican non-freshman House incumbent whose race has a "Likely" competitiveness rating. All other values are set at their mean.

criticizing his or her record. More important to the argument of this book, the results here indicate that much of the focus on incumbents—whether positive or negative—is on their past actions and experiences. When incumbent campaigns talk about their candidate, they use candidate-centered appeals. When challenging campaigns talk about the incumbent, they also use candidate-centered appeals.

a. In an Ad Analysis

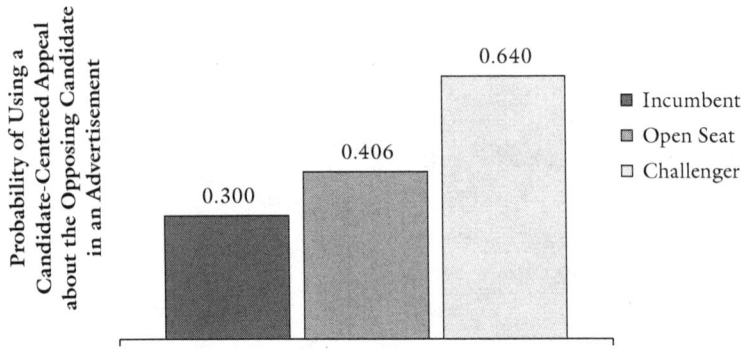

b. In a Phrase Analysis

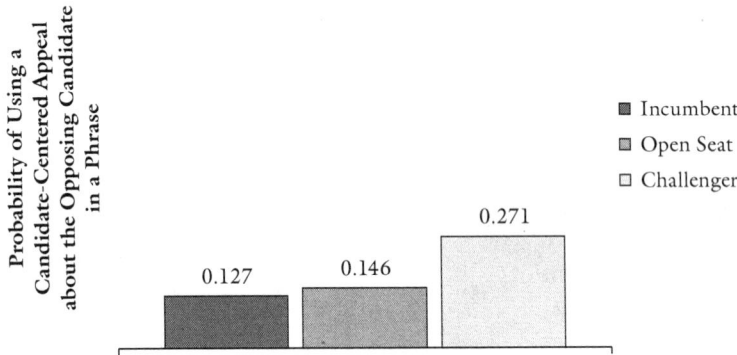

Figure 4.9 Predicted Probabilities of Use of Candidate-Centered Appeals about Opposing Candidate, 2004 House & Senate Campaigns.

Note: Data and coding calculated by author using data from the Wisconsin Advertising Project. Dataset count each airing of each advertisement. The candidate here is a Republican non-freshman House incumbent whose race has a "Likely" competitiveness rating. All other values are set at their mean.

Conclusion

At the beginning of the chapter, I discussed how the Elizabeth Warren campaign used candidate-centered appeals to develop the credibility of their candidate. The Warren campaign's advertisements focused on the candidate's working-class background in an effort to shield their candidate from Republican attacks on her status as a professor at Harvard. Appeals focusing on Warren's biography also provided the campaign a way to build credibility for their candidate's issue stands opposing Wall Street and focusing on middle-class economic reforms. In this chapter, I showed that the strategy of the Warren campaign is not an isolated phenomena. Campaigns for candidates from a wide variety of backgrounds, from both parties, and running for different offices employ the same strategy—using candidate-centered appeals as a means of developing the credibility and likeability of their candidate.

For the most part, the use of candidate-centered appeals by political campaigns fits with my expectations. Campaigns use candidate-centered appeals as a regular part of their campaign strategy, as these appeals are present in the vast majority of advertisements they air. The "in a phrase" analysis shows that campaigns seek to connect candidate-centered appeals to other types of appeals. Campaigns also tend to use candidate-centered appeals about their candidate early—both in terms of the date of the message and its placement inside an advertisement. That campaigns use candidate-centered appeals early is consistent with my argument that campaigns use candidate-centered appeals to develop the credibility and likeability of their candidate. Finally, I showed that candidate status is the most important factor in determining what type of candidate-centered message is used, as incumbent campaigns focus more on their candidate, while challenging campaigns focus more on the opponent.

In general, these results show the importance of understanding candidate-centered appeals by political campaigns. Political campaigns do not feel that they can simply tell voters what their candidate will do if he or she wins election to the subsequent term; voters are skeptical of these claims. Instead, campaigns feel compelled to tell voters about who their candidate is, primarily by discussing what their candidate has done. In order for campaigns to make prospective appeals, they must start by making retrospective appeals. I provided evidence that campaigns make candidates themselves a key focus of their messages to voters, using a wide variety of content to discuss the candidate's background. In other words, campaigns try to develop the credibility of their candidates and use candidate-centered appeals as the means to meet this goal.

This chapter treated all candidate-centered appeals as equal. But a review of the text of the various advertisements quoted in this chapter demonstrates that campaigns use different types of candidate-centered appeals. Why and how do campaigns use candidate-centered appeals that revolve around the character, the issue position, and the expertise of their candidate and their opponent? I address this question in the next chapter.

CHAPTER 5

THE TYPES OF
CANDIDATE-CENTERED APPEALS

From a partisan standpoint, the campaign for incumbent governor Chris Christie faced a difficult task in winning reelection in 2013. New Jersey is a Democratic state. President Obama won the state by 17 points in 2008, and, during the middle of the 2013 governor's election, the state held a special US Senate election to choose a successor to the deceased Frank Lautenberg. Democrat Cory Booker won easily, but expectations of the state's blue hue (in addition to Booker's charismatic personality) were so high that conventional wisdom regarded the margin as disappointing. The Christie campaign would have to convince many voters who normally marked the Democratic line to choose a Republican.

Christie's record as a governor demonstrated his bipartisan appeal. Christie brokered deals with Democrats who controlled the state legislature to cut pension and health-care benefits for state employees and to increase barriers to tenure for public school teachers (Portnoy and Rizzo 2013). These laws, combined with Christie's hectoring, get-it-done-or-I-get-angry personality proved popular in the state, and he sported mostly positive approval ratings throughout his term. But the big boost to Christie's political fortunes was his performance during Hurricane Sandy, which battered the state's shoreline. Christie was a constant media presence during the storm and the recovery. He worked closely with President Obama on the recovery, praised the president's efforts to assist the state, and toured hard-hit Atlantic City with Obama (Haberman 2013). While Christie's embrace of President Obama during the recovery played poorly among national Republicans worried about the 2012 presidential election, it played extremely well in New Jersey, boosting Christie's approval ratings to above 60 percent.

For the 2013 Christie campaign, the imperative was simple: keep it up. Voters were happy with Christie and gave him wide leads in the polls over Democratic state senator Barbara Buono. The job for the Christie campaign was to remind voters of why they liked Christie and the job he had done in office.

Not surprisingly, the advertisements from the Christie campaign touted his accomplishments as governor (Celock 2013). Here is the first advertisement aired by the Christie campaign:

> They said it couldn't be done. New Jersey was too broken—too partisan. But they never met Chris Christie. Working with both parties, he made tough decisions: four balanced budgets, no new taxes for anyone, wasteful spending cut, a cap on property taxes that's working, the best job growth in a decade, and the most education funding ever. And when tragedy struck, he was there every step of the way. Chris Christie: the governor.

Another Christie ad focused on a Christie program to reduce drug addiction:

> Announcer: Drug addiction: it's a sad fact of life. It tears apart families. It ruins lives.
>
> Christie: We can't forget that what we're dealing with here is an illness. And we need to treat it that way. Because I believe that no life is disposable and that everyone deserves a second chance.
>
> Announcer: So Governor Christie worked with both parties to pass a law that gives nonviolent drug offenders rehab, instead of jail time. It's a compassionate plan that helps people with addiction. Chris Christie: the governor.[1]

These two advertisements are very different. The first focuses on a broad set of bread-and-butter issues in the state and tells Christie's version of the story of his first term as governor. The second focuses on a more obscure issue, but one that the Christie campaign wants to tout (Portnoy 2013).

Unsurprisingly, there is one thing that these ads have in common—they both use candidate-centered appeals. One focus of candidate-centered appeals is the political record of a candidate, and, as demonstrate in chapter 4, campaigns for incumbent candidates frequently discuss their candidate's previous actions in office.

But the candidate-centered appeals in the two advertisements are different in nature. The first ad highlights two elements of Christie's record as governor. One is his issue stands, emphasizing Christie's accomplishments in balancing budgets and holding the line on taxes and spending, which led to a positive jobs record. But what introduces these appeals based on Christie's issue positions are appeals that focus on his competence. Noting that "they" said the state was too broken or partisan to make major changes, Christie's skills as governor ("tough decisions," "working with both parties") produced the accomplishments. The ad argues that not only does Christie have the right issue positions, but he also has the competence to enact his policy preferences into law and to produce good results for the state.

The second ad is titled "Compassion," and it approaches Christie's record in a completely different way. The ad does tout Christie's issue position on drug offenders and notes the rehabilitation program that Christie helped to create. But framing this set of issue positions are arguments about Christie's character. Christie notes his belief in second chances, and the ad calls the plan "compassionate." Instead of the tough-minded decision maker, this advertisement highlights Christie's character. Because he believes that "no life is disposable," he was willing to create this drug rehabilitation program for nonviolent offenders. Christie has an understanding of the problems of those addicted to drugs and has shaped a policy response based on that understanding.

These two advertisements represent the three different ways in which campaigns employ candidate-centered appeals. Further, campaigns use these different types of appeals for different reasons. The Christie campaign wanted to show voters that their candidates had the right issue positions, and to do this, they employed position-based appeals that focused on his policy accomplishments as governor. In the advertisement on drug rehabilitation, they emphasized the governor's compassion and understanding through character-based appeals. And in the "They Said" advertisement, the Christie campaign made competence-based appeals, discussing the tough obstacles Christie overcame to accomplish his policy vision.

In this chapter, I take up the question of what type of candidate-centered appeals campaigns make. Just as the Christie campaign did in their advertisements in the 2013 election, I find that campaigns make character-based, issue-based, and competence-based appeals. I define each of these types of appeals and then assess their use in campaign messages. As discussed in chapter 2, I expect to find that character-based appeals are most common; these appeals focus on developing the credibility of a candidate as a person, and campaigns for all types of candidates, regardless of circumstance, must achieve this goal. This chapter also analyzes which types of campaigns use each type of candidate-centered appeal.

Types of Candidate-Centered Appeals

This chapter differs from chapter 4 by examining not just whether a campaign makes a candidate-centered appeal, but also what type of candidate-centered appeals campaigns make. I have identified three ways in which campaigns can use personal messages to win votes.

1. Highlighting Character: Campaigns use personal messages to overcome the natural skepticism voters have about the intentions of those who seek office. The messages try to communicate the values and character of the candidate running for office.
2. Creating Certainty on Issue Stands: Campaigns employ candidate-centered appeals to reduce uncertainty that voters may have about what the candidate will do once elected to office. More specifically, campaigns emphasize past issue stands by the candidates, often from previous terms in office. These appeals allow voters to infer that these past actions will be repeated in the future.
3. Demonstrating Competence: Campaigns demonstrate the knowledge or competence of the candidate. These messages emphasize the particular knowledge, skill, or insight that candidates have gained previously, whether in the private sector or in elective office.

None of these types of appeals are mutually exclusive in an advertisement. Campaigns can and do combine any of these three candidate-centered appeals with other appeals, such as issue stands and discussions of broader values. In fact, such a combination should be more persuasive, as the personal focus of the issue message should increase the credibility of the candidate.

I now sketch out why campaigns use each of these types of candidate-centered messages. I also discuss which types of campaigns would be most likely to use each of these types of appeals, developing hypotheses about the uses of candidate-centered appeals.

Highlighting Character

Voters are skeptical of all politicians. Also, voters think that the selfish motives of elected officials keep our government from solving its problems (Hibbing and Theiss-Morse 2002). If voters think all politicians are two-faced, corrupt, selfish, and the cause of problems, the solution for a campaign is to make voters think their candidate is not a typical politician (and thus is not two-faced, corrupt, selfish, etc.). Campaigns have two methods to do this. First, they can show that their candidate represents a set of exceptional qualities. Examples of this are relatively rare, and the archetype is John McCain. In previous chapters I have detailed how his 2008 presidential campaign emphasized his heroism as a POW in Vietnam as well as issues such as national security, which easily connected to his service.

In other words, McCain was using his past actions as a naval fighter pilot and prisoner of war to show his desire to win office was rooted in a love of country, not a love of power or self-aggrandizement. As such, McCain was not the typical politician who sought office for his own gain. Other candidates employ the same strategy, telling stories about their achievements in public service, in charitable endeavors, and even in business, to show that they have lived a life of service to others and not to themselves.

The more common way that campaigns highlight their candidate's character is by emphasizing that the candidate has common values. That is, the candidate shares the values of the average person in a state or district, not the values of a party or of Washington (which is what typical politicians do). In fact, this is the most common way that campaigns highlight their candidate's character. Often these appeals use the candidate's biography and upbringing to demonstrate the values he or she learned as a child and how those values have stayed with the candidate throughout his or her political career. As an example, take this ad from Sen. Harry Reid (D-NV):

> Reid: I'm Harry Reid, and I approved this message.
> Woman 1: Welcome to Searchlight, Nevada, where Harry Reid and I grew up.
> Man: His dad was a hard-rock miner, right here in my grandfather's mine.
> Woman 2: His mom took in wash for a little extra money.
> Woman1: His nickname was "Pinky."
> Man: Pinky.

Woman 2: Pinky.

Various people: There were no doctors, no hospitals . . . but he always loved this place. And he still lives here. He eats here at the Nugget.

Woman 2: He's never forgotten where he comes from.

Woman 1: And we see it every day.

Reid: I'm Harry Reid, and this is my home.[2]

Both of these methods focus on the character of the candidate and showing voters that the candidate is not like a typical politician. Campaigns try to show the best side of their candidate and attempt to present a narrative of selfless action by their candidate, which demonstrates his or her nonpolitician qualities to voters.

What types of campaigns will use character-based appeals? I discussed in detail the theoretical rationale for each type of appeal in chapter 2. To briefly summarize, all campaigns must develop the credibility of their candidate and use character-based appeals to do so. Thus, I expect that character-based appeals will be the most common type of candidate-centered appeals. Second, the issue of character and credibility should be most pressing for the campaigns whose candidate is unfamiliar to voters. Therefore, challenging candidates, especially those who are newcomers to politics, will use character-based appeals most frequently.

Creating Certainty

Voters are uncertain of what candidates will do if elected to office. Theoretical (Alvarez 1997, ch. 3; Hinich and Munger 1997, ch. 6) and empirical evidence (McGraw, Hasecke, and Conger 2003; Glasgow and Alvarez 2000) show that voter uncertainty about the issue positions or traits of a candidate produces reduced vote share (Alvarez 1997; Bartels 1986; Gill 2004). How do campaigns reduce uncertainty? One method is to emphasize issue positions (Franklin 1991). But the incentive for campaigns to reduce voter uncertainty conflicts with another incentive—to remain ambiguous in their issue stands (Shesple 1972; Page 1976, 1978; Enelow and Hinich 1981). The desire to remain ambiguous means that campaigns want to avoid making clear issue stands known to voters.

I argue that candidate-centered messages provide campaigns with a way to solve the dilemma of whether to provide specific policy information to voters. In particular, talking about a candidate's past acts to achieve policy goals provides certain information about the candidate's past while maintaining future ambiguity. Rather than saying, "Tom Latham (R-IA) supports tax cuts," his campaign said that you will "find Congressman Tom Latham . . . voting for lower taxes that have helped grow our economy and create new jobs." Instead of just hoping voters will believe that David Wu (D-OR) will protect Social Security, his campaign said that "on every one of these votes, Wu voted to protect Social Security."[3] An appeal that discusses the past political action of the candidate shows not only that the candidate advocates the particular position, but that he or she backs up that position through actions—either votes in a legislature or policy accomplishments in executive office. In showing voters what candidates themselves have done, such messages are more credible and trustworthy to voters.

Who will use these position-based appeals? The campaigns of politically experienced candidates have the most material to work with when it comes to position-based appeals. On the other hand, it is much more difficult for the campaign of an inexperienced candidate to relate their candidate's background to issue stands in a credible way. Thus, I expect that the campaigns of experienced candidates will use issue-based appeals most frequently.

Demonstrating Competence

Voters want to elect candidates who are not only sincere, trustworthy, and credible, but they also want officeholders to know how to do the job. In other words, voters prize competence in their elected officials. Samuel Popkin (1994, 61) argues that "voters care about the competence of the candidate, not just the candidate's issue positions, because they do not follow most government activity and because they care about what the candidate can deliver from government."

Voters want competent candidates who can successfully deliver government benefits to them and their local community, who can manage the country effectively, and who can use knowledge and judgment to solve problems. Thus, voters want candidates with the appropriate experience, knowledge, and expertise for the office they seek. So a campaign may highlight that their candidate "delivers . . . He's brought millions to our classrooms . . . He founded the Education and Research Consortium, bringing the latest technology to over one thousand classrooms right here in western North Carolina," or that their candidate's "seniority on the Ways and Means Committee means clout for the people of Louisiana and jobs for our district," or that "we needed to reopen that bridge to two-lane traffic. Sweeney came though."[4]

Which type of campaigns will be most likely to use competence-based appeals? The obvious hypothesis is for incumbency. Incumbents, by definition, have more experience than their opponents, and often that experience has produced knowledge and expertise on how to pass legislation and win localized benefits. Incumbent campaigns can argue that their candidate's experience in the job has given their candidate wisdom and insight that will produce results in the subsequent term. Challengers and open-seat candidates cannot. Thus, I expect incumbent campaigns will use more competence-based appeals than other types of campaigns.

Coding for Types of Candidate-Centered Appeals

As described in chapter 4, I divided advertisements from the 2004 general election House and Senate candidates into phrases and coded each phrase for whether it included a candidate-centered appeal. Again, I define *candidate-centered appeals* as those that discuss the past actions by the candidate. For the phrases that included a candidate-centered appeal, I also coded for the type of candidate-centered appeal.

As noted above, there are three ways in which a campaign can discuss a candidate's background. I coded whether the appeal focused on the candidate's character. In these types of appeals, campaigns make reference to a candidate's parents or grandparents, the values their candidate learned as a child, the candidate's commitment to his or her own family, or the candidate's actions to promote a set of shared community values. The second way campaigns can use background appeals is to provide more credibility to issue stands. Here, campaigns discuss the past actions the candidate has taken to enact policy goals. The third type of candidate-centered appeal involves noting the competence or expertise of the candidate. These appeals discuss the candidate's experience, mastery of legislative procedure, or knowledge and wisdom acquired in the private sector. I coded each background appeal to determine which of these three methods (if any) was used to make the background appeal.

As in chapter 4, my data set is general-election advertisements from House and Senate candidates from 2004, using all aired advertisements available from the Wisconsin Advertising Project. Again, I use two types of analysis to determine how often campaigns use each type of candidate-centered appeal. The "in an ad" analysis measures whether an ad contains a character-based, a position-based, or a competence-based appeal. The "in a phrase" analysis examines each phrase in the text of an advertisement and whether it contains each type of candidate-centered appeal.

THE USE OF CHARACTER-, POSITION-, AND COMPETENCE-BASED APPEALS

What types of candidate-centered appeals do campaigns use, and in what frequency? Figure 5.1 provides the answer and shows that, despite my expectations, candidate-centered appeals focus most on issue positioning. Of all ads under study, 63.0 percent discussed the candidate's background from an issue-positioning standpoint. There were 1,139,771 different phrases in ads airing in the 2004 cycle that used position-based appeals, which is 22.9 percent of all phrases in the sample. Character-based appeals, which I thought would be most common, were the second most common type of candidate-centered appeal. They appeared in 130,482 advertisements (40.8 percent) and in 260,256 phrases (11.0 percent). The least common type of candidate-centered appeal was competence-based appeals. They appeared in less than a quarter of all advertisements and less than 5 percent of all phrases (4.9 percent to be exact).

I also analyzed the mean number of phrases per advertisement that used each type of candidate-centered appeal. Table 5.1 shows that, again, position-based appeals were most common, used in a mean 5.5 phrases when mentioned in an advertisement. Character-based appeals were used in 4.2 phrases, and competence-based appeals showed up in a mean 2.7 phrases.

How do campaigns use position-based candidate-centered appeals? They do so primarily by highlighting past votes or accomplishments in office. For example, take this advertisement from the campaign of Rep. Chris Van Hollen (D-MD):

> Named outstanding new Congressman by the largest nonpartisan education group. To him, making a difference on issues has always been the way to make a difference for people. To help families afford college, he's passed reforms stopping lenders from taking big profits off student loans. To preserve the environment, he's fighting to expand clean energy and protect the Chesapeake Bay. And with bipartisan support, he's working to pass promised health benefits for veterans.
>
> Van Hollen: I'm Chris Van Hollen, and I approve this message.[5]

a. In an Ad Analysis

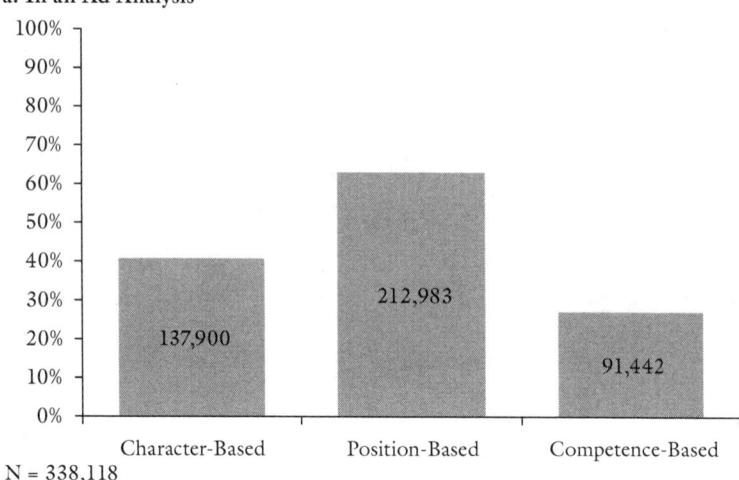

N = 338,118

b. In a Phrase Analysis

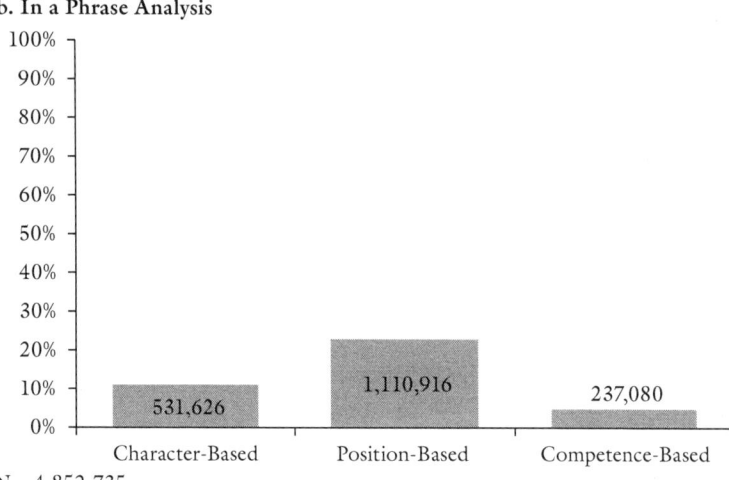

N = 4,852,735

Figure 5.1 The Use of Each Type of Candidate Centered Appeal.

Note: Data and coding calculated by author using data from the Wisconsin Advertising Project. Dataset includes each airing of each advertisement.

In this message, the Van Hollen campaign makes no promises about what Van Hollen will do if he wins another term in office. Instead, they discuss the actions that Van Hollen has taken in the previous term. This strategy is not limited to incumbents. For example,

Table 5.1 Phrase by Type of Candidate-Centered Appeals

	Character	Position	Competence
Means Phrases	1.7	3.5	0.6
(Standard Deviation)	(3.0)	(3.7)	(1.3)
Mean Phrases, if	4.2	5.5	2.3
Mentioned	(3.4)	(3.2)	(1.5)

Note: Data and coding calculated by author using data from the Wisconsin Advertising Project. Dataset includes each airing of each advertisement.

this advertisement from the campaign of Jim Costa (D-CA) sounds very similar to Van Hollen's, despite the fact that Costa was running in an open-seat election:

> Costa: What am I proudest of? I'm proudest of a ton of jobs that I've been able to create to improve the economy of this valley. I've worked hard to get health insurance for the kids of working poor, and I'm proud of that too. When the LA politicians tried to deny us our fair share of special education funding, I stood up to them and fought them, and I won. I'm Jim Costa, and I approve this message.[6]

This sounds like a great argument for reelecting Costa to the California State Senate. What does it have to do with him seeking a new job in the U.S. Congress?

Like Van Hollen's message, the Costa campaign is arguing that the past performance of their candidate will be indicative of future actions. Voters are supposed to infer that if elected to Congress, Costa will continue to create jobs, improve the economy of the San Joaquin Valley, get health insurance for children, and beat urban politicians for distributive benefits. Campaigns refer to a candidate's past actions in an attempt to reduce voter uncertainty about what their candidate will do if elected to office. But by emphasizing past actions, these campaigns can use very general descriptions of the policies pursued by their candidates to allow voters to increase their certainty about what the candidate will do in office without making explicit and specific promises.

My expectation was that the character-based appeals would be the most common type of candidate-centered appeal; they were not. Instead, they were the second most common type of appeal. Character-based appeals discuss the values that are important to candidates and make the argument that those values will guide their decisions in office. Here is an advertisement from Cathy McMorris (R-WA):

> McMorris: While I'm someone that has had some tremendous opportunities in my life, I was born and raised by a family who understood and appreciated the values of hard work and perseverance. And they weren't afraid to instill those values in their children. And I was raised on an orchard and fruit stand. And I spent thirteen years working in that family-owned business. And it's an experience that has forever grounded me in the principles of the free enterprise system and capitalism. My background is in agriculture and small business. That's the economic backbone of this district. And we need someone in Congress that understands that. I've served in the state legislature now for 10 years. And I was a Republican leader. I worked to keep taxes down, to cut waste, and to ease the regulatory burden—both on small businesses and farmers. And these should be the priorities in Congress too.[7]

The bulk of this advertisement features McMorris discussing the lessons she has learned from her life experiences in childhood and working for her family's farm and business. What lessons do they teach voters about what she will do in office? From a policy standpoint, this discussion of McMorris's background tells us little about how she will vote in the U.S. Congress or which policy proposals she will champion. Instead, this description of her upbringing makes the case that McMorris was "raised right" by her parents and implies that McMorris, unlike a typical politician, has the best interests of her rural eastern Washington district at heart. Her description of her policy achievements in the state legislature demonstrates how she has put these values into practice as an elected official.

McMorris's opponent Don Barbieri (D-WA) made similar types of claims about the lessons he learned from running a business:

> Employee: Don Barbieri is an old-fashioned individual running an old-fashioned company.
>
> Barbieri: If you don't have a happy, well-educated employee, you're not going to have a successful bottom line.
>
> Friend: As a business person, he takes the long-term view
>
> Barbieri: I think a caring company is about looking after the essentials—the things that make up a good community.

Employee: He does care about every single member of our company.

Barbieri: We started a corporate day care. We recognize that education is a backbone, and that health care is critical to families and critical to the success of businesses.

Mother: He's really thinking of the people with whom he is working.

Barbieri: I helped grow our family business from five to five thousand employees.

Another Friend: What he could do for us on a national level for this region is limitless.

Barbieri: I'm running for Congress because I love our community. I want my kids and my grandkids to have the same opportunities that I had, and that's a future. I'm Don Barbieri, and I approved this message.[8]

Just as with McMorris, Barbieri discusses the lessons he has learned about how to treat employees. Voters can assume that his practical caring about his employees will extend to practical caring about his constituents if he wins election.

The third form of candidate-centered appeal is competence-based appeals. And they are third not just in my list, but also in frequency. Despite being the least used type of candidate-centered appeals, campaigns in the right circumstances want to highlight their candidate's abilities to enact favored policies and steer government benefits to their constituents. Frequently, these appeals come in the form of quotes from newspaper endorsements, such as this advertisement from the Charles Schumer (D-NY) campaign:

"Hardworking." "Principled." "A leader." From the *New York Times* to the *New York Post* to the *Buffalo News* and everywhere in between, newspapers all across New York endorse Chuck Schumer. The *Times*, the *Post*, the *Westchester Journal-News*, the *Staten Island Advance* all endorse Chuck Schumer, praising his leadership, energy, and outstanding record. Keep New York's hardworking senator Schumer. Hard at work and getting results. Reelect Senator Chuck Schumer. Hard work. Results for New York.

Schumer: I'm Chuck Schumer, and I approve this message.[9]

This advertisement uses the endorsements of the various newspapers in the state to show the effectiveness of Senator Schumer in his first term in office and implies that he will be similarly effective in his next term.

As noted, campaigns are not limited to a single type of candidate-centered appeal in a single advertisement. They are able to combine the use of all three types of appeals in an advertisement. Table 5.2 shows how often they do this. Campaigns discussed the candidate's background in terms of both character and position in 23.4 percent of the advertisements under study.[10]

Advertisements that include both character-based and position-based appeals often use the character-based appeals first to develop the candidate' credibility and sincerity before moving on to the position-based appeals. This advertisement from the campaign of Sen. Jim Bunning (R-KY) uses the importance of family to explain his issue stands in his term in the Senate:

> I'm Jim Bunning. Mary and I approve this message. Family is important to me. My wife, Mary, and I and our nine great kids, our wonderful grandchildren, tossing the ball with my grandsons—these are the values I work for as your senator. I'm proud of what we have accomplished. Delivering the tobacco buyout, fighting higher taxes, protecting Social Security, and standing up with President Bush to support our troops in the war against terrorism: our work is not done, and I would appreciate your vote on November 2.[11]

The advertisement starts with character-based appeals, having Bunning discuss the importance of family. This establishes that Bunning's interest in the Senate is to protect his family and their values. Voters can infer that through protecting his own grandchildren, he will

Table 5.2 Combinations of Candidate-Centered Appeals, 2004 House & Senate Campaigns

	Character	Position	Competence
In an Ad Analysis			
With Character	—	79,071 23.4%	70,359 20.8%
With Position	79,071 23.4%	—	39,591 11.7%
With Competence	70,359 20.8%	39,591 11.7%	—

N = 318,249 ads;

Note: Data and coding calculated by author using data from the Wisconsin Advertising Project. Dataset includes each airing of each advertisement.

protect everyone's family and grandchildren. This helps establish Bunning's character not as a politician out for his or a special interest's benefit. Then, the advertisement pivots to the fruit of Bunning's good character—his accomplishments as senator. He lists a series of policy achievements, and while he notes that "our work is not done," he does not specify what that work is. Instead, voters should trust that this kindly grandfather who accomplished good things in his previous term in office will do so in the next term.

Advertisements that combined character and competence made up 20.8 percent of all advertisements aired, nearly as many as the combination of character and position. Such appeals show that candidates not only care about the same values as their constituents, but that they are also able to implement policies that build on those values. One example is from this advertisement by the Chris Chocola (R-IN) campaign:

> Veteran 1: The current VA clinic is one provider.
>
> Veteran 2: It was almost impossible to get an appointment. One provider: that's not enough—not after you've served your country.
>
> Announcer: Then Chris Chocola and community leaders stepped in and demanded better care for veterans.
>
> Veteran 1: We have a VA clinic coming to the 2nd District because of Chris's leadership.
>
> Veteran 2: I don't think the clinic would've happened without Chris Chocola.
>
> Veteran 1: That's getting things done.
>
> Veteran 2: Yeah, he's just a great leader.
>
> Veteran 1: I'll always be grateful to Chris Chocola.
>
> Chocola: I'm Chris Chocola, and I approved this message.[12]

This message implies that Chocola is different from ordinary politicians. An ordinary politician would not have cared enough about these veterans to build the clinic, nor had the skill and determination needed to win the funding to get it built.

The least common combination was position-based and competence-based appeals, which made up only 11.7 percent of all aired advertisements. Yet campaigns do find it effective to note that not only does their candidate hold the right positions on issues, but he or she has the wherewithal to enact those positions into law. Consider this advertisement from the Roy Blunt (R-MO) campaign:

Blunt: I'm Roy Blunt, and I approved this message.

Announcer: Our Congressman Roy Blunt: Working through the night, Roy was able to bring people together to pass the largest tax cut for working Americans in a generation. And Roy Blunt played a lead role in the passage of four economic stimulus packages, trying to keep America and southwest Missouri on the job. Roy Blunt: making government work for us.[13]

The Blunt ad has several statements that any incumbent member of Congress, looking to claim credit for a particular policy, would say ("the largest tax cut for working Americans in a generation," trying to keep America . . . on the job"). But the argument of the ad is that Blunt didn't just vote for these bills, he led the efforts to pass them. Blunt was House majority whip when this commercial aired, so his claim to leadership was not idle. As such, his ad conveys that his accomplishment was more than just supporting a popular policy; he was one of the people who made it happen.

I also analyzed the mean number of phrases used for each type of appeal when used in combination with another type of appeal. Table 5.3 shows the results—campaigns make relatively longer and more detailed competence-based appeals in combination with other types of appeals. Campaigns use a greater number of phrases based on character when combined with competence (1.7 phrases) than when combined with position (1.4 phrases). This pattern holds for position-based appeals. Campaigns use a mean 3.7 phrases on position when they combined it with competence, more than the 2.7 phrases when they combine position and character. Apparently being smart and

Table 5.3 Mean Phrases Used In Combination with Other Candidate-Centered Appeals, 2004 House & Senate Campaigns

	Character	Position	Competence
With Character	—	1.4	1.7
		(2.6)	(2.9)
With Position	2.9	—	3.8
	(3.4)		(3.6)
With Competence	0.7	0.7	—
	(1.3)	(1.5)	

N = 818,249 ads;

Note: Data and coding calculated by author using data from the Wisconsin Advertising Project. Dataset includes each airing of each advertisement.

knowledgeable is not enough for candidates; campaigns perceive an advantage in showing voters that their candidate is smart, knowledgeable, and sincere.

When Is Each Type of Candidate-Centered Appeal Used?

The analysis in the chapter to this point has been descriptive, examining how often campaigns make each type of candidate-centered appeal and providing examples of them doing so. Now the analysis turns to questions of who uses each type of candidate-centered appeals and when. Answering questions about when and who provides leverage on the question of why.

I start with the question: when do campaigns use each type of candidate-centered appeal? Just as I did in chapter 4, I examined this question in two ways. First, I examined the date when campaigns used each type of appeal. Figure 5.2 shows the percentage of all advertisements aired each day from Labor Day to Election Day that are character-, position-, and competence-based appeals respectively. Panel A shows the results for each type of candidate-centered appeal across all advertisements. Just as it did in chapter 4, this measure shows little variation across the course of a campaign.

But just as I did in chapter 4, I also broke the results down based on which candidate is mentioned in the advertisement. Panels B, C, and D show the results for character-, position-, and competence-based appeals respectively. There are separate lines for appeals that discussed the sponsoring candidate exclusively, the opposing candidate exclusively, and both candidates. Breaking out the advertisements by their target produces recognizable patterns. Character-based advertisements about the sponsor are most common at the beginning of the campaign, appearing in over 30 percent of all advertisements aired in the first weeks of September. These appeals dip in late September and have a slight increase through October. Character-based appeals in advertisements that mention the opponent or both candidates are never featured in a large percentage of advertisements, and the rate of these appeals does not change much over time.

Position-based appeals show great variation over time. Position-based appeals about a sponsoring candidate are quite common in the first few weeks of a campaign, appearing in a majority of all advertisements up through September 29. These appeals remain quite common through the rest of the campaigns and increase over the last two weeks of the campaign. Fewer advertisements about the

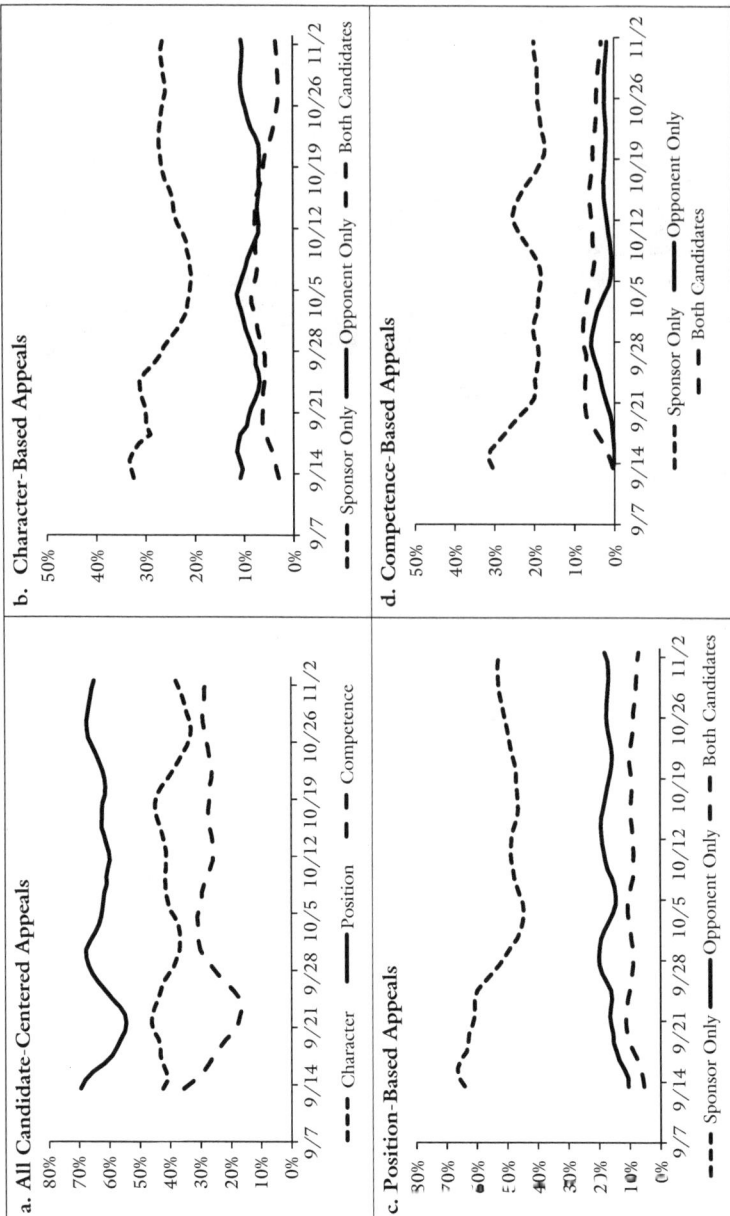

Figure 5.2 Type of Candidate-Centered Appeals by Date.
N = 318,249 ads;
Note: Data and coding calculated by author using data from the Wisconsin Advertising Project. Dataset includes each airing of each advertisement.

opponent include position-based appeals. But after appearing in fewer than 15 percent of advertisements in the first few weeks in September, these appeals increase in the last half of September and are used in 15 to 20 percent of advertisements for the rest of the campaign. The use of position-based appeals in advertisements that mention both candidates appear in fewer than 10 percent of all advertisements, a pattern which changes little over the course of the campaigns.

As discussed above, competence-based appeals focus almost exclusively on the sponsoring candidate. As such, competence-based appeals appear rarely in advertisements that discuss the opposing candidate. In fact, campaigns are more likely to employ competence-based appeals when they discuss both candidates in the same advertisement. This finding indicates that campaigns employ competence-based appeals when they think their candidate has an advantage in experience over their opponent. Panel D shows that competence-based appeals about both candidates are more common in September and trail off slightly in October. Competence-based appeals in advertisements that feature the sponsoring candidate only occur in between 20 and 25 percent of all advertisements. The exception is in the days immediately preceding Labor Day (not shown in the figure), when such appeals are used in over 30 percent of all advertisements.

Overall, there is relatively little movement in the types of candidate-centered appeals used across the course of the campaign. What changes there are come primarily from position-based appeals. Position-based appeals about the sponsoring candidate decrease over the course of the campaign, while position-based appeals about the opponent increase. This is weak, if supportive, evidence of my argument that campaigns use candidate-centered appeals early to develop the credibility of their candidate.

The second way to assess when campaigns use each type of candidate-centered appeal is by position in the advertisement. Just as in chapter 4, the results here are based on my coding of the placement of each phrase in an advertisement. The results in Figure 5.3 show the percentage of aired advertisement in which the first, second, and so on phrases are character-based, position-based, and competence-based appeals, respectively.[14] For example, campaigns discuss character-based appeals 11 percent of the time in the first phrase of an advertisement.

The results in Figure 5.3 show that campaigns tend to use character- and position-based appeals early in an advertisement. Character-based appeals make up over 10 percent of the first nine phrases of an advertisement and then under 10 percent for all subsequent phrases. Character-based appeals also peak early, in the second through fifth

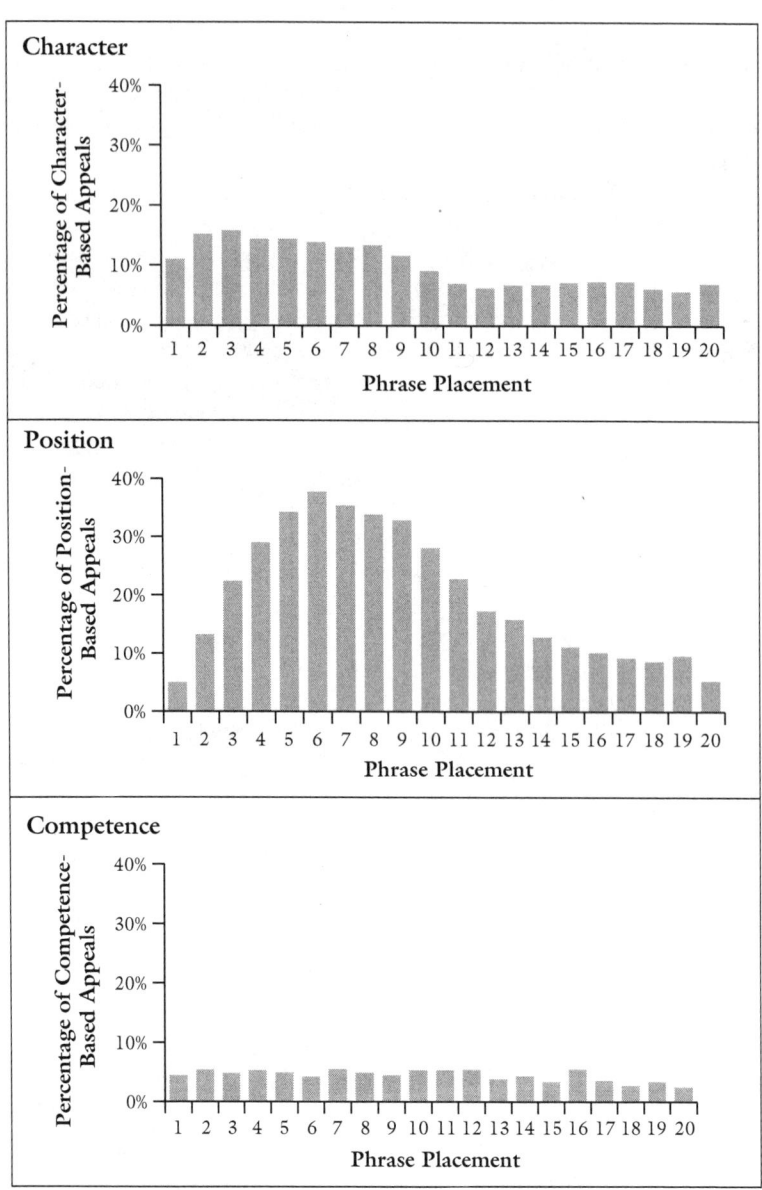

Figure 5.3 Candidate-Centered Appeals by Phrase Placement.

N = 318,249 ads;

Note: Data and coding calculated by author using data from the Wisconsin Advertising Project. Dataset includes each airing of each advertisement.

phrase of an advertisement. Position-based appeals show a pattern most similar to the overall pattern shown in chapter 4. They are not as common in the first couple of phrases, but then reach a peak between the sixth and ninth phrases. There is no pattern for when campaigns use competence-based appeals in an advertisement.

The evidence from both character-based and position-based appeals fits well with my argument that campaigns use candidate-centered appeals as mechanisms to develop the credibility of their candidate. Campaigns first establish their candidate's trustworthiness and sincerity before moving on to talk about the issue stands, and they do so by first focusing on the character of their candidate and then on previous actions in political office.

When do campaigns use different types of candidate-centered appeals? Between the two measures, there is little evidence of any pattern for the use of competence-based appeals. But the data do show that campaigns tend to use character-based and position-based appeals in the first half of the phrases in an advertisement. And when discussing their candidate, campaigns are more likely to make these types of appeals toward the beginning of the campaign. My argument is that campaigns use candidate-centered appeals as a means of establishing the credibility of their candidate, and the evidence here supports this argument.

WHAT CAMPAIGNS USE EACH TYPE OF CANDIDATE-CENTERED APPEALS?

Now the question moves to what campaigns use different types of candidate-centered appeals. Different types of campaigns have different imperatives for establishing the credibility of their candidate, primarily based on the status of a candidate. Incumbent campaigns have a different set of incentives than the campaigns of open-seat and challenging campaigns. As a result, I expect that incumbents will be most likely to use position- and competence-based appeals, while inexperienced candidates will be most likely to use character-based appeals. Here I test these assumptions.

Different campaigns use different types of candidate-centered appeals and use them for different purposes and in different contexts. Also, campaigns can use different types of appeals when discussing their opponent than they do when discussing their own candidate. As discussed in chapter 4, I coded the context of candidate-centered appeals by coding each phrase for how it discussed the background of the candidates.[15] Table 5.4 is similar to Table 4.3 in that it has rows

Table 5.4 Use of Candidate-Centered Appeals in Political Advertisements, 2004 House and Senate elections

	All (%)	Position (%)	Character (%)	Competence (%)
Any Background Mentioned		62.2	39.8	27.3
Sponsor's Background Mentioned	68.1	32.5	47.1	25.1
As Incumbent:	40.1	28.5	13.0	13.3
In Other Political Office:	10.8	16.1	11.7	10.3
In the Private Sector	6.3	5.7	7.7	3.9
General Appeals to Experience	1.4	5.3	3.6	5.7
Biography	9.5	7.9	15.7	4.8
Opponent's Background Mentioned	31.9	12.1	24.9	6.6
As Incumbent:	9.0	8.3	3.0	2.3
In Other Political Office:	13.1	14.8	6.8	3.6
In the Private Sector	7.6	1.7	3.3	0.8
Observations	958,741	210,171	134,540	92,398

Note: Individual advertisements can use the candidates' records in various ways, so percentages do not add up to 100%. Data and coding calculated by author using data from the Wisconsin Advertising Project. Dataset includes each airing of each advertisement.

that measure how many phrases use candidate-centered appeals in that context. But it has three columns, one for each type of candidate-centered appeal. Thus, the percentages in the table are the percentage of total phrases that use each type of candidate-centered appeal in each particular context. For comparison purposes, the "Candidate-Centered Phrases" column from Table 4.3 is included as the "All" column.

Position-based appeals are the most commonly used candidate-centered appeal, and they are used in over twice as many phrases as are character-based appeals. Position-based appeals tend to focus on a candidate's actions in office. Nearly 11 percent of all phrases discuss position-based actions by incumbents, and another 3.7 percent discuss the sponsoring candidate's actions while holding another political office. Candidate-centered appeals about the opponent make up 12 percent of all phrases. Of these, over two-thirds are position-based appeals about the opponent's actions in public office (4.4 percent as incumbent, and 3.8 percent in another political office). Position-based statements reflect the past political actions taken by a candidate and are used to encourage voters to presume that past actions by the candidate will result in similar actions again in the future. Thus, position-based appeals focus on actions in recent political office.

The frequent negativity of position-based appeals stands in contrast to the infrequent use of negativity for character-based appeals. Relatively few negative appeals are character-based, though the character-based negative appeals are disproportionately used about opponent's actions in other political offices and in the private sector. This fits well with the notion that campaigns use character-based appeals to develop their candidate's credibility. Character-based appeals tend to be positive appeals, which highlight the strengths and values of the sponsoring candidate. Not surprisingly, almost all biographical appeals are character-based. In fact, appeals about the prepolitical biography of candidates make up over half of all character-based appeals. When campaigns talk about the character of their candidate, they want to demonstrate that their candidate does not have the aberrant values of a typical politician. Emphasizing the lessons learned from his or her upbringing or family serves to humanize a political candidate, making it seem like the candidate has learned the same lessons as the average voter in the state or district and that he or she will bring (or has brought) these lessons to Washington. It is also worth noting that references to a candidate's actions in the private sector (good or bad) are most commonly character-based.

Competence-based appeals are most tilted toward sponsoring candidates (and thus tilted toward positive messages). Only 0.7 percent of all appeals focus on the opponent's competence, while 4.3 percent of all phrases discuss the sponsoring candidate's competence. Further, competence-based appeals frequently deal with the candidate's actions as an incumbent. Of the 4.3 percent of phrases that are competence-based appeals about the sponsor, nearly half (2.1 percent) are about the candidate as an incumbent. Only 0.5 percent of all phrases are general appeals to the experience of the candidates.

Who Uses Each Type of Appeal?

What type of campaign uses each type of candidate-centered appeals? Again, I argue that the key factor that explains what type of candidate-centered appeal a campaign will use is the experience of the candidate.

Campaigns for lesser known candidates should use character-based appeals more frequently because they must introduce their candidate to voters, and campaigns for more experienced candidates should use more position- and competence-based appeals.

Just as in chapter 4, I used multivariate analysis to test these expectations. I created separate logistic regression models for the use of character-based, position-based, and competence-based appeals. That is, the dependent variable was coded "1" if there was a position-/character-/competence-based phrase in an advertisement or phrase, and "0" otherwise. I ran separate models for "in an ad" and "in a phrase" analysis.[16] The independent variables were the same as those used for the analysis presented in chapter 4. I measured candidate experience via candidate status, with variables for "Incumbents" and "Open Seat" candidates. There are control variables for candidate partisanship, competitiveness, office sought (Senate or House), and district ideology. A description of the measurement of these variables and the rationale for their inclusion was given in chapter 4. And just as in chapter 4, I present the predicted probabilities in graphic form, focusing on the probabilities for different types of candidate status. The candidate was a Republican House candidate (modal values) in a district rated at the "Likely" level of competitiveness (mean) and a mean level of district ideology.

Figure 5.4a shows the results for the "in an ad" analysis (full results are presented in Table A5.1). The expectation is that incumbent campaigns will use more position-based appeals ceteris paribus. This expectation is met as the figure shows that incumbent campaigns are nearly 20 percent more likely to use position-based appeals in an advertisement than open-seat or challenging campaigns. The expectations are not met in the character-based appeals model. There is a modest but insignificant increase in the use of character appeals by challengers over incumbents. The competence models look similar to the position-based model; incumbent campaigns are twice as likely to employ competence-based appeals as challenging campaigns. But contrary to my expectations, open-seat candidates used competence-based appeals at a similar rate to incumbent candidates.

Similar patterns exist in the "in a phrase" analysis, which is shown in Figure 5.4b. Incumbent campaigns use position-based appeals more frequently than do challenging or open-seat campaigns. Again there is no significant pattern, however, in the character-based model; incumbent, open-seat, and challenging campaigns use character-based phrases at a similar rate. The competence-based model shows that

THE TYPES OF CANDIDATE-CENTERED APPEALS   117

incumbents are indeed more likely to use these appeals than challenging campaigns. But just as in the "in an ad" analysis, open-seat campaigns defy my expectations, as these campaigns use competence-based phrases at a similar rate to incumbent-based campaigns.

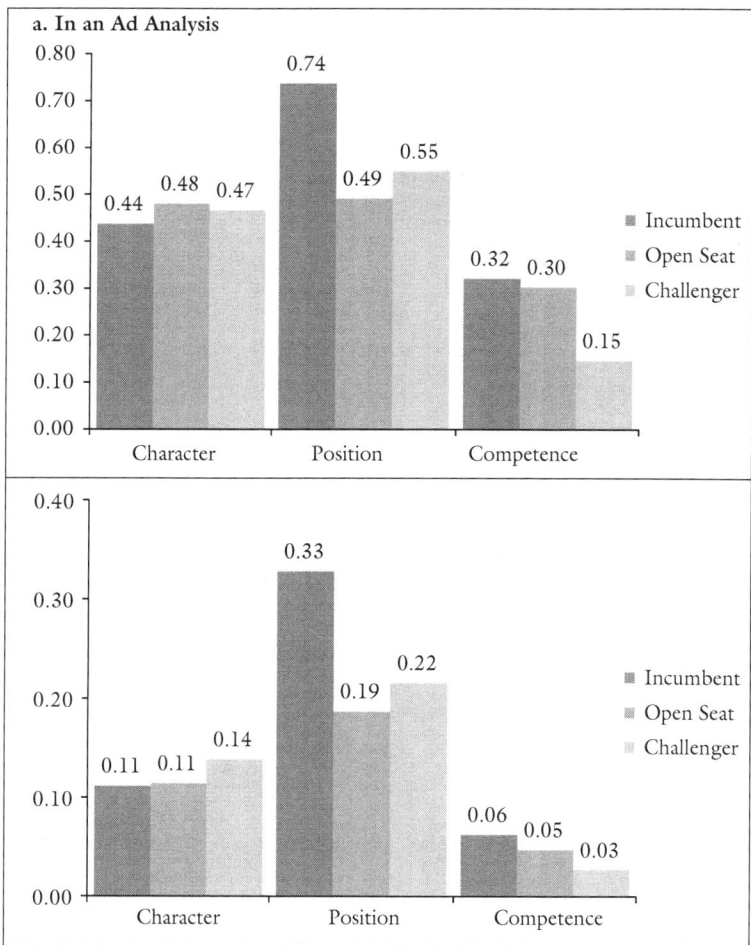

Figure 5.4 Predicted Probabilities of Use of Different Types of Candidate-Centered Appeals, 2004 House & Senate Campaigns.

Note: Probabilities are the post-estimation calculation of the difference between the probability of using that type of background appeal with the independent variable of interest coded at 1. Calculations are for a Republican in a district rated at the "Likely" level of competitiveness. The *District Conservatism* is calculated at its mean. Post-estimation calculations conducted in Stata on the S-Post program.

Overall, these results confirm that the status of the candidate is the key explanation of what type of candidate-centered appeal is employed. Incumbent campaigns are much more likely to use position- and competence-based appeals than are challenging campaigns. Of course, incumbent candidates have developed a substantial record of votes on key issues and passing key bills through the Congress. As such, their campaigns can more credibly make position- and competence-based appeals. Incumbent campaigns also hold a large credibility advantage on position- and competence-based measures over their opponent who, by definition, has experience less proximate to the job being sought. On the other hand, there are few differences between different types of candidates for the use of character-based appeals. Of course, all candidates must convince voters of their character, and neither incumbents, challengers, nor open-seat candidates have, by definition of their status, an advantage over their opponents.

Conclusion

In this chapter, I showed how the reelection campaign of New Jersey governor Chris Christie used their candidate's record to show not only his issue positions to voters, but also his compassion and competence. In discussing Christie's accomplishments in balancing the state's budget and reforming education, the Christie campaign used position-based appeals to show how their candidate's record matched with the preferences of New Jersey voters. In discussing how Christie's concern for those addicted to drugs caused him to beef up rehabilitation alternatives for nonviolent offenders, his campaign made character-based appeals. And in arguing that Christie overcame perceptions that New Jersey was too broken and partisan to create reforms, the campaign made competence-based appeals.

These are the three different types of candidate-centered appeals that campaigns make to voters. Position-based based appeals focus on the past actions and votes of the candidates in their previous political work and are the most common type of candidate-centered appeal. Character-based appeals discuss the candidate's core values, often by discussing the lessons learned from parents, family, or the local community. These are the second most common type of candidate-centered appeal. Third, there are competence-based appeals, which discuss how the past experience of the candidate provides him or her with some expertise to bring to the job being sought. Most commonly, competence-based appeals focus on the legislative experience or clout of a long-serving incumbent.

This chapter helps us understand the contours of candidate-centered appeals. Campaigns analyze different components of their candidate's past actions and experiences, their candidate's particular strengths and weaknesses, to determine what type of appeals will be most effective in wooing voters. For incumbent congressional campaigns, their candidate has a significant number of votes in the legislature, which provides them the opportunity to discuss the positions of their candidate and use these votes as evidence of the sincerity of his or her position. Challenging candidates may not have the credibility to state position-based appeals as effectively, so their campaigns choose to use these appeals less frequently. The results in this chapter show that campaigns are not just discussing their candidate willy-nilly, but are making specific types of candidate-centered appeals. Campaigns identify the elements of their candidate's background that are most amenable to a credible argument that their candidate understands the issues that face the state or district and have solutions to these problems.

Of course, when I say that a candidate has solutions to the problems of his or her district, this is another way of saying that the candidate has a series of issue positions and policy proposals. Issues have been absent up to this point in the book, save for my argument that political science's understanding of campaign messages is too heavily reliant on issue agendas and positioning. This chapter joins the previous two in demonstrating that campaigns analyze the strengths and weaknesses of their opponent to identify the most credible way to present that candidate to voters and that the presentation of the candidate's personality and values are vital to that presentation. This chapter also shows that in addition to the importance of the presentation of the candidate, campaigns make a substantial number of position-based appeals, connecting the issue stands of their candidate to the past actions of their candidates. In this next chapter, I take up the question of issue agendas and candidate-centered appeals, examining how the past actions and experiences of candidates affect what issues their campaigns choose to emphasize.

CHAPTER 6

CANDIDATE-CENTERED APPEALS
AND PERSONAL ISSUES

The Ken Salazar for Senate campaign faced a stiff challenge in 2004. Republicans held both Senate seats in Colorado and the governor's chair. The state's Republican lean was evident in presidential elections, as George W. Bush had won the state by 9 points in the 2000 election. There were some positive signs for Salazar. The state had a growing Hispanic population and a growing population of high-tech and professional workers. Both were pushing the state toward the Democrats.

The most daunting challenge Salazar faced that year was his opponent. Pete Coors was not just willing to spend the millions of dollars he earned in business to win a Senate seat, his business was the most iconic in the state of Colorado. Coors was not only the Chairman of the Coors Brewing Company, but he was the great-grandson of Adolpf Coors, the brewery's founder. The company's success was built off of marketing its connections to Colorado. Ads would feature Pete Coors walking through the snow on a mountain, extolling the virtues of "Rocky Mountain water" in the Coors brewing process. Coors even held the naming rights to the baseball stadium of the Colorado Rockies. In other words, Coors had a huge advantage financially, a huge advantage because of the state's Republican lean, and a huge advantage in terms of public image.

The Salazar campaign needed to win over Republican-leaning swing voters in the state, boost turnout among their base, and successfully contrast their candidate to their wealthy businessman opponent. How did they manage this daunting task? By using candidate-centered appeals.

An introductory ad told Salazar's story. In the ad, a cowboy-hatted Salazar drives his pickup truck and then meets with cattlemen and school children. Images are shown of a church and Salazar riding a horse and meeting with police officer. The audio intersperses Salazar's voice with that of a voiceover announcer:

> Salazar: When you grow up on a ranch, hard work is a way of life.
>
> Announcer: He's been to all 64 Colorado counties many times, and he's on the road again.
>
> Salazar: I was raised to help people—that deeds, not words, are what matter.
>
> Announcer: His values run deep: from his faith, from the land, from his family.
>
> Salazar: My parents always said they couldn't give us riches, but they could give us some education.
>
> Announcer: Their ranch had no power or telephone lines until 1981, but all eight Salazar children went to college. It's the classic American story. As attorney general, he's been a champion for people, prosecuted criminals who prey on children and seniors. Gone after those who pollute the land and water he loves. Now he's running for the United States Senate.
>
> Salazar: For too long there have been two Colorados.
>
> Announcer: He's talking about what Colorado can be.
>
> Salazar: No matter who you are, no matter where you're from, you ought to be able to live the American dream.
>
> Announcer: Ken Salazar: from the people, for the people."[1]

The Salazar campaign obviously liked much of the text of this advertisement: they used the phrases "I was raised to help people—taught that deeds, not words, are what matter" and "Ken Salazar's values run deep: from the land, from his faith, and from his family" in subsequent ads. These subsequent ads combined these biographical appeals with policy appeals on issues ranging from crime and the environment to taxes and health care. The character-based focus on Salazar's humble roots worked not only to demonstrate who Salazar is and demonstrate his concern for the average Coloradan, but they also served as an excellent contrast to the privileged life and upbringing of Coors.

Another Salazar campaign ad focuses not on Salazar's upbringing and parents, but on more contemporary biographical details. The ad then connects those details to his issue priorities.

> Ken Salazar still works weekends at his family's ranch. His wife, Hope, runs a Dairy Queen. Their values run deep: work, faith, family. As our attorney general, Ken Salazar fought to protect our land, water, and people. In the Senate, he'll focus on cutting the deficit, on helping families, with affordable health care and quality education, tax cuts for the middle class, and not for millionaires. He'll always be a champion for people.
>
> Salazar: I'm Ken Salazar, and I approve this message.[2]

Similar to the previous advertisement, this Salazar campaign ad focuses on character-based appeals about the candidate, noting how he and his wife's work keeps them rooted to their values. The ad then transitions to discussing Salazar's issue stands, with the candidate-centered appeal at the beginning of the advertisement serving to validate these views.

Salazar's campaign focused not just on character-based appeals, but also used position- and competence-based appeals to woo Colorado voters. Another advertisement focuses on Salazar's record as attorney general.

> Announcer: Attorney General Ken Salazar has fought to protect our land, water, and people. He won the longest jail term against an environmental polluter in our history, wrote the law to create Great Outdoors Colorado, protected Colorado water from out-of-state interests—an extraordinary record of accomplishment. So what are these attack ads against Ken Salazar?
>
> [Screen shows cutouts from newspaper articles: "Slime." "Sleazy." "Slur."]
>
> Announcer: Ken Salazar for Senate: experience money can't buy.
>
> Salazar: I'm Ken Salazar, and I approve this message.[3]

This ad focuses entirely on Salazar's record in office and uses it to demonstrate Salazar's effectiveness and to insulate him from attacks by Coors and Republicans. These Salazar appeals were effective. On election night, despite a 4-point victory for George W. Bush, Salazar reversed that result and won his own 4-point victory.

The diversity of the Salazar campaign's appeals helps to demonstrate the effectiveness of candidate-centered appeals. As demonstrated last chapter, campaigns can use candidate-centered appeals for different purposes. Here we see the Salazar campaign making effective appeals about their candidate's character ("words, not deeds matter"), political record ("the longest jail term against an environmental polluter"), and competence ("an extraordinary record of accomplishment"). Highlighting different parts of Salazar's background allows his campaign to make different types of appeals while developing their candidate's credibility and likeability.

The Salazar ads demonstrate another element of how candidate-centered appeals work. Campaigns highlight particular elements of their candidate's background as key elements of their campaign strategy. In this case, the Salazar campaign highlights their candidate's biography, his political record, and his political values as key elements of these advertisements. The campaign uses these elements just as persuasively as they use their focus on issues such as taxes and the environment. In this chapter, I examine the use of what I call "personal issues"—biography, political record, personal values, and so forth—in campaign messages. How often do campaigns highlight these issues for voters, and do they highlight them more or less frequently than they discuss more substantive policy issues? The Salazar campaign also combined particular personal issues with particular policy issues—for example, biography with taxes and the economy, political record with the environment. I also investigate how campaigns combine personal issues with policy issues. Do campaigns use the same set of issues for this, or do they use a specific set of issues that map more easily into personal appeals?

What Are Personal Issues?

This discussion of the use of personal issues in political campaigns stands in contrast to the main thrust of political science research on campaign messages. These studies have focused heavily, if not exclusively, on the issue agendas of political campaigns. Campaigns want to highlight favorable issues, and political scientists have developed a series of models that assess why campaigns use particular issues (e.g., Downs's median voter theorem and John Petrocik's theory of issue ownership). Yet the study of issue agendas by political scientists is attenuated. The focus of issue-agenda research has been on the use of policy issues by political campaigns. For example, Table 1 of John Sides's article "The Origins of Campaign Agendas" (418) "presents the total volume of advertising—that is, the number of airings—that mentioned an issue" in the 1998 election. The coding for the table is based on those done by the Wisconsin Advertising Project. But the table includes policy issues and ignores issues listed in the

"Personal Characteristics of Candidate(s)" category. These issues are background, political record, attendance record, ideology, personal values, honesty/integrity, and special interests.[4] Sides work is similar to other models of issue agendas, which ignore these personal issues, such as background and personal values, for a focus on policy issues (cf. Kaplan, Park, and Ridout 2005; Arbour 2013).

In focusing on policy issues and ignoring personal issues, political scientists have unnecessarily limited our understanding of issue agendas. Table 6.1 provides evidence for this. The left-hand panel follows the description of the Sides table given above—it includes the percentage of advertisements that mentioned a policy issue. The data come from general election US House and Senate campaign advertisements from 2000 to 2004 and were coded by the Wisconsin Advertising Project.[5] The right-hand panel of Table 6.1 includes the same results, but also includes data from the seven personal issues listed in the previous paragraph. The results show that these personal issues are quite important to political campaigns. "Political Record" is the most commonly discussed issue; it appears in 28.1 percent of all aired advertisements across the three election years. "Biography" is the third most common issue, appearing in 22.0 percent of all aired advertisements. "Personal Values" is the eighth most common issue (12.4 percent of all advertisements) while "Honesty and Integrity" is the eleventh most common issue (8.3 percent of all aired advertisements). Discussions of "Ideology" (7.0 percent) and "Special Interests" (4.8 percent) happen on a regular basis, while mentions of an incumbent's work in "Constituent Service" are not very common (1.7 percent of all aired advertisements).

These results demonstrate that personal issues are a very common part of campaign strategy. Campaigns use biographical appeals more frequently than they do health-care appeals, discuss personal values more often than they do Medicare, and appeals to honesty and integrity are more common than those about national defense. These personal issues are an important and vital part of campaign rhetoric, and we, as political scientists, should try to understand how and why campaigns use these appeals. In this chapter, I take up this challenge. I examine the use of these personal appeals. I first assess what type of campaigns use each type of personal appeal in an effort to understand why campaigns choose to use these appeals. I then examine how campaigns use these appeals, assessing what other issues campaigns combine with personal appeals.

Table 6.1 Campaign Issue Agendas; US House & Senate Campaigns, 2000–2004

Policy Issues Only					Personal and Policy Issues				
Issue	Total (%)	2000 (%)	2002 (%)	2004 (%)	Issue	Total (%)	2000 (%)	2002 (%)	2004 (%)
Taxes	24.1%	22.6%	22.6%	26.4%	*Political Record*	28.1%	16.0%	36.2%	28.5%
Health Care	20.3%	27.2%	14.0%	21.4%	Taxes	24.1%	22.6%	22.6%	26.4%
Education	18.6%	30.4%	19.2%	11.1%	*Background*	22.0%	22.6%	21.6%	22.1%
Jobs & the Economy	17.6%	4.9%	15.6%	26.8%	Health Care	20.3%	27.2%	14.0%	21.4%
Social Security	14.3%	23.7%	18.5%	5.3%	Education	18.6%	30.4%	19.2%	11.1%
Prescription Drugs	9.4%	0.0%	16.0%	9.4%	Jobs & the Economy	17.6%	4.9%	15.6%	26.8%
Medicare	9.1%	21.2%	7.9%	2.9%	Social Security	14.3%	23.7%	18.5%	5.3%
Defense	7.4%	1.9%	8.3%	10.0%	*Personal Values*	12.4%	5.2%	16.2%	13.4%
Terrorism	5.2%	0.0%	3.1%	10.1%	Prescription Drugs	9.4%	0.0%	16.0%	9.4%
Environment	4.0%	4.9%	4.2%	3.4%	Medicare	9.1%	21.2%	7.9%	2.9%
Deficit/Budget	4.0%	8.7%	2.1%	2.7%	*Honesty/Integrity*	8.3%	7.0%	8.5%	8.8%
Government Spending	3.6%	3.9%	2.7%	4.2%	Defense	7.4%	1.9%	8.3%	10.0%
Abortion	3.4%	2.6%	2.1%	4.9%	*Ideology*	7.0%	1.6%	10.6%	7.2%
Trade/NAFTA	2.9%	0.1%	2.2%	5.1%	Terrorism	5.2%	0.0%	3.1%	10.1%
Crime	2.8%	4.5%	2.5%	2.0%	*Special Interests*	4.8%	6.1%	4.0%	4.6%
Children's Issues	2.6%	4.5%	2.7%	1.4%	Environment	4.0%	4.9%	4.2%	3.4%
Corporate Pensions	2.6%	0.0%	7.0%	0.4%	Deficit/Budget	4.0%	8.7%	2.1%	2.7%

Policy Issues Only

Issue	Total (%)	2000 (%)	2002 (%)	2004 (%)
Veterans	2.5%	1.0%	2.5%	3.4%
Gun Control	2.4%	5.1%	2.4%	0.9%
Moral Values	1.8%	1.5%	2.0%	1.7%
Business	1.7%	0.2%	1.7%	2.7%
September 11 Attacks	1.7%	0.0%	1.1%	3.2%
Local issues	1.4%	0.0%	1.7%	2.1%
Bill Clinton	1.2%	0.0%	2.8%	0.5%
Farming/Agriculture	1.0%	1.7%	0.9%	0.8%

Personal and Policy Issues

Issue	Total (%)	2000 (%)	2002 (%)	2004 (%)
Government Spending	3.6%	3.9%	2.7%	4.2%
Abortion	3.4%	2.6%	2.1%	4.9%
Trade/NAFTA	2.9%	0.1%	2.2%	5.1%
Crime	2.8%	4.5%	2.5%	2.0%
Children's Issues	2.6%	4.5%	2.7%	1.4%
Corporate Pensions	2.6%	0.0%	7.0%	0.4%
Veterans	2.5%	1.0%	2.5%	3.4%
Gun Control	2.4%	5.1%	2.4%	0.9%
Moral Values	1.8%	1.5%	2.0%	1.7%
Constituent Service	1.7%	0.0%	2.1%	2.5%
Business	1.7%	0.2%	1.7%	2.7%
September 11 Attacks	1.7%	0.0%	1.1%	3.2%
Local issues	1.4%	0.0%	1.7%	2.1%
Bill Clinton	1.2%	0.0%	2.8%	0.5%
Farming/Agriculture	1.0%	1.7%	0.9%	0.8%

Note: Values represent the percentage of advertisement that discussed the issue at hand. Advertisements come from general election advertisements aired by US House and Senate campaigns from 2000–2004. Data coded by the Wisconsin Advertising Project. Dataset includes each airing of each advertisement. N = 823,419.

Who Uses Personal Issues?

To understand why campaigns use candidate-centered appeals, it is necessary to understand who uses these appeals. By leveraging the variation in who uses each of these different types of candidate-centered appeals, one can assess why campaigns use them.

To address this issue, I use multivariate logistic regression. As discussed in chapters 4 and 5, multivariate analysis allows for the measurement of a specific variable while controlling for the other variables in the model. Once again, the key variable to test is candidate status—"Incumbent," "Open Seat," and "Challenger." Campaigns have different imperatives based on their candidate's status. Open-seat and challenging campaigns must introduce their candidate to a new set of voters, while incumbent campaigns should seek to highlight their candidate's actions in office. Discussions of personal values and honesty and integrity should affect all candidates, but would seem to be most important for nonincumbents, whose virtues and values are less well known to voters.

I run a logistic regression for six of the seven personal issues identified above (biography, political record, personal values, honesty and integrity, ideology, and special interests).[6] To account for candidate status, I include dichotomous variables for "Incumbent" and "Open Seat" (Challengers arethe excluded category). A multivariate test allows me to examine whether any differences in the use of candidate-centered advertisements between incumbent, challenging, and open-seat campaigns are based on candidate status or the result of a correlation between these variables and another variable in the model. In addition, I include a variable for "Republican." Issue-ownership theory would lead one expect significant coefficients for this variable in a model that tested substantive issues such as health care and taxes. There is no theoretical reason to expect that one party *owns* a particular personal issue, but this variable tests for that possibility. Lipsitz (2011, 57–59) finds that competitive elections change the nature of issue agendas, prompting campaigns to focus on the same issue. To account for this potential impact, I include a measure of the competitiveness of each race.[7] I also include a variable to account for the conservatism of each district or state. [8]

As I did in chapter 4, I present the predicted probabilities of the results in graphic form in Figure 6.1 (the full results of the model are available in Appendix Table A6.1). The results of the "Biography" model demonstrate the greatest variation. Incumbent campaigns use biographical appeals in only about 17 percent of their advertisements, which is significantly less than challenging candidates (.2253).

Open-seat campaigns use biographical appeals in significantly more advertisements; the results show that over 28 percent of open-seat ads include biography appeals. These results meet my expectations; incumbents are relatively well known to voters, and there is little reason to introduce them via discussions of their biography. That being said, biography still plays an important part in the message strategy of incumbent campaigns, appearing in nearly one-sixth of all aired advertisements. Challengers and open-seat campaigns discuss their candidate's biography more frequently, though open-seat campaign use these appeals more frequently.

Campaigns use appeals about the candidates' political record with great frequency, but there is no significant variation between incumbent, challenging, and open-seat campaigns in their use of this personal issue. In fact, the only variable in the model that is significant is district conservatism. As the district becomes more conservative, campaigns are more likely to talk about their candidate's political record. I have no good explanation for why this occurs. More relevantly, it is important to note that incumbent and challenging campaigns use appeals about the candidates' political records at similar rates. This suggests that all campaigns, regardless of the status of their candidate, are equally likely to focus on the actions of their candidate in public office in their messages to voters. Similarly, incumbent, open-seat, and challenging campaigns were all just as likely to discuss personal values. There are few differences (and no significant ones) in the predicted probabilities for each type of candidate. Similarly, there were no significant differences in the use of appeals about candidates' honesty and integrity.

Overall, the use of these personal issues is spread relatively evenly across candidates of different statuses. Whether a candidate is an incumbent, a challenger, or an open-seat candidate, campaigns are equally likely to highlight a personal issue in their messages to voters. Because campaigns use these personal-issue appeals with great frequency, I conclude that personal-issue appeals are important to all campaigns, regardless of context.

How Campaigns Use Personal Issues

The results so far show that campaigns use personal issues with great frequency and with little pattern. All campaigns seek to use these issues, almost regardless of context or status. In other words, all campaigns see an advantage to highlighting personal aspects of their candidates to voters. The question moves to how campaigns choose to highlight personal issues for voters.

One way to examine how campaigns use personal appeals is to examine what issues campaigns combine with a personal issue. By assessing what issues campaigns combine with personal issues, I can assess what type of narratives campaigns find most effective. Campaigns may use the same set of issues when discussing personal appeals as they do when they focus entirely on policy issues, but they may focus on particular sets of issues that connect most easily with their candidate's biography, record, or values.

To examine how campaigns combine personal issues with other issues, I took all advertisements that discussed biography and then determined the percentage of those advertisements that discussed each of the other issues. Of course, one would expect that campaigns would be more likely to use more popular issues more frequently, so I decided to assess the relationship via the ratio between the percentage of ads that discussed biography and a particular issue and the percentage of all advertisements that discussed that issue. I then repeated this process for ads that discussed political record, personal values, and honesty and integrity.

Table 6.2 shows these ratios. There is a column for each of the four issues under study, and the results are sorted from the highest to lowest ratios. For example, take personal values. This issue appears in 12.4 percent of all advertisements. But when campaigns discuss biography in an ad, they are more eager to discuss personal values, doing so in 18.7 percent of these advertisements. Divide the 18.7 percent by 12.4 percent, and you get a ratio of 1.51. You can see in Table 6.2 that "Personal Values" has the highest ratio in the "Biography" column. A number greater than 1 indicates that a campaign aired a higher percentage of advertisements in ads combined with the particular personal issue under study than they did in all advertisements that they aired.

It is worth noting that many campaign advertisements do not combine different issues; 8.12 percent of all aired advertisements discuss "Biography" and no other issue. Campaigns can do this by focusing on a candidate's upbringing and parents. An example is provided in this advertisement from the Inez Tenenbaum (D-SC) for Senate campaign:

> Tenenbaum: My mother was an elementary school teacher; she was a leader in our church. She taught Sunday school class. My father was a farmer when I was born, but shortly thereafter he went back into the navy. My father was a career navy man. I learned from my parents about responsibility, about commitment to one's community and one's nation. I learned about patriotism and commitment. I'm Inez Tenenbaum, and I approved this message.[9]

Table 6.2 Ratio of Use of an Issue When Combined With a Personal Issue to All Uses of That Issue

Biography		Political Record		Personal Values		Honesty	
Personal Values	1.51	Corporate Pensions	1.77	Moral Values	1.78	Special Interests	1.43
Business	1.42	Constituent Service	1.24	Honesty/Integrity	1.41	Corporate Pensions	1.35
Honesty/Integrity	1.28	Crime	1.14	Ideology	1.30	Ideology	1.34
Ideology	1.25	Local issues	1.14	Background	1.15	Moral Values	1.33
Terrorism	1.11	Prescription Drugs	1.10	Local issues	1.14	Personal Values	1.26
Environment	1.06	Government Spending	1.08	Abortion	1.12	Political Record	1.08
Moral Values	1.03	Taxes	1.04	Crime	1.07	Background	1.01
Corporate Pensions	1.00	Environment	1.03	Constituent Service	1.06	Business	0.88
Education	0.97	Honesty/Integrity	1.00	Political Record	1.05	Government Spending	0.86
Jobs & the Economy	0.97	Veterans	1.00	Defense	0.95	Taxes	0.75
Crime	0.94	Bill Clinton	1.00	Government Spending	0.94	Veterans	0.72
Defense	0.87	Business	0.94	Terrorism	0.94	Local issues	0.71
Special Interests	0.81	Special Interests	0.94	Taxes	0.80	Social Security	0.71
Political Record	0.77	Ideology	0.91	Veterans	0.72	Defense	0.69
Veterans	0.73	Terrorism	0.85	Jobs & the Economy	0.72	Environment	0.65
Taxes	0.72	Other Children's Issues	0.85	Environment	0.70	Prescription Drugs	0.56
Health Care	0.72	Medicare	0.82	Farming	0.70	Health Care	0.52
Bill Clinton	0.71	September 11 Attacks	0.82	Other Children's Issues	0.69	Medicare	0.51
Trade/NAFTA	0.70	Education	0.82	Corporate Pensions	0.69	Abortion	0.50

(*continued*)

Table 6.2 Ratio of Use of an Issue When Combined With a Personal Issue to All Uses of that Issue (*continued*)

Biography		Political Record		Personal Values		Honesty	
Gun Control	0.67	Jobs & the Economy	0.81	Trade/NAFTA	0.69	Terrorism	0.46
September 11 Attacks	0.64	Defense	0.81	Education	0.60	September 11 Attacks	0.41
Prescription Drugs	0.64	Trade/NAFTA	0.76	Gun Control	0.58	Education	0.39
Local issues	0.64	Personal Values	0.74	Bill Clinton	0.58	Jobs & the Economy	0.38
Social Security	0.62	Health Care	0.71	Business	0.53	Other Children's Issues	0.35
Other Children's Issues	0.54	Abortion	0.71	Health Care	0.50	Farming	0.30
Abortion	0.49	Moral Values	0.67	Social Security	0.49	Trade/NAFTA	0.28
Deficit/Budget	0.46	Social Security	0.66	Deficit/Budget	0.48	Deficit/Budget	0.28
Constituent Service	0.39	Deficit/Budget	0.65	Special Interests	0.42	Bill Clinton	0.25
Government Spending	0.36	Background	0.56	Prescription Drugs	0.41	Gun Control	0.13
Farming	0.31	Farming	0.50	September 11 Attacks	0.41	Crime	0.07
Medicare	0.30	Gun Control	0.42	Medicare	0.34	Constituent Service	0.00

Note: Values represent ratio between the percentage of ads that discussed biography, political record, personal values, or honesty/integrity as well as the specific issues and the percentage of all advertisements that discussed that issue. Advertisements come from general election advertisements aired by US House and Senate campaigns from 2000–2004. Data coded by the Wisconsin Advertising Project. Dataset includes each airing of each advertisement. N = 823,419.

Other biographical appeals focus on the actions of candidates as adults in their lives before they entered politics. This is demonstrated by this ad from the Jeanne Patterson (R-MO) for Congress campaign:

> Patterson: I'm Jeanne Patterson, and I approve this message.
>
> Announcer: Rodney was born with fused ribs.
>
> Mother: His lungs were not given enough proper space to grow.
>
> Announcer: An insurance company denied him a life-saving treatment, so Jeanne Patterson and the First Hand Foundation stepped in.
>
> Mother: Jeanne just stepped right up and said, she told me, "All right, we'll take care of him."
>
> Announcer: Jeanne Patterson: putting people first.
>
> Mother: I thank them every day with every breath my son takes."[10]

Another way that campaigns talk about their candidate's biography is by emphasizing the candidate's family. This ad from the Baron Hill (D-IN) for Congress campaign does just that:

> Hill: There's no place quite like southern Indiana. I've lived here in Seymour all my life. Born and raised here, and we love it here. It's why I return home every weekend from Washington, DC. Our three daughters are here in Indiana. Our youngest daughter is still in high school.
>
> Betty Hill: And there's a lot of things that I miss about not living in DC, but I'd miss a lot more if I wasn't here. Just being here when the older daughters call.
>
> Hill: You learn to appreciate home when you are away. This is where we knew we wanted to live.
>
> Betty Hill: It's home.
>
> Hill: I'm Baron Hill, and I approved this message.[11]

These three ads have different topics and focus on different time periods in the candidates' lives, but what unites them is not only their focus on the lives of the candidates, but also their attempt to enhance a candidate's likeability and make known his or her common values.

Most advertisements about a candidate's biography, however, combine the biographical appeal with appeals about other issues. The most common way that campaigns combine biographical appeals with other appeals is through other personal issues. The data show that campaigns were more likely to discuss their candidate's personal values, honesty and integrity, and ideology when discussing their candidate's biography than during other advertisements. The policy issues that campaigns use in high ratios with biographical appeals include "Business," "Terrorism," "Environment," and "Moral Values." These are issues in which a candidate's personal experience with the issue is seen as particularly relevant.

The Brad Carson (D-OK) for Senate campaign was able to combine four different personal issues ("Biography," "Personal Values," "Honesty and Integrity," and "Ideology") into a single advertisement:

> I'm Brad Carson, and this is Stillwell, where I learned growing up what Oklahoma is all about. I knew as a boy that Oklahomans treated each other with respect and that we do what we say we'll do. Well, I also know from my years in Congress that neither national party has a monopoly on the truth, and they don't care much about Oklahoma. I approve this message because in the United States Senate, my loyalty will be to you, and I will never back down. To me, Oklahoma's worth fighting for.[12]

The ad avoids any discussion of specific policies that Carson wants to achieve and focuses on the values Carson learned as a child and contrasts those values to what he has learned as a member of Congress. Those experiences shape Carson's ideology ("neither national party has a monopoly on the truth"), and he uses this to try to connect with voters.

Other campaigns strike similar personal themes without combining as many issues. In this ad, the Rick Boucher (D-VA) for Congress campaign has their candidate discuss his biography, personal values, and honesty and integrity in the same ad.

> Boucher: Growing up in Washington County, our community's values were deeply learned: the values of hard work and playing by the rules, pride in our country. A promise made was a promise kept. Years have gone by since then. Now the pace is faster, and the world is a more complicated place. But my values are the same ones I grew up with. I'm Rick Boucher, and I approve this message because I'm proud to take southwest Virginia's values to Washington.[13]

Ads like the Boucher and Carson ads try to emphasize the common values of the candidates and use biography, primarily focused on the candidate's upbringing, as the means to do this.

Other campaigns try to combine a candidate's biography with policy issues. As suggested by the table, campaigns are more likely to

Candidate-Centered Appeals and Personal Issues 135

discuss biography with issues such as business. For example, in this ad, David Wu (D-OR) connects his work in high tech with his position on Social Security:

> I'm David Wu, and before I went to Congress, I worked with high-tech businesses. So I believe in the power of investing. But unlike my opponent Goli Ameri, I don't believe in putting Social Security money into the stock market. She and George Bush think that's a great idea. I don't. Privatizing Social Security is about as risky as, well, jumping off a bridge. That's why I'll never vote for it in Congress. I approve this message, and I do my own stunts. [Wu then bungee jumps off of a bridge.][14]

Wu's background in high tech gives him credibility to object to the Social Security plans of his opponent. Other campaigns discuss how a candidate's experience and biography will help them fight the threat of terrorism. Consider this ad from the John Gibbons (R-NV) for Congress campaign.

> Announcer: What we in American hold most dear is under attack. Terrorists try to strike fear in our hearts. Now America needs leadership. Now, America needs heroes. Jim Gibbons served America in two wars, winning 19 medals, including the Distinguished Flying Cross for bravery. In Congress, Jim Gibbons is a leader in homeland security and always fights to put Nevada first.
>
> Gibbons: I'm Jim Gibbons, and I approve this message, and I'm asking for your vote.
>
> Announcer: Jim Gibbons for Nevada.

This ad claims that Gibbon's military service qualifies him to deal with terrorism effectively. And certainly military experience allows a campaign to claim that their candidate has the toughness to deal with enemies such as al-Qaeda.

Advertisements that focus on a candidate's political record try to do something different than ads about biography. In these advertisements, campaigns try to demonstrate the competence and experience of their candidate. The argument is that their candidate is an accomplished person and that these accomplishments demonstrate why their candidate will be effective if elected to office. Some of these advertisements can focus entirely on a candidate's political record without touching on policy issues. This advertisement from the George Voinovich (R-OH) for Senate campaign summarizes newspaper endorsements of the candidate without discussing his issue positions:

> Announcer: Ohio newspapers overwhelmingly agree: George Voinovich's "decades of experience make him the better choice." He's "one of the few Republicans who cares about deficit reduction." Senator Voinovich "has established himself as a tenacious and independent voice for Ohio." "By far a better choice." Voinovich is "the savvy, level-headed leader you would want protecting your well-being in a dangerous time which our nation now faces."
>
> Voinovich: I'm George Voinovich, and I approve this message to keep fighting for Ohio families.[15]

The ad uses the authority of the newspaper endorsements to note Voinovich's accomplishments, but the only rationale for Voinovich's election spelled out in the ad is basic approval of Voinovich's previous term in office and his "decades of experience."

This advertisement from the congressional campaign of Nancy Naples (R-NY) does give a rationale for her election—she wants to focus on keeping jobs in the area—and uses her résumé as evidence of her competence to do so.

> Announcer: We know her as our comptroller, rooting out waste and fraud in government. But Nancy Naples is also an accomplished businesswoman who was a senior executive on Wall Street, then ran a family business here at home. So she knows how to create jobs. Those are the skills she will bring to Congress.
>
> Naples: My first priority will be creating jobs here in western New York because, for too long, we've not only lost jobs, but our young people move away to seek opportunity. And I want to change that. I'm Nancy Naples, and I approve this message.

The message of the Naples ad is that she knows what she is doing, and her record in both the public and private sector demonstrates this.

When campaigns combine appeals about a candidate's political record with policy issues, the effect is a little different. In these messages, the appeals to résumé are appeals that focus on the compassion and concern of these candidates. Rather than demonstrating that concern through biography, the political actions of the candidates provide the evidence. This advertisement from the Dave Reichert (R-WA) campaign demonstrates how this works.

> Woman: It's frightening.
>
> Woman 2: You never recover from this.
>
> Woman 3: It's unforgivable.

Reichert: Domestic violence is a crime that violates every shred of human decency.

Announcer: As sheriff, Dave Reichert didn't just talk about these offenders: he went after them. One day, he nearly lost his life stopping one.

Reichert: As sheriff, we've toughened our approach. In Congress, we'll toughen federal law to stop the violence. I'm Dave Reichert, and I approved this message because talk alone never protected a wife, mother, or child.[16]

Of course, campaigns can be just as willing to use a candidate's political record to attack an opponent as they can to build up their candidate. An opponent's political record can provide excellent evidence of his or her misplaced priorities or bad decision making, and thus, increase the credibility of the attack. An example is provided here by the Rick Renzi (R-AZ) for Congress campaign.

Paul Babbitt: a career of high taxes and big spending. While he was a Flagstaff councilman, the city budget doubled. When he moved on to Coconico County, spending skyrocketed there too, forcing the county into debt for the first time since 1894. The *Arizona Daily Sun* said: "Babbit has not provided the kind of representation and leadership that is essential." They're right.[17]

Discussions of a candidate's political record are direct appeals to the credibility of a candidate, regardless of whether the appeal is used to support your candidate or attack an opponent.

Two personal issues directly deal with the character of candidates—"Personal Values" and "Honesty and Integrity." Both of these personal issues attempt to show voters who the candidate is. They try to demonstrate the inner values of the candidate. Campaigns of course hope that by showing the character of their candidate through these appeals, voters will regard their candidate as more likeable and more trustworthy. Often these appeals are made in the voice of other people describing the candidate. Take for example this advertisement from the Steve Pearce (R-NM) for Congress campaign.

Paul Borunda: I'm a Democrat, and I'm supporting Steve Pearce.

Laurie Kincaid: I'm a Democrat, and I support Congressman Pearce.

Announcer: Steve Pearce is bringing us together.

Kincaid: He has made a difference for all of us.

Yolanda Roybal: It's not about Democrat or Republican; it's about what's best for the people.

Kincaid: I don't think anyone can question his honesty, his integrity.

Announcer: Steve Pearce: our congressman.

Roybal: I'm a Democrat, and I'm very proud to support Steve Pearce.

Pearce: I'm Steve Pearce, and I approved this message.[18]

This advertisement tells us nothing about Pearce's accomplishments in his previous terms in Congress or Pearce's plans in the upcoming term. It simply tells us that he has a particular worthwhile set of values—bringing people together, caring about what's best for the people, honesty, integrity.

Table 6.2 shows that campaigns are very likely to combine "Personal Values" and "Honesty and Integrity" with other personal issues. Campaigns were more likely to discuss "Honesty and Integrity," "Ideology," and "Biography" in an ad featuring "Personal Values" than in the average advertisement (ratios of 1.41, 1.40, and 1.15 respectively). Campaigns were more likely to discuss "Ideology," "Personal Values," and "Biography" when combined with "Honesty and Integrity."

Campaigns also combine these two character-based personal issues with a number of policy issues. A common issue to combine with these two personal issues was abortion. Many view abortion as the ultimate personal issue, and campaigns want to develop the connection between a candidate's personal values and views on abortion. Take this ad from the campaign of Congressman Chet Edwards (D-TX), which defends the candidate from attacks against him:

> Announcer: Arlene Wohlgemuth and her Washington, DC, friends are distorting Chet Edwards's record again. The truth: Chet is a true Texas conservative, a Christian man who bucks his party leaders to oppose partial-birth abortion. And he opposes gay adoption. But above all, Chet Edwards believes in telling the truth. Chet Edwards: Texas values.[19]

The Edwards campaign seamlessly includes honesty along with opposing abortion rights and homophobia as "Texas values." You could well argue that one of these is not like the other, but the Edwards campaign does not believe that voters will do so.

Not surprisingly, there is an easy connection between "Personal Values" and "Moral Values." That is, campaigns were likely to use discussions of a candidate's personal moral values to enhance their argument about policy issues that deal with moral values. This Robert Aderholt (R-AL) for Congress ad helps to demonstrate this:

Aderholt: I'm Robert Aderholt, and I approved this message.

Woman: You can trust Robert Aderholt to do the right thing.

Man: Robert believes in our traditional values, and he fights for them.

Man 2: Congressman Aderholt's a man of principle and integrity.

Announcer: A new prescription drug benefit for seniors, federal funding for rural hospitals, lower taxes for working families—that's Congressman Robert Aderholt, always fighting for our conservative Alabama values.

Woman 2: He's done a lot for Alabama.[20]

According to the ad, Robert Aderholt is a man of principle and integrity who you can trust to do the right thing, like stand up for traditional values (which usually means opposing abortion and gay rights). Aderholt's personal values give credence to his policy stands on issues of moral values and issues such as prescription drugs and taxes.

Looking over all of these advertisements and the results from Table 6.2, two clear patterns emerge. First, campaigns are most likely to combine personal issues with other personal issues. For each of the four issues under study, there are several personal issues with ratios of greater than 1.0. For example, campaigns talk about "Personal Values" over 50 percent more often in advertisements featuring "Biography" and 25 percent more often in ads featuring discussions of the candidate's "Honesty and Integrity" than in all ads. Similarly, discussions of "Ideology" are more common when combined with "Biography," "Personal Values," and "Honesty and Integrity" than in the average advertisement. Such a finding should not be that surprising. Campaigns often run ads that focus entirely on the personal aspect of their candidate. As shown here, an ad might highlight a candidate's upbringing and the values the candidate learned from his or her parents. Or an ad will feature constituents and/or friends discussing the values and integrity of the candidate. Different personal issues provide different points of evidence for the credibility and likability of the candidate.

The second pattern is that the issues that campaigns are more likely to combine with personal issues are not the most common and thus most salient issues. The most common policy issues are "Taxes" and "Health Care," followed by "Education," "Jobs and the Economy," and "Social Security." Among these five issues, only one has a ratio of 1.0 for any of the four personal issues under study. When it comes to issues that are highly salient among voters, campaigns do not need to combine them with personal issues to demonstrate the candidate's concern about these issues. Instead, the issues with high ratios are ones that are aired less frequently, such as "Corporate Pensions" or "Crime." Here, the personal connections of the candidate provide evidence of the candidate's interest and concern in the issue. Campaigns want to combine issues such as "Crime" or the "Environment" because the credibility provided by the personal issue is needed to enhance the appeal on the policy issue.

Conclusion

At the beginning of this chapter, I discussed the advertising strategy used by the Ken Salazar for Senate campaign in 2004. In that campaign, the Salazar campaign used a wide variety of candidate-centered appeals to successfully sell their candidate to Colorado voters. Some focused on the candidate's humble upbringing and the values it taught him. These appeals were combined with discussions of the candidate's views on bread-and-butter issues, like taxes. Other candidate-centered appeals discussed Salazar's record as attorney general and in the state's cabinet. These appeals focused on environmental issues. These pairings were intentional. Salazar's humble biography helps to demonstrate his understanding of the struggles of common people in Colorado, and his campaign thought that these appeals would enhance their message on taxes. Salazar's work in public office focused heavily on the environment. His campaign could use their candidate's record to make credible appeals about the environment.

This chapter demonstrates that the strategies used by the Salazar campaign are common. Campaigns seek to combine their discussion of personal issues with other issues. Campaigns weigh the strengths and weaknesses of their candidate's biography, background, and political record in an effort to craft the most effective message. The results in the chapter show that campaigns make these choices carefully and deliberately, identifying the elements of the candidate's background and the issue that they can combine most effectively.

CHAPTER 7

THE EFFECT OF CANDIDATE-CENTERED APPEALS

John Barrow was in political trouble in 2012. Of course, as a white Democrat who represented a rural and small-town Southern district, Marshall was always in political trouble. But in 2012, Marshall was running under new district lines that had been drawn by Republicans in the Georgia legislature for the specific purpose of defeating Barrow. Polls in August showed a neck-and-neck race between Barrow and his Republican opponent, Lee Anderson, a state representative (Kerr-Dineen 2012).

The Barrow campaign needed a message that stood out from the national Democratic Party (Barack Obama had won only 44 percent of the vote in Barrow's district) and connected to voters in the district. The Barrow campaign found one based on Barrow's endorsement by the NRA and his own family's guns:

> I'm John Barrow. And long before I was born, my grandfather used this little Smith & Wesson here to help stop a lynching. And for as long as I can remember, my father always had this rifle real handy [Barrow cocks the rifle] just to keep us safe. That's why I support the Second Amendment, and that's why I'm proud to be endorsed by the NRA. I approve this message, because these are my guns now and ain't nobody gonna take them away.[1]

The Barrow campaign's advertisements throughout the campaign emphasized their own candidate, putting their candidate front and center, letting him make a direct-to-camera appeal (Sullivan 2012). These advertisements tried to walk a fine line between supporting traditional liberal and Democratic themes while establishing Barrow's independence from his national party and its leaders. This ad, where Barrow brandishes his family's guns, achieves these goals. His grandfather's Smith and Wesson stopped a lynching, which is a nod to African American and white liberal voters in the district. At the same time, the emphasis on guns and the NRA endorsement demonstrates how Barrow is different from the national Democratic Party.

But what made this advertisement so effective were the candidate-centered elements of it. Barrow shows his guns, the ones he inherited from his father and his grandfather. Barrow loads and cocks the shotgun during the advertisement, which demonstrates his familiarity with the weapons and emphasizes their value. The ad demonstrates that Barrow does not just happen to support gun rights. His support for guns is rooted in family and personal experience. The personalization of these values in the advertisement indicates to voters that these values will not erode quickly.[2]

Barrow succeeded at contrasting himself to the national Democratic Party and carved out an independent profile. A writer in the Elections section of the liberal website DailyKos reviewed Barrow's returns in comparison to Barack Obama and praised "Barrow's 8 years of building a centrist image . . . He was able to sell himself to the Dixiecrat southern Georgia counties that the Republicans counted on turning him out of office" (KingofSpades 2013). The gun ad was given wide credit for this accomplishment. Barrow's chief of staff noted at a postelection academic conference that the campaign was able "to get our message out that Rep. Barrow is a different kind of Democrat—a moderate, Blue Dog Democrat. The surprise success of the campaign was our 'Gun Ad,' which linked Rep. Barrow's NRA endorsement with a personal story about why Second Amendment rights mattered to him" (Vote View 2012).

The Barrow ad fits into the pattern that I have established throughout this book—candidate-centered appeals are quite common. Campaigns account for candidate-centered factors in their campaign plans and use these in a majority of the advertisements they air. Campaigns use several different types of candidate-centered appeals and connect policy appeals with personal issues. Left unanswered so far is the question of the effectiveness of candidate-centered appeals. Campaigns behave like these appeals help their candidate on Election Day, and the credit given to the guns ad from Barrow provides an example where a staffer clearly believes that a specific ad did help her candidate. But do they? In the chapter, I try to answer that question, isolating the impact of a candidate-centered appeal and testing its effectiveness.

Candidates and Source Credibility

The argument of this book is that campaigns employ candidate-centered appeals with great frequency in an effort to develop the credibility of their candidate in the minds of voters. To this point, I have examined the use of candidate-centered appeals and explanations for why these appeals are so common. To do this, I have focused on the strategies used by political campaigns, using perceptions of voter preferences to create behavioral expectations about campaign behavior and then have empirically tested those expectations about the use of candidate-centered appeals. This chapter shifts the focus away from campaigns and their behavior and moves it to voters and their actual behavior. Do candidate-centered appeals enhance the perceptions of the candidates in the eyes of the voters?

The premise of my argument is that the credibility of a candidate matters to voters. Extensive research in psychology, communications, and marketing shows that the more an individual believes in the trustworthiness and expertise of the source of a communication, the more likely that recipient will accept and be persuaded by the source's message (Hovland and Weiss 1951; Hovland, Janis, and Kelley 1953; Sternthal, Phillips, and Dholakia 1978). The content of the source's messages does not have to vary for a respondent to change his or her opinion, only the respondent's perception of the source.

A wide body of literature has taken these insights from other disciplines and applied them to political information. Individuals are more likely to believe a source they consider sincere. As such, elements such as trustworthiness (Popkin 1991), party reputation (Iyengar and Valentino 2000), and ideology (Zaller 1992) can affect an individual's perception of political information. The credibility of a source is also dependent on perceived expertise, with factors such as candidate status (Page, Shapiro, and Dempsey 1987) and public approval (Mondak 1993, Mondak et al. 2003) affecting perceptions. Thus, a source's credibility can vary. Individuals react differently based upon the perceived commonality between the source and the recipient (Lupia and McCubbins 1998, Druckman 2001). What are the components of credibility? Again, researchers have examined this question in communications, marketing, and psychology, and these dimensions "have been commonly identified to consist of expertise and trustworthiness" (Pornpitakpan 2004, 244).

Candidate-centered information can influence perceptions of both of these elements. Candidate-centered appeals can affect perceptions of trust because, as shown in chapter 5, many issue-based appeals focus on the candidate's issue priorities and voting record. Such a message implicitly argues that since the candidate has demonstrated concern about an issue in the past, voters can trust him or her to continue to care about that issue in the future. Since voters tend to distrust political messages a priori, candidate-centered information can thus serve to assure voters that the candidate's commitment to the issue is credible and not mere campaign rhetoric.

Candidate-centered appeals can also improve perceptions of the candidate's expertise. Much like a job applicant who presents a résumé to a potential employer, a campaign message that highlights the past accomplishments of a candidate indicates the skill level that a candidate will bring to elective office. If a candidate has passed legislation or implemented a government program in the past, voters can assume he or she would be able to accomplish similar tasks in the future. In fact, voters view incumbents more favorably because they regard them as more competent (Kahn 1993). For nonincumbents, highlighting the experience of a candidate in a particular field indicates the candidate's knowledge about the issues facing that profession, which he or she could better address if elected. Regardless of whether a candidate-centered appeal improves perceptions of a candidate's competence or sincerity (or both), these appeals should improve the standing of a candidate in the eyes of voters.

Candidate-centered appeals should therefore help campaigns in their efforts to woo voters. As shown previously, political consultants certainly behave as if they do. Thus, I expect that candidate-centered appeals will improve perceptions of a candidate. Research into credibility posits that trust and expertise are two factors that credibility can influence. In addition to testing the effect of background on overall perceptions of the candidate, I will also test its effect on trust and expertise. I expect to find a positive relationship between both factors and candidate-centered appeals.

An Experimental Test

To test my expectations, I used an experimental design that varied the use of a candidate-centered appeal in a mock message to voters. The experimental design isolated the value of candidate-centered appeals separate from other confounding factors. As shown in chapter 6, real-world campaigns connect a candidate's reputation and personal experiences to particular issue positions and trait characteristics. This complicates to the point of nullity the task of isolating the effect of background in an observational study.

Front

Back

Figure 7.1 Mock Direct Mail Piece, Version "Both Democrat."

In the experiment, I held the issue position of the candidate constant, while varying the candidate's occupational background and the candidate-centered appeal based on that background. Respondents viewed a mock direct-mail piece from a mock congressional campaign. Then, respondents gave their overall impressions of the candidate, as well as their opinions of his sincerity and potential effectiveness. Figure 7.1 shows one version of the direct-mail piece for the "Sam

Kelley for Congress" campaign. Kelley's statement on the front, "My Number One Goal: Improve Our Health Care," and his pledge on the back to "wait no longer" to fix the nation's health-care system are constant across each treatment group.

Variation comes from Kelley's occupational background and the candidate-centered appeal based on this background (for the text of each experimental manipulation, see Table A5.1), summarized as follows:

- "A doctor and surgeon at Memorial St. Joseph Hospital." He knows "firsthand what quality and affordable health care means to our families." He will "never forget that in Washington."
- A state legislator who "passed the Patient's Bill of Rights Act of 2004. It guarantees that patients can see the doctor of their choice." He has "fought hard here to provide quality and affordable health care to our families." And he will "fight just as hard for them in Washington."
- A "small business owner," who "knows firsthand how far the cost of health care has skyrocketed. And how hard it is for families to afford health care." He will take his "experience and commitment to Washington to make sure that all our families can get the quality and affordable care they need."
- Kelley can have both of the first two backgrounds together.
- Kelley can have no occupational background mentioned and thus no candidate-centered appeal (the control group).

These backgrounds represent the range of background appeals that a nonincumbent campaign might make. Some ("Doctor," "Politician") feature a close connection between the actions in a candidate's past and plans for the future. The "Both" treatment examines whether there is a cumulative effect between two connected backgrounds. Finally, the "Businessman" treatment is employed to test whether a background that is tenuously related to the issue affects perceptions of the candidate in a similar way to more obvious connections.

In addition to testing the effect of background on voter perceptions, I also examine its relationship to partisanship. Partisanship serves as a credibility mechanism for a candidate, connecting candidates to a set of stereotypes that affect voter perceptions of them (Rahn 1993). These stereotypes are based on a wide range of factors—the party's history, issue stands (Lodge and Hamill 1986), major constituents, issue handling advantages (Petrocik 1996), party-associated traits (Hayes 2005), and symbols (Philpot 2004). While I do not have an assumption about how particular occupational backgrounds might interact with the candidate's party, the strong influence of partisanship and party stereotypes means that such an interaction is possible. Thus, I vary candidate Kelley's partisanship, in addition to varying his occupation.[3]

The random sample of 959 respondents comes from the University of Texas module of the Cooperative Congressional Election Study. The online survey was conducted by Polimetrix between late September and late October 2006. Respondents were randomly assigned into 1 of 15 different experimental groups, with each group viewing a different version of the direct-mail flyer. Respondents then answered questions about their impressions of Sam Kelley, the candidate in the flyer. Respondents were also asked to evaluate their feelings toward Mr. Kelley on a 100-point feeling thermometer rating (on a traditional 0 to 100 scale).[4] Respondents were asked to include their perception of the candidate's sincerity and effectiveness on an 11-point rating (on a 0 to 10 scale).[5]

No Party Results

Did respondents have a better impression of the candidate when he made a candidate-centered appeal? I begin by assessing the 331 respondents who received no information on the candidate's party affiliation. Figure 7.2 presents the descriptive results for the difference in mean thermometer ratings between the experimental treatment groups and the control group for these respondents. The "Candidate-Centered" category combines each of the four noncontrol groups into a single variable.[6] Respondents regarded the candidate 5.18 "degrees warmer" when they learned about his occupation than respondents in the control treatment, who gave Kelley a mean 52.7 rating;[7] this difference is statistically significant ($t = 1.98$; $p = .02$).[8] These results provide supportive evidence that appeals centered around a candidate and his or her occupation specifically serve to enhance the credibility of a candidate. When candidate Kelley did not have an occupation, respondents did not have a particularly favorable view of him. When they learned that the candidate was an accomplished professional, they increased their evaluation of him.

The effect is relatively constant regardless of the candidate's occupation. Respondents in the "Businessman" treatment gave the candidate a mean rating of 59.4, which is significantly warmer than the control group ($t = 2.10$; $p = .02$). Respondents also regarded the candidate as 5.52 "degrees" warmer as a "Doctor" and 4.44 "warmer"

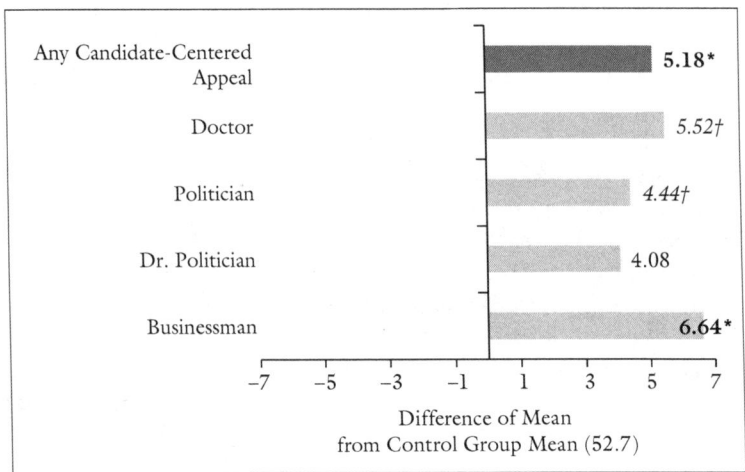

Figure 7.2 Difference in Mean Thermometer Ratings from Control Group. No Party for Candidate.

p < .05; † = p < .10. Any Candidate-Centered Appeal variable combines the four occupational treatments. Dependent variable: Respondents' thermometer ratings of the candidate on a 101-point (0 to 100) scale. Chart shows difference in the mean value for each treatment group with the mean value for the control group (52.7)

as a "Politician." Both are statistically significant at the p < .10 level ("Doctor": t = 1.61; p = .06; "Politician": t = 1.31; p = .096). Respondents did regard the "Dr. Politician" as 4.08 "degrees warmer" than when candidate Kelley had no occupation; this difference is not statistically significant.

The positive effects of candidate-centered appeals did not apply to perceptions of the candidate's sincerity and had an insignificant effect on perceptions of his competence. Figure 7.3 shows that respondents gave lower sincerity ratings after viewing a candidate-centered appeal about the candidate. That is, respondents give the highest sincerity ratings to the candidate when they did not learn about his occupational background (mean rating of 5.93). This finding was true across all occupational categories. These differences are not statistically significant, except for the "Doctor," which reached the p < .10 level of significance. Figure 7.4 shows the effectiveness ratings that respondents gave candidate Kelley. These results fit expectations, in that respondents gave him more favorable ratings when Kelley had an occupation than in the control group, when he did not. However, these differences are not statistically significant in any experimental condition.

The Effect of Candidate-Centered Appeals 149

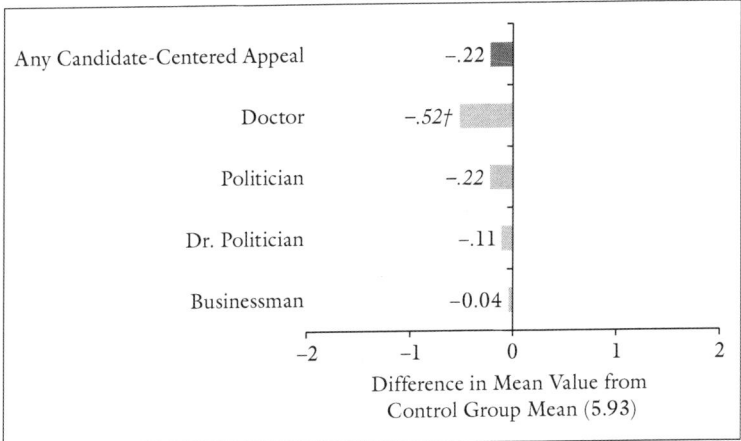

Figure 7.3 Difference of Mean Sincerity Ratings from Control Group. No Party for Candidate.

Note: n = 331; * = p < .05; † = p < .10. Background Variable combines the four occupational treatments. Dependent variable: Respondents' sincerity ratings of the candidate on an 11 point (0 to 10) scale. Graph shows difference in the mean value for each treatment group with the mean value for the control group (5.93).

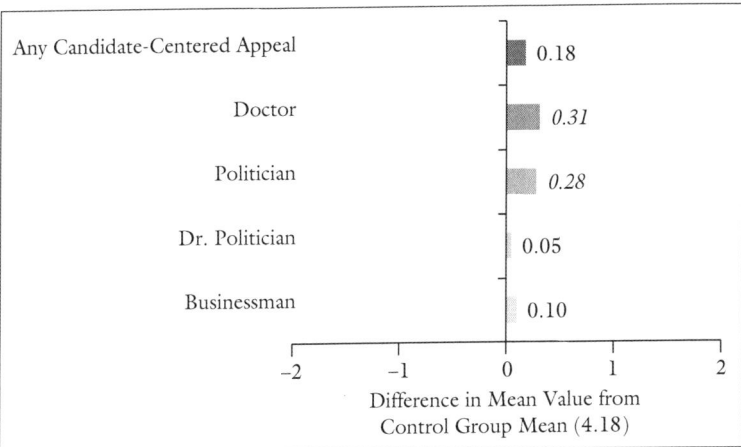

Figure 7.4 Difference in Effectiveness Ratings from Control Group. No Party for Candidate.

Note: n = 331; * = p < .05; † = p < .10. Background Variable combines the four occupational treatments. Dependent variable: Respondents' effectiveness ratings of the candidate on an 11 point (0 to 10) scale. Graph shows difference in the mean value for each treatment group with the mean value for the control group (4.18).

Overall, the results presented here show that there is a benefit, albeit modest, to employing a candidate-centered appeal. Respondents gave higher thermometer ratings when they read about the background of the candidate, and they particularly liked the "Politician" and the "Doctor." These results are tempered though by the results in the sincerity and effectiveness models, which show no background benefit.

With Party Labels

In addition to varying the occupation of the candidate, the experimental design also varied candidate Kelley's party label between "Democrat," "Republican," and a "No Party" condition. The reason for this is simple—party is far and away the most important voting cue used by voters; the party label itself allows voters to infer much about the issue stands, image, and traits of the candidate in question. Including the party label of the candidate provides a check on whether the effect of candidate-centered information gets washed out by the overwhelming cue provided by party affiliation.

So what effect did adding a party label have to perceptions of the candidate? First, I examined whether the party labels themselves have some effect on how respondents viewed the mock candidate. Figure 7.5 shows the difference in overall, sincerity, and effectiveness ratings based for the two party-label conditions in comparison to the "No Party" condition (combining all occupational treatments). Overall, little difference exists in perceptions of the candidate based on his party label. Respondents gave statistically indistinguishable responses for all three measures, with the exception of the sincerity of the candidate as a Republican. Here, candidate Kelley was regarded as .31 less sincere (again on an 11-point scale) than the "No Party" candidate, which is significant at the $p < .10$ level. There is a clear pattern in all three measures—respondents gave slightly more favorable ratings to the candidate when he was a Democrat and slightly less favorable ratings to the candidate when he was a Republican. Considering the experiment was conducted during the 2006 campaign, when the image of the Democratic Party was on the upswing and image of the Republican Party declining rapidly, this result is not surprising. But the key conclusion from this figure is that the presence of a party label for the mock candidate does not create a different set of perceptions of that candidate from the candidate when he had no party label.

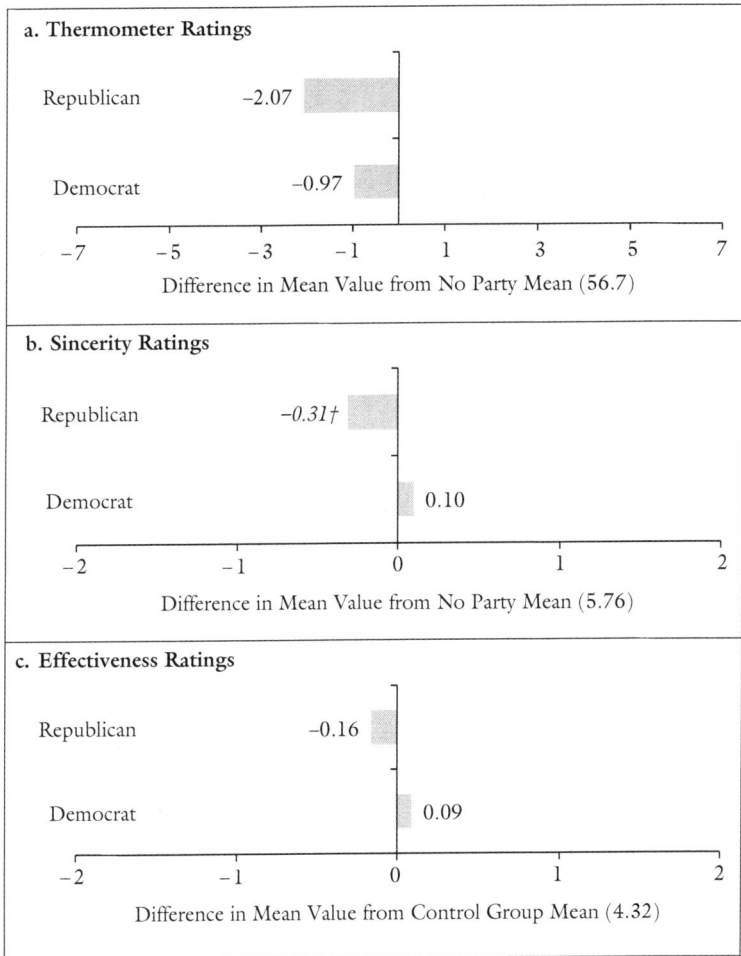

Figure 7.5 Difference in Ratings for Party Labels from No Par Group. No Party for Candidate.

Note: n = 331; * = p < .05; † = p < .10. Background Variable combines the four occupational treatments. Dependent variable: Respondents' sincerity ratings of the candidate on an 11 point (0 to 10) scale. Graph shows difference in the mean value for each treatment group with the mean value for each control group.

While there may not be an overall effect from the use of a party label, it is worth exploring how the combination of party labels and occupational treatments work. Figure 7.6 shows the results of the thermometer ratings for each of the 15 individual experimental conditions.

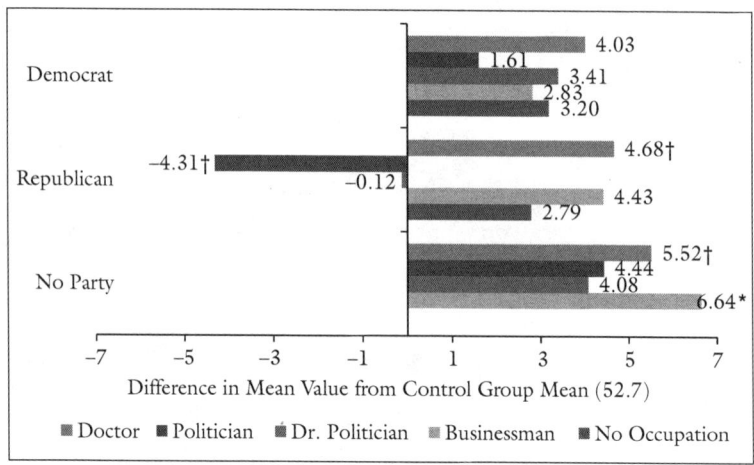

Figure 7.6 Difference in Thermometer Ratings from Control Group. All Parties for Candidate.

* = p < .05; † = p < .10. Dependent variable: Respondents' thermometer ratings of the candidate on a 101-point (0 to 100) scale. Graph shows difference in the mean value for each treatment group with the mean value for the control group (52.7).

Again, the measure is the difference from the control group ("None No Party"). In general, the data show that some combinations worked better than others. In general, Kelley was regarded more positively as a Democrat, though none of these ratings are significantly different from the "None No Party" category. In the "No Party" condition, Kelley was regarded more favorably in each condition than he was as a Democrat. In fact, Kelley's ratings are significantly different than the control group in the two conditions where he is not a politician—"Doctor and CEO."

While perceptions of candidate Kelley are relatively constant across occupation in the "Democrat" and "No Party" treatments, there was a wide variation among different occupations when Kelley was a Republican. Respondents viewed him more favorably as a "Republican Doctor" or a "Republican Businessman" than respondents in the control group. When Kelley was a "Republican Dr. Politician," voters viewed him almost the same as if they had learned nothing of his party or occupation. But when Kelley was a "Republican Politician," voters viewed him significantly less favorably than the control group. In fact, respondents gave the "Republican Politician" a mean favorability of 48.4, the only "cool" rating among the 15 different treatment groups. In a difference of means tests, the thermometer rating for "Republican Politician" is significantly "cooler" than each of the other 14 treatments. These results show just how unpopular Republican politicians were in the fall of 2006.

The results show that the effect of candidate-centered appeals is contingent upon a candidate's partisanship. The results for both the "Democrat" and "No Party" treatment have a relatively consistent effect across the various occupation treatments. The results for "Republican," though, are highly contingent upon the candidate's

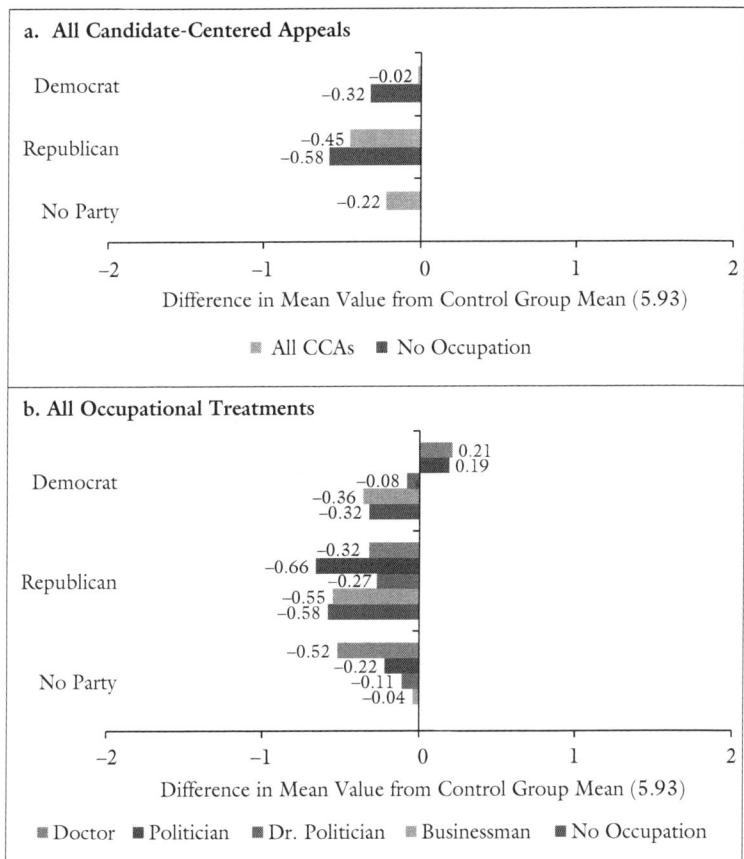

Figure 7.7 Difference in Sincerity Ratings from Control Group. All Parties for Candidate.

* = p < .05; † = p < .10. Dependent variable: Respondents' thermometer ratings of the candidate on a 101-point (0 to 100) scale. Graph shows difference in the mean value for each treatment group with the mean value for the control group (5.93).

occupation; respondents regarded the "Doctor" and "CEO" quite favorably, but disliked the "Politician." While information about the candidate's background was a positive signal to respondents in the "No Party" and "Democrat" treatment, different backgrounds had different effects for "Republicans."

I also examined sincerity and effectiveness ratings in the same way. Figure 7.7 shows sincerity ratings, with Panel A comparing the mean results for all occupational treatments combined into the "All CCAs" category and comparing the results to the control group. As discussed above, respondents gave lower ratings to the candidate when

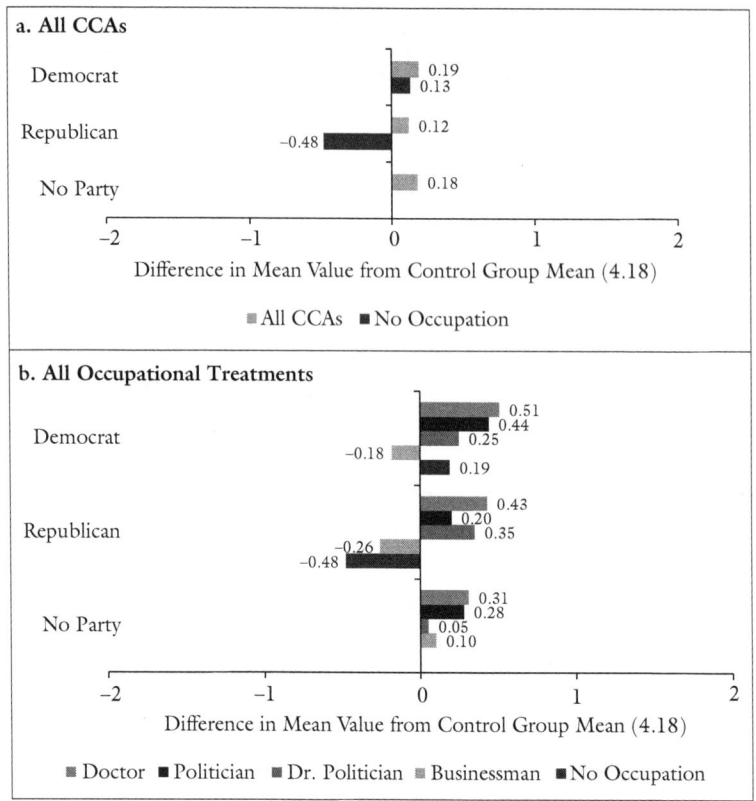

Figure 7.8 Difference in Sincerity Ratings from Control Group. All Parties for Candidate.

* = p < .05; † = p < .10. Dependent variable: Respondents' thermometer ratings of the candidate on a 101-point (0 to 100) scale. Graph shows difference in the mean value for each treatment group with the mean value for the control group (5.93).

shown a candidate-centered appeal. However, when there was a party label attached to the candidate, his thermometer ratings improved. Panel B breaks up each occupational treatment. It shows that respondents found the candidate more sincere as a "Democratic Doctor" or "Politician" than in the control group. Among Republicans, the candidate receives his highest marks as a "Doctor" and his lowest as a "Politician."

Figure 7.8 shows a similar pattern for perceptions of the candidate's potential effectiveness in office. Among all three partisan conditions (Panel A), candidate Kelley was regarded as more effective when the respondent viewed a candidate-centered appeal. The difference was slightest for the candidate as a Democrat and most distinctive when Kelley was a Republican. Panel B shows that Kelley was regarded as most potentially effective as a doctor or politician, and least effective as a businessman.

Overall, these differences are small (and statistically indistinguishable), so any conclusions about these differences should be regarded skeptically. That being said, these results provide modest evidence that candidate-centered appeals help candidates, especially in a partisan context.

Modest but Positive Effect

The results demonstrate a modest but consistently positive effect from the use of candidate-centered appeals. The candidate received a four- to six-point mean bump in his thermometer ratings after respondents viewed a candidate-centered appeal. On the other hand, the results show that the reason for this increase in the overall perception of the candidate is not an increase in perceptions of his sincerity or his potential effectiveness. There were no significant differences in ratings of the candidate's sincerity or effectiveness in comparison to the control group.

I also varied the candidate's party affiliation. This enhances external validity by providing the most commonly used voting cue to respondents. Despite the use of this easily accessible cue, candidate-centered information still produced a modest but positive effect, just as it did when the party cue was absent. The effect of party varied depending on whether the candidate was a Republican or a Democrat. The Democratic Party was better regarded than the Republican Party when the experiment took place, and the candidate received better ratings when his party affiliation was Democrat rather than Republican. Interestingly, the candidate's ratings were sensitive to his occupational background when he was a Republican, as he was regarded quite favorably as a "Doctor" or a "CEO," and less favorably than the control group when a "Politician."

It is worth noting that it is rare for campaigns to include candidates' party affiliation in television advertisements and other campaign communications (Vavreck 2001). Instead, as shown in the previous chapters, the focus is on candidates themselves. The results here provide supportive evidence that voters view a candidate-centered appeal and update their impression of a candidate in a positive fashion. Campaigns use information about candidates themselves in a way consistent with these findings, emphasizing their candidate's personal characteristics and values in an effort to enhance the candidate's likeability and credibility.

The results here should be interpreted cautiously. There are several reasons for this. First, as with any experimental design, there are issues of external validity. Presenting a flyer in the context of an Internet survey will lead respondents to pay more attention to it than a mailed flyer, which competes with other pieces of mail and other elements of life for attention. And respondents were exposed to only one piece of information about the candidate, rather than a whole campaign's worth of campaign messages and media reports. Further, campaigns will shape the issue agenda of their campaign to the reputation of their candidate (Arbour 2013). Here, I held the issue agenda constant regardless of a candidate's occupational background. Also, a real-life campaign has a wide variety of mechanisms to build their candidate's credibility (e.g., party issue ownership, party images, endorsements, and connections to local party leaders) beyond candidate-centered appeals.

There are also reasons to worry about the pool of respondents. As noted, respondents were more politically aware than the average citizen.[9] Those who are the most politically sophisticated are the most able to screen out messages contrary to their own political views (Zaller 1992). On the other hand, having more politically sophisticated respondents means they likely would have spent more time analyzing the flyer than respondents of average levels of political sophistication. In addition, it is worth noting that because the candidate is running for legislative office, voters may have different expectations for relevant experience than they do for candidates for executive office.

Each of these cautions is worthwhile to consider in light of the findings in this chapter. But regardless of these objections, the results show that campaigns such as John Barrow's do indeed benefit from candidate-centered appeals. Of course, not every campaign has the vivid and stark connection between their candidate's past and a specific issue as the Barrow campaign did with guns. But the results here show that using more common candidate-centered appeals under the right circumstances can help campaigns win votes on Election Day. The frequent use of candidate-centered appeals by political campaigns does seem a productive strategy.

Chapter 8

Candidate-Centered Appeals and Citizens

The most consistent criticism leveled at the Mitt Romney campaign in 2012 was the need for Romney to "define himself." Republican consultant Rob Stutzman said that voters "have soured on the president. The question is: Are they willing to turn the keys over? There's an important element that lies ahead for Gov. Romney, who has to tell people what he'll do [as president], and do so with his own voice in his own ads" (West 2012). Obama advisor David Axelrod said that "[Romney] hasn't been very successful in defining himself to voters. And he's left himself vulnerable to a whole range of questions . . . whether he'll be the kind of advocate for the middle class, an advocate for their interests in this economy that they're looking for in this election" (Slack 2012). The scrupulously neutral political analyst Charlie Cook (2012) argued that "Romney's poor numbers go back to his campaign's obsession with talking only about the economy and not attempting to define who Romney is as a person, as a way to build trust and strong positive personal feelings toward their candidate."

Each of these diagnoses of the Romney campaign had a similar prescription—focus on candidate-centered appeals. A postmortem of the Romney campaign in his hometown *Boston Globe* found that "one of the gravest errors, many say, was the Romney team's failure, until too late in the campaign, to sell voters on the candidate's personal qualities and leadership gifts." The *Globe* also reported that in an effort to spur the Romney campaign to focus on his father's personality, Mitt's son Tagg created a list on 12 individuals who "had been helped by [Mitt] in ways that were publicly unknown but had been deeply personal and significant" (Kranish 2012). Yet the Romney campaign chose not to focus on the biography and background of their candidate, focusing instead on attacking the record of Barack Obama in an effort to make the election a referendum on Obama's performance in his first term. Even the Romney campaign's attempts to discuss their candidate's biography ran up against a combination of poor decision making and bad luck. The Romney campaign was scared off of a plan to run a biography video of their candidate during primetime network coverage of the Republican National Convention,[1] and a series of testimonials about Romney's charitable efforts and character were pushed out of the network coverage window in order to highlight the disastrous "empty-chair speech" by actor and director Clint Eastwood (Balz 2013).

Instead, Romney's opponents filled in details of his biography and record, particularly his work as CEO of the venture capital firm Bain Capital. The attacks on Romney's business record began with his fellow Republicans. Texas governor and Republican primary opponent Rick Perry labeled Bane's tactics "vulture capitalism" (Sherman 2012), and the super-PAC-supporting Newt Gingrich aired a documentary during the South Carolina primary titled *The King of Bain*, which attributed Romney's venture capital work for job losses in the companies it bought (Coll 2012). Democrats piled on in the general election. A particularly resonant ad from PrioritiesUSA, the Obama-supporting superPAC, aired testimony from workers who were tasked with building a stage where executives from Bain would soon announce that the plant was closing: "turns out that when we built that stage, it was like building my own coffin" (Haberman 2012). An ad from the Obama campaign featured Mitt Romney singing "America the Beautiful" over images of shuttered factories while text pilloried Romney for his work at Bain Capital (Sonmez 2012).

The negative ads about Romney's record in the business world portrayed Romney as someone who cared only about making money and had little understanding of the plight of the employees who worked for the companies that Bain Capital bought and sold. Rather than being portrayed as someone whose business expertise gave him the knowledge and skill to create economic growth, Romney's image was that of a heartless and distant boss. When the infamous 47 percent video was unearthed in September 2012, it only sealed in that reputation for Romney. Romney had little to no personal credibility among voters on which to fall back. The Romney campaign shows the perils of failing to develop the credibility and likeability of your candidate. Thus the absence of candidate-centered appeals from the Romney campaign demonstrates the power and effectiveness of candidate-centered appeals.

If the absence of candidate-centered appeals by the Mitt Romney campaign demonstrates the power and effectiveness of such appeals, the ubiquity of candidate-centered appeals by the John Kerry campaign demonstrates their limits. Kerry's 2004 campaign was notable for its heavy focus on Kerry's record of naval service during the Vietnam War. John Kerry began his acceptance speech at the 2004 Democratic Convention by saying, "I'm John Kerry, and I'm reporting for duty."[2] Ads for the Kerry campaign focused on this service in Vietnam and included testimonials from others who served in his unit (Lizza 2004). The rationale for Kerry's nomination in the Democratic primary was that his service in Vietnam would give him greater credibility than his opponents to challenge George Bush over the conduct of the war in Iraq. By focusing on Kerry's biography, his campaign wanted to demonstrate Kerry's devotion to his country and his willingness to shed blood for it (Yglesias 2008). In the context of the war in Iraq and in the shadow of the September 11 terrorist attacks, Kerry's military background was the key asset to his campaign.

Yet much like Mitt Romney, Kerry also lost the presidential election. Kerry lost in large part because of the issue-ownership advantage Republicans traditionally possess on national security. But he also suffered because biography itself is not sufficient to convince voters of your electable qualities. Background serves an entry point for voters, but background must be combined with issue positions and policy proposals. John Kerry's appeal seemed to be "I served in Vietnam: trust me to figure out something in Iraq." Further, the overreliance on biography by Kerry made him vulnerable to attacks on his biography. When the Swift Boat ads came out, Kerry had only established credibility on his personality and biography and had not used that credibility to establish a set of policy views among voters. Character and confidence may have mattered to voters, but such appeals proved ineffective because they were not prepared with a clear policy vision.

In this chapter, I assess the findings of this book and place them in context. Doing so suggests a Goldilocks analysis: not too few candidate-centered appeals (like the Romney campaign), not too many (like the Kerry campaign), get them *just right*. Campaigns can benefit from employing candidate-centered appeals, and, as I show in this book, they do so with great frequency. But candidate-centered appeals serve to enhance the credibility and likeability of candidates. Credibility means that candidates can then present their issue positions and policy proposals with reduced levels of skepticism from voters. But present future oriented plans they must.

This chapter places the findings of this book in context, assessing their importance for political campaigns, for political scientists, and for the conduct of American elections. I find that political campaigns use candidate-centered appeals with great frequency as a means of developing the credibility and likeability of their candidate. I also find that candidate-centered appeals have a modest but positive impact on perceptions of a candidate. For political science, my findings demonstrate the importance of candidates themselves to the campaign message process. Our models of campaign issue agendas and strategies should do more to incorporate candidate-centered factors. For campaigns, these findings suggest that candidate background and biography are essential elements of campaigns, which means the decision of a potential candidate to enter or avoid a race is one of the most important elements of a campaign.

I suggested earlier that the use of candidate-centered appeals by political campaigns follows a Goldilocks approach—not too much, not too little, get it *just right*. It should be similar for the democratic value of candidate-centered appeals—not too much (not enough policy information is presented), not too little (officeholders are free to be corrupt or dishonest), get them *just right*. My read of the evidence suggests that we have not been getting the role of candidate-centered appeals *just right*. Instead, candidate-centered appeals play too great of a role in contemporary American elections, and this role is coming at the expense of policy information. More importantly, the rationale for the use of candidate-centered appeals is based on faulty and incorrect assumptions voters make about the political world. Campaigns are employing these appeals to overcome voter skepticism about politicians. But research shows that skepticism is misplaced—the best predictor of what politicians will do in office is the policy proposals and issue stands they take during the campaign. Voters should thus focus more on issue positions and policy proposals during the campaign. Voters are electing policymakers, not neighbors or friends.

Implications for Political Science

This book finds that candidates themselves are central to the message strategy employed by political campaigns. This stands in stark contrast to the major thrust of political science research on campaign messages—which focuses heavily (if not exclusively) on issues. As discussed in chapter 1, political scientists have placed a heavy emphasis on the issue agendas employed by campaigns. This book argues in favor of the need for political scientists to take candidates more seriously as a source of campaign strategy. Political consultants sure do.

As demonstrated in chapter 3, political consultants consider candidate background to be at least equally important to the issue agenda as the national issue environment or district demography in determining the message strategy of their campaigns. Accounting for a candidate's background, biography, or political record can give more context to some of the findings in the campaign issue literature.

Take for example the concept of issue ownership. There is an extensive debate over whether campaigns are more likely to highlight the issues owned by their party (Brasher 2003; Budge and Farlie 1983; Kahn and Kenney 1999; Spiliotes and Vavreck 2002; Sulkin and Evans 2006; Druckman, Kifer, and Parkin 2009) or are willing to talk about the same issues regardless of which party "owns" it (Damore 2004, 2005; Kaplan, Park, and Ridout 2006; Sides 2006; Sigelman and Buell 2004). Regardless of where one stands in this debate, it is clear that campaigns are willing (at least on occasion) to discuss issues owned by the other party, even in expensive forms of communications such as television advertising (cf. Sides 2005; Arbour n.d.). From a strict issue ownership perspective, such trespassing is unwise, as the opposing party's reputation on their issue reduces the effectiveness of such an appeal (Norpoth and Buchanan 1992). But let us suppose that campaigns take into account not only the reputation of their political party, but also the reputation of their candidate on specific issues. If their candidate has a position reputation on an issue, a campaign is more likely to highlight that issue for voters (Arbour 2013). In other words, campaign issue agendas are larger than presumed by the models used by political scientists. Incorporating candidate-centered information, such as a candidate's issue reputation, helps us to understand more fully the variety of factors that go into producing the wide diversity of campaign issue agendas (Sulkin and Evans 2006).

The findings in this book also indicate that campaigns do not worry about positioning their candidate at the ideal place on the Downsian spectrum as political science findings might suggest (cf. Wright and Berkman 1986; Burden 2004; Ansolabehere, Snyder, and Stewart 2001; Brady, Cogan, and Canes-Wrone 2002). The consultants I interviewed argued for the importance of "passion" and "authenticity" for their candidates. If passion and authenticity are the key values for candidates, then the attempt to properly position a candidate on the ideological spectrum can enhance voter skepticism of the candidate. The lack of specific policy information in political advertising indicates that campaigns do not try to find the ideal place on the ideological spectrum. Political campaigns take their candidate's issue positions as a given and identify the best way to sell the issue priorities of their candidate to voters.

Instead of positioning candidates on the ideological spectrum, campaigns want to prime issues and traits on which voters have favorable considerations for their candidate. The importance of candidate-centered appeals in political campaigns fits well with the idea that campaigns try to increase the weight voters give to particular issues or traits. Previous work in this vein (outside of the notable exception of Sellers 1998) identifies only national or partisan rationales for emphasizing favorable issues (e.g., Ansolabehere and Iyengar 1994 and Brasher 2003 on national issue salience; Spiliotes and Vavreck 2002; and Simon 2002 on partisan issue ownership). Campaigns wish to highlight the strengths of their candidates, and candidate-centered appeals provide an important method to do so.

My argument here is not that issues are unimportant in political campaigns. To do so would be to overlook mounds of evidence that show the important role that issues play in campaign strategy and voter decision making. But the relationship between candidates and voters is not the simple utility calculation of the Downsian model. Voters are not calculating their "Euclidean distance" from a political candidate and choosing the smaller one. Instead, voters want to know what a candidate is like, and campaigns are quite eager to tell them. The relationship is centered on likability and credibility. Instead of focusing on what specific policies candidates propose or specific votes in the legislature, voters focus on their ability to trust candidates to solve problems. This relationship is more emotional than assumed by political science models.

The short shrift given to the role of candidate-centered appeals in political campaigns means that our understanding of how issues work is incomplete. Campaigns must sell voters on both the personal characteristics of their candidate as well as policy proposals. The results here suggest that campaigns use their candidate's background, biography, and record to determine the issue agenda for their campaign, in combination with district demographics and the national issue agenda. Future studies can examine how candidate background affects the choice of issues in campaign advertising and how background interacts with the national issue agenda and district demographics to influence issue choices for political campaigns.

Implications for Campaigns

The results here also show the importance of certainty to voters. The unchanging past, rather than the unclear future, provides the certainty that voters seek. Campaigns thus want to talk about their candidate's political record or biography in an effort to let voters know "who their candidate is" and to present that candidate in a way similar to a neighbor or a friend. Candidate-centered appeals work to demonstrate the authenticity of a candidate. Campaigns start with the premise that voters regard anything their candidate says with intense skepticism. The ability to convince voters that their candidate's views are more than mere campaign rhetoric is essential to winning electoral victory. And to do that, campaigns must make appeals based on their candidate's past.

Campaigns can reduce uncertainty through emphasizing policy stands (Franklin 1991) or by emphasizing partisan and ideological themes (Popkin 1994). But I find that the primary method campaigns use to reduce uncertainty is candidate-centered appeals. By using information about the candidate in place of specific policy appeals, campaigns can avoid angering those who disagree with their candidate's policy stands, partisan affiliation, or ideological views. Thus, candidate-centered appeals hold a particular appeal to political campaigns, allowing them to meet their incentives for uncertainty and ambiguity. If a candidate's biography, record, or background is not appropriate for the office sought or is not one that easily creates credibility and likeability among voters, then a campaign will have a much more difficult time wooing voters.

The importance of "who a candidate is" suggests that candidate entry is vital to determining the shape of an election. If a candidate whose background can credibly connect to the issues of the day and the people of a district enters a race (either as an incumbent or a challenger), that candidate's chances of winning are substantially greater than if a less credible candidate enters. The importance of candidate entry decisions is the central insight of congressional elections literature. Incumbents should win most elections, but when a "quality challenger" enters, who has organizational support, fund-raising capacity, name identification, and political skills to present messages to voters, a competitive race will develop (Jacobson and Kernell 1983; Jacobson 1989, 1990, 2007). In addition to organizational skills and familiarity to voters, the centrality of the candidate to campaign messages is an essential element of what a "quality challenger" brings to the table when deciding to run for office.

In the current day, campaigns are "candidate centered," and the fate of the candidate is the primary, if not the solitary, factor in campaign decision making. No longer do local party leaders control the campaigns of all their nominees. Instead, a team of personal advisors, consultants, and staffers join with the candidate to autonomously guide and manage the campaign. (Ehrenhalt 1991). Candidates, not parties, are at the center of campaign organizations, starting such organizations at the beginning of the campaign and keeping them going between elections (Herrnson 2011).

The results here show we can add campaign message to this long list of campaign elements where the candidate is central. Political consultants are trying to sell the candidate. Other message elements—district demography, the national issue agenda, party reputations, and so forth—interact with the candidate's own personal background, reputation, and skills to determine the message. But essential to each of these other elements is the candidate. A nationally important issue can be important in a particular U.S. House election, but only if that issue can be personalized to the candidate.

The ability to make candidate-centered appeals is not equal across all candidates. One group of candidates who are particularly advantaged by this are incumbents. For example, legislative incumbents have usually taken a long series of votes on a wide variety of issues, allowing them to establish a past position on an issue, even if this issue is not high on their list of priorities. If the national issue agenda changes, incumbent campaigns can use these past votes as part of a background appeal. Certainly, the voting record of an incumbent candidate is a double-edged sword. Their opponent can use obscure votes to trump up attacks against a candidate. But voting records allow incumbent campaigns more flexibility in changing their issue agenda to fit with the changing times because their voting record allows them to make background appeals on a wide variety of issues. Challenging campaigns often do not have such a luxury.

The results also say much about who runs for office. As mentioned above, the entry decisions made by potential candidates—whether an incumbent runs for reelection, whether "quality" challengers or open-seat candidates emerge—plays the largest role in determining the competitiveness and intensity of a congressional election. The need for a credible background also affects who can run for office. In particular, campaigns for candidates who were not successful in previous jobs, whether in previous elected office or in the private sector, face a steeper climb to electoral victory. The bias toward successful background is a positive. The correlation between job success and other worthy attributes, such as knowledge, leadership skill, and judgment, means that officeholders tend toward the most qualified. In many ways, it is heartening that those who fail (or even hover at the middle) at other professions have a difficult time moving into elective office as a means of personal advancement.

The prominence of candidate-centered information during a campaign also has consequences long after Election Day. Campaigns often use candidate-centered information rather than policy-based information in an effort to better relate their messages. Using candidate-centered information rather than policy-based information also brings specific advantages to a candidate in subsequent runs for reelection. That candidates do not have to commit to particular policy proposals during a campaign provides them flexibility when they enter office and attempt to represent their constituents. Officeholders whose campaigns used candidate-centered appeals to reduce uncertainty among voters, rather than specific policy proposals, have not precommitted to particular policy options. They are able to adapt to new information and changing circumstances. Representatives who have not made specific policy commitments can more easily seek compromise with other stakeholders.

Implications for Democracy

Democracies place the ultimate repository of political power with the *demos*. In the ideal, "the people" know not just the names of the candidates, but also their issue positions and policy priorities. Elections should connect the opinions of the public with the policy choices of their elected representatives. This connection, though, is tenuous if voters lack knowledge about the policy positions of the candidates they are choosing for office.

The question of how much political knowledge is possessed by the electorate has been at the heart of the study of political behavior from its outset. In many ways, the question of voter knowledge has been the central question in the study of political behavior, and it certainly animated the early studies of political behavior from both the Columbia (Lazersfeld, Berelson and Gaudet 1948; Berelson, Lazarsfeld and McPhee 1954) and Michigan schools (Campbell et al. 1960). The seminal studies are united in finding low levels of political knowledge among the American electorate (see Delli Carpini and Keeter 1997 for a review). At the same time, scholars find that voters use different sets of information shortcuts—from party identification (Campbell et al. 1960) to retrospective evaluations of incumbent party performance (Fiorina 1981) and economic conditions (Kieweit 1983) to elite cues (Zaller 1992) to symbolic events (Popkin 1994)—to make sense of the political environment and to decide for whom to vote.

These studies have examined the question of voter knowledge from the perspective of what voters learn. In this study, I turn the question around and ask, what information do political campaigns provide to voters? The answer is that campaigns tend to provide a great deal of information about candidates themselves, focusing on biography, background, and political record. But those who advocate for increased campaign knowledge and voter deliberation (see Lipsitz 2011, 23–29) want to hear not only issue positions from candidates, but also their rationale for that position (Guttman and Thompson 1996).

My findings here indicate that, for many voters, the policy positions of candidates (much less the rationale for those positions) are in many ways beside the point: their focus is on the personality of the candidates. Do they like and trust a candidate? Does the candidate look and act similar to how their friends or neighbors do? Would they trust this person to babysit their children or fix their car? Campaigns must then respond to a public-opinion environment in which voters reward candidates with more impressive biographies, regardless of what their stand on an issue is. In this environment, campaigns emphasize the personal characteristics of their candidate, focusing on past accomplishments in office and biographical and family details in campaign advertisements.

In many ways, this is a logical information shortcut for most voters. Policy problems are notoriously complex and require a great deal of knowledge, not only about the problem, but a technical understanding of how government can address the problem. There are intense debates over the most important policy issues, and much of those debates involve obscuring an opponent's points rather than clarifying your own. In the face of such confusion, voters often opt to identify an individual in whom they trust to (1) understand these complicated problems and (2) to find the solutions that will fix them.

So voters do have some good reasons for focusing on the personality and résumé of candidates. But, the biggest reason that voters focus on a candidate's personal characteristics is their skepticism about those who run for office. The consultants I interviewed in chapter 3 saw this as the biggest thing their campaign message had to overcome. Voters see politicians as duplicitous and two-faced and regard most of their rhetoric as nothing but cheap talk and empty promises, and I show how campaigns feel compelled to use candidate-centered information in an effort to overcome this skepticism. But this skepticism possessed by voters is not needed. Political scientists who examine campaign promises find that if you want to know what an elected official will do in office, the campaign rhetoric provides far and away the best guide (Sulkin 2009; Fishel 1985; Krukones 1984). In other words, politicians, for the most part, keep their promises. Yet, for a variety of reasons (high-profile examples of promise breaking, a bias toward negative information by both citizens and the media, failure to understand the fractured nature of power in America's system of separate institutions sharing power, an association of bad results with broken promises), voters have not absorbed the idea that politicians do indeed keep their promises.

If politicians keep their promises, then voters should seek more promises from those running for office. They should seek promises with as much detail as possible about the issue positions and policy proposals of candidates. Voters could use this information to assess how a candidate will vote on key issues if elected to a legislative body and to understand what policy solutions he or she might implement if elected to an executive position. In other words, voters should seek information that would provide them the ability to assess what a candidate will do in the job being sought. Through this information, voters can assess how close or far they are from the candidate's issue stands and can evaluate the potential effectiveness of the candidate's policy stands.

There is another important reason why voters should focus on policy information for a basic reason: enacting policy is the job of elected officials. Legislators vote on policy proposals (bills) and develop their own bills that encompass their policy proposals and pass them into law. Executives not only proposal new laws and persuade legislators to pass those laws, but they also implement the laws and administer a large bureaucracy to do so. What is not in this job description? Being a friend and neighbor to the thousands (if not millions) of constituents that an elected official might have. The job of an elected official is to identify and solve problems. Political candidates, with rare exceptions, are not the friends and neighbors of voters.

By emphasizing the importance of personal characteristics, by judging candidates based on how much they like and trust them, by evaluating candidates similarly to how one would evaluate a new neighbor or potential friend, voters are promoting evaluative criteria for candidates that are not essential elements of the job description. Voters are unlikely to ever meet their representative or senator, and when they do, it will almost always be in an official or campaign context, not that of friends or even companions. No matter how much one likes a politician, one is not going to be his or her friend, and that affection you have for the candidate will not be returned directly. Yet the lack of contact between individuals and their elected officials does not stop campaigns from focusing on the personal—which presumably means that voters continue to focus on the personal.

The inability of voters to focus on policy information actually exacerbates the issue they hope to solve. Voters are worried that political candidates will break their campaign promises, and thus, they try to evaluate the trustworthiness of the candidates. In response, campaigns focus on personal information and, as a result, present less information on a candidate's policy positions and proposals than they might otherwise. Voters would like to know what a candidate plans to do in office and punish candidates when they are uncertain of their plans in office (Alvarez 1997). Instead, campaigns are able to successfully use candidate-centered information in the place of policy commitment, wearing down voter's natural aversion to ambiguous positions.

As I suggested earlier, there is a Goldilocks nature to candidate-centered appeals. The amount of candidate-centered appeals should not be too much or too little, but just right. Voters have good reason to want to know about who their candidate is; they want their elected officials to be upright and to avoid corruption. In addition, voters care about the management of the country, state, city, or county in which they live and are voting on, and will extrapolate information about a candidate's competence from personal information and presentations about the candidate's resume (Popkin 1994, 62–65). More importantly, elected officials must work with others to achieve their goals—to persuade legislators to support their policy proposals, to bargain with other policymakers and stakeholders to find an appropriate compromise on bills and policy proposals, and to understand the problems of the public. Voters want to evaluate how well a candidate might interact with others and bargain with other key actors. Personal information about a candidate can help a voter assess what kind of colleague and bargainer the representative might be. All of that being said, the most important element of the bargaining position of someone involved in a negotiation is their initial position. In politics, the initial bargaining position is a candidate's policy preferences. While it is important to evaluate the bargaining skills of a candidate, it is more important to understand his or her policy positions and issue plans; these provide the best insight into what a candidate will do in office.

My personal normative preference for less personal and more policy information stands athwart many observations of the behavior of humans. People seem to want to identify people similar to neighbors or friends in all sorts of different contexts, even when it makes little sense to do so. Take, for example, entertainment news: the focus here is relatively rarely on the acting or musical skills of the performer, or any element of the creative process. Instead, much entertainment coverage focuses on gossip about a particular celebrity, with deep examinations of the star's love life and charitable endeavors and little focus on the craft of the job. Take Angelina Jolie as an example. She is an actress who is both successful and serious at her job. Yet, the elements that dominate media coverage of her are her high-profile and long-term relationship with Brad Pitt, her adoption of a large number of children from around the world, and her charitable efforts in Africa. None of these have to do with what is officially her job. Questions about her acting—what roles she chooses, what choices she makes as an actress, how she approaches her roles—are asked rarely and usually covered in a superficial way. Celebrity coverage focuses on the personal presumably because that is what consumers want, and media outlets, facing a competitive media marketplace, aim to give customers what they want. If you do not believe me, examine the newsstand the next time you are waiting for a cashier at a grocery store: all gossip and personality.

We can see this situation repeated in other avenues. Sports coverage asks us to get "up close and personal" with people with whom we have never met. News presenters and personalities are judged on their ability to relate to the audience first and their journalistic skills second (if at all). The lesson of this is that humans are intrinsically interested in the personal and are likely to assess people as potential friends and neighbors. That one does not know a person does not stop one from evaluating people like one might one day.

It is also worth noting that, in recent years, straight-ticket voting has increased. Fewer and fewer voters are choosing to vote Republican for president and Democrat for Congress, and vice versa (Jacobson 2013; Silver 2012). If we assume that party serves as a proxy for the ideological preferences of voters, then an increase in straight-ticket voting is consistent with the notion that voters are relying more on policy information in making their decisions. Obviously, there are still congressional districts where incumbents carve out their own "personal vote" through developing a moderate political profile, bringing pork back to the district, and having an outstanding constituent service. But the number of these districts is greatly reduced from, say, the 1970s or 1980s, when there seemed to be a passel of Southern and midwestern Democrats who easily won congressional districts that voted Republican at the top of the ticket. The lack of split-ticket voting does not in and of itself prove a hypothesis that voters are weighing policy more than personality in contemporary elections, but it is consistent with that hypothesis. From my standpoint, this is encouraging news.

You Are the Message

At the beginning of this book, I discussed the story of Bill Clinton's 1992 presidential campaign. Weighed down by Clinton's "slick Willie" nickname and voter belief that he came from a privileged background, the Clinton campaign fought back by highlighting Clinton's life story for voters. Clinton's acceptance speech at the Democratic National Convention and the video that proceeded discussed Clinton's humble upbringing as the son of a widowed nurse in a small Arkansas town. Clinton's background was nothing like what the voters assumed, and by showing voters "who he was and where he came from," the Clinton campaign succeeded not only in overturning voters' incorrect perceptions of their candidate, but focusing attention on Clinton's credibility at addressing jobs and the economy, the big issues in that year's election (Matalin and Carville 1994).

Such strategies are not limited to Democrats. Roger Ailes, who served as the one of the chief political consultants on George H. W. Bush's successful 1988 presidential campaign, has argued that individuals themselves are the key to the success of communication. Ailes has written, "The principle here is not to change yourself because the environment changes, but rather to become totally comfortable with yourself wherever you are. Once you realize that *you* are the message, you can transmit that message to anyone and be pretty successful at it" (Ailes with Kraushar 1988, 5).

This book shows that a generation later campaigns, both Republican and Democrat, agree. Campaign after campaign, case study after case study, table after table, and figure after figure in this book has shown the same thing—campaigns use candidate-centered appeals with great frequency, and they do so as a means of developing the credibility and likeability of their candidate.

The best campaigns match the story of their candidate's life to the issues of concern to the people of a particular district. Such campaigns do not transform their candidates to meet the political contours of a district. Instead, campaigns demonstrate who their candidate is and transmit that message to voters. Political campaigns can offer candidates a way to package themselves in a more positive light. But they can only change the candidate around the margins, identifying the best stories and best evidence about their candidate's biography, background, résumé, and political record, and then use the techniques of modern media to highlight their message.

This book has also shown that candidate-centered appeals are not limited to gauzy positive messages about the candidate's biography.

Campaigns also want to use candidate-centered appeals to demonstrate the political record of their candidate, demonstrating to voters the actions their candidate has taken in office. This retrospective examination helps sell voters on the future. Of course, not all looks at the past are positive. Campaigns use candidate-centered appeals to attack their opponents. These appeals almost always focus on the political record of the candidate. Just like positive appeals about a candidate's actions in public office, these negative appeals imply that if a candidate made these decisions in the past, voters can expect these same types of decisions in the future.

Campaigns must take all of these factors into account when they craft their message to voters, and calibrate the strengths and weaknesses of their candidate against other factors, such as the national issue environment, the demographic makeup of the district, and the partisan composition of voters. Most political science models focus only on these exogenous factors. What I show in this book is that those models are incomplete. It matters greatly to campaigns who their candidates are. And who a candidate is shows up in the messages that voters receive on a regular basis.

Appendix

Table A4.1 Use of Candidate-Centered Appeals, 2004 U.S. House and Senate Candidates

a. In an Ad Analysis

	All	Sponsor	Opponent
Incumbent	0.452	1.493***	−1.421***
	(.371)	(.268)	(272)
Open Seat	−.324	.799**	−.953***
	(.298)	(.236)	(.262)
Competitiveness	−.036	−.096	.002
	(.013)	(.083)	(.103)
Bush %	−.032*	−.015	.005
	(.013)	(.010)	(.010)
Freshman	.531	.556	.063
	(.497)	(.321)	(.340)
Held Office	.532	.298	−.469
	(.496)	(.249)	(.249)
Republican	.219	.110	.115
	(.225)	(.181)	(.187)
Senate	.146	.142	.372
	(.255)	(.186)	(.195)
Constant	−3.08***	.324	−.193
	(.717)	(.528)	(.521)
PsuedoR^2	.044	.070	.039
Observations	338,118	338,118	338,118

b. In a Phrase Analysis

	All	Sponsor	Opponent
Incumbent	0.439***	1.214***	−0.942***
	(0.134)	(0.180)	(0.237)
Open Seat	−0.0327	0.541***	−0.781***
	(0.130)	(0.182)	(0.216)

(continued)

b. In a Phrase Analysis (*continued*)

	All	Sponsor	Opponent
Competitiveness	−0.0718	−0.149*	0.156*
	(0.0463)	(0.0583)	(0.0764)
Bush %	−0.0184***	−0.00740	−0.0210*
	(0.00530)	(0.00660)	(0.00878)
Freshman	0.142	0.257	−0.213
	(0.160)	(0.173)	(0.317)
Held Office	−0.0543	0.222	−0.281
	(0.129)	(0.167)	(0.197)
Republican	0.291***	0.0465	0.631***
	(0.0873)	(0.107)	(0.160)
Senate	0.0610	−0.0440	−0.0765
	(0.0939)	(0.109)	(0.182)
Constant	0.297	−1.321***	−0.633
	(0.283)	(0.346)	(0.479)
PsuedoR^2	.027	.048	.037
Observations	4,613,350	4,744,655	4,744,655

* = $p < .05$; ** = $p < .01$; *** = $p < .001$.

Dependent Variable is coded 1 if the advertisement mentions each type of candidate-centered appeal, 0 otherwise.

Robust standard errors clusters on each produced advertisement.

Table A5.1 Types of Candidate-Centered Appeals, 2004 U.S. House and Senate Candidates

a. In an Ad Analysis

	Position	Character	Competence
Incumbent	0.831***	−0.114	1.020***
	(0.211)	(0.197)	(0.246)
Open Seat	−0.235	0.056	0.934**
	(0.233)	(0.230)	(0.297)
Competitiveness	0.0002	0.075	−0.216
	(0.090)	(0.087)	(0.112)
Republican	−0.093	0.180	0.344
	(0.179)	(0.169)	(0.211)
Senate	0.047	−0.327*	.274
	(0.174)	(.167)	(.186)

(*continued*)

Appendix

a. In an Ad Analysis (continued)

	Position	Character	Competence
District Conservatism	0.006	−0.012	−0.002
	(0.010)	(0.010)	(.012)
Constant	−0.031	0.198	−1.72**
	(0.535)	(0.491)	(0.599)
PsuedoR²	0.039	0.006	0.037

b. In a Phrase Analysis

	Position	Character	Competence
Incumbent	0.459**	−0.245	0.883***
	(0.155)	(0.171)	(0.222)
Open Seat	−0.179	−0.221	0.584*
	(0.182)	(0.189)	(0.258)
Competitiveness	−0.020	0.053	−0.169
	(0.056)	(0.076)	(0.102)
Republican	0.318*	0.130	0.426
	(0.121)	(0.161)	(0.219)
Senate	−0.117	−0.062	.285
	(0.120)	(.150)	(.190)
District Conservatism	0.006	−0.014	−0.011
	(0.006)	(0.009)	(.012)
Constant	−1.145**	−1.298***	−3.27***
	(0.383)	(0.424)	(0.609)
PsuedoR²	0.023	0.002	0.026

N = 330,973; * = p < .05; ** = p < .01; *** = p < .001.

Dependent Variable is coded 1 if the advertisement mentions each type of candidate-centered appeal, 0 otherwise.

Robust standard errors clusters on each produced advertisement.

Table A6.1 Use of Personal Appeals, 2004 U.S. House and Senate Candidates

	Biography	Political Record	Ideology	Personal Values	Honesty	Special Interests
Incumbent	−0.361**	−0.00793	−0.139	−0.0856	−0.137	−0.840***
	(0.141)	(0.120)	(0.212)	(0.177)	(0.191)	(0.289)
Openseat	0.304**	−0.269*	0.485**	−0.00971	0.480**	−0.400
	(0.147)	(0.143)	(0.204)	(0.192)	(0.190)	(0.276)
Senate	−0.389***	0.0876	−0.531***	−0.0785	−0.150	0.287
	(0.126)	(0.108)	(0.195)	(0.150)	(0.162)	(0.224)
Republican	0.186	0.206	0.318*	0.242*	−0.108	−0.800***
	(0.118)	(0.109)	(0.171)	(0.137)	(0.172)	(0.235)
District	0.00231	0.0195***	0.0358***	0.0385***	0.00360	0.00539
Conservatism	(0.00584)	(0.00606)	(0.00996)	(0.00755)	(0.00880)	(0.0101)
Competitiveness	0.0236	0.000881	0.0427	0.0425	0.116	0.219
	(0.0570)	(0.0494)	(0.0893)	(0.0684)	(0.0697)	(0.133)
Constant	−1.470***	−1.965***	−4.649***	−4.024***	−2.763***	−3.129***
	(0.317)	(0.315)	(0.584)	(0.458)	(0.451)	(0.638)
PsuedoR^2	0.0172	0.00958	0.0383	0.0221	0.0164	0.0464

N = 832,419 Robust standard errors in parentheses; *** p < 0.01, ** p < 0.05

Notes

Chapter 1

1. Salazar's ad is titled "Intro 60." Davis's ad is titled "Military Bio." The titles are provided by the Wisconsin Advertising Project and do not reflect the name given to the ad by the campaigns and their consultants.
2. The classic in this genre is of course from Will Rogers: "I don't make jokes. I just watch the government and report the facts." A Google search of "politician joke" returns over 8.23 million results; "politicians joke" gives 11.4 million results; "Congress joke" returns a whopping 57.8 million results (though, to be fair, a number of them are serious articles with titles like "Congress Is a Joke").

Chapter 2

1. The author of this book, who started going bald at age 17, is a strong believer in the proposition that great hair is a massive asset in modern communications.
2. These models build off the traditional Downsian perspective, beginning with the assumption that voters view themselves and the candidates on a single ideological dimension. The models assume that voters, however, view the candidate's position as a distribution over a series of points. When a voter is certain about the true position of a candidate, the distribution is concentrated over a small area. But when the voter is not sure what a candidate will do if elected to office, the distribution is over a much larger area.
3. Similarly, campaigns cruising to a landslide victory rarely discuss controversial issues in their messages to voters, to avoid providing fodder for opposition attacks (Kahn and Kenney 1998).

Chapter 3

1. Thus, these are general, media, or direct-mail consultants. I did not include as potential interview subjects consultants who specialize in other campaign elements—polling, fund-raising, mobilization, and so forth.
2. The sample is primarily a convenience sample, developed from personal contacts. Other subjects I identified via Internet and Lexis-Nexis searches for "political consultants." The majority of the interview subjects live and

work in Texas. Some of these consultants work exclusively in Texas races, but most have direct experience outside of the state. I also interviewed six consultants based in other states; the similarities between their answers and the Texas-based consultants indicate a lack of bias in the Texas interviews. I should note that I observed very few differences in message strategies between Republican and Democratic consultants. Both agreed that they key to winning votes was to make voters like their candidate and convince voters of their candidate's sincerity and credibility.

3. In an effort to ensure candor, I told each subject that I would stop recording at their behest at any point in the interview. I also told interview subjects that I would not ask any questions about particular clients (nor did I). While some willingly discussed examples from particular campaigns, I have chosen not to include any of that information in this work.

4. A list of interview subjects is available from the author on request.

5. Some examples (each quote is from a different consultant; emphases mine):

"As you bring issues up . . . it has to do with *who your candidate is* and their background."

"A message is who the campaign is and *who the candidate is* and how they're going to be effective in moving certain issues."

"You need that context—*who the candidate is*, what strength or weaknesses they have—and see how that fits with the thematic."

"You have to stay true to *who the candidate is*."

"A lot of what we're spending time on is how do we do a great job of communicating *who the candidate is*."

"You have to start with *who the candidate really is* at the core for the campaign to be a credible and a believable campaign."

"You need to have a deep and thorough understanding of *who that person* [the candidate] *is*."

"Because these are the issues that are going to dominate, and you have to try to tailor it so it fits. It just . . . It just depends on *who your candidate is*."

Chapter 4

1. A Kennedy—John, from 1953 to 1961, and Ted, from 1963 to his death in 2009—had held that Senate seat for 56 years before Brown's election. The only time a Kennedy did not hold the seat was after John's ascension to the presidency. A placeholder named Ben Smith, who was John's roommate at Harvard, held the seat until Ted was old enough to run in the 1962 election.

2. Transcript from Lybio.net. Available at http://lybio.net/tag/elizabeth-warren-who-i-am-text/.

3. Transcript was from *USA TODAY*'s and FactCheck.org's analysis of the ad, which is available online at http://usatoday30.usatoday.com/news/politics/political-ad-tracker/video/786863/elizabeth-warren-kids-like-me-mass.

4. Baron Hill (D-IN), "Tax Cuts." Connie Mack (R-FL), "Freedom." The names of the advertisements listed here and below are those provided by the Wisconsin Advertising Project. They are usually different than the names given by media consultants.
5. Mark Kennedy (R-MN), "Seniors." Dan Boren (D-OK), "Oklahoma Values." I'll note that the claim that a candidate will represent a distinct and unique set of local values is common. The 2004 data set includes appeals about Minnesota, Oklahoma, Maine, Connecticut, Kansas, Kentucky, North Carolina, and New Hampshire values, in addition to more regional values (e.g., "Southwest Virginia values," "really represents the heart and soul of the [California Central] Valley"). Of course, many campaigns talk about "our values." Despite the appeal to distinctive local values, my read of these advertisements is that these values are pretty universal—rejection of special interests and concern for the voice of middle-class Americans who feel lost in Washington. The frequent use of these appeals indicates that politicians certainly do not fail to listen to the voice of middle-class Americans, despite the implication of this rhetoric that other politicians do.
6. Alternatively, I could examine the speeches given by candidates for candidate-centered appeals. Outside of the major party presidential nominees, no comprehensive database (or really any database) exists of such speeches, making analysis limited at best. I could also examine newspaper accounts of congressional campaigns for candidate-centered discussion or candidate-centered statements by candidates. Newspaper accounts are filtered through the perspective of the reporter and editors. As such, it may reflect the views of the reporter more than those of the campaign. In addition, journalistic practices will allow for a similar number of statements between the two candidates, rather than reflecting the intensity of the campaign. For these reasons, I chose not to use either of these methods.
7. I note one other advantage to studying congressional campaigns. As a legislative body dealing with all pertinent national issues, Congress is relatively neutral on providing advantages to particular types of experiences or backgrounds. In races for executive office, possessing executive experience is often an advantage for a candidate. Also, in running for down-ballot executive races at the state (attorney general, treasurer, insurance commissioner) or local (sheriff, district attorney, judge) level, particular types of experience are prized over others.
8. These conditions are not met in presidential elections. In presidential campaigns, the role of the national media in setting the agenda and reporting on campaign events reduces the importance of advertising to campaigns. Further, the small numbers of presidential candidates do not provide enough variation for appropriate study.
9. The 2004 database includes the one hundred largest markets. While there are over two hundred media markets in the United States, the data set covers the largest, giving coverage to 80 percent of the nation's

population. The Wisconsin Advertising Project is the most comprehensive database of campaign advertising available.
10. Advertisements that discuss a candidate's background have more phrases than ads without. Ads that mention the candidate's background have 15.1 phrases, while those without have 14.1. The difference is statistically significant even before weighting for the number of ads aired (t = 2.70; p < .01). The biggest reason for the difference is that the handful of 60-second advertisements in the data set almost always include candidate-centered appeals and, of course, always include more phrases.
11. Steve Pearce (R-NM), "Father."
12. Charles Schumer (D-NY), "End Oil Dependence." Doug Walcher (R-CO), "The Two Johns."
13. An occasional phrase discusses both candidates in the same message. There are 56,029 aired phrases that mention both candidates. I include them in the chart but do not label them.
14. By tradition, Labor Day is regarded as the traditional kick-off of the campaign season. The data reflect this, as the number of advertisements run by campaigns spikes the day after Labor Day, which is 63 days before Election Day in both years. Only 8.8 percent of the advertisements in the two elections aired before Labor Day, too small to add to the figure. These advertisements do fit into the broader pattern—80 percent of these advertisements used candidate-centered appeals about the sponsoring candidate; 18 percent focused on the opposing candidate.
15. I choose to use a moving average to normalize the noise is a daily dataset. I use a seven day average because campaigns tend to purchase advertisements by weeks (i.e. they buy 1,000 Gross Ratings Points in a market by week) (Shaw 2006; Johnson 2001).
16. I limit the number of phrases that I analyzed to 20. I chose 20 because it equals the mean number of phrases plus one standard deviation (mean 15.50; standard deviation 4.55). There are not enough twenty-first, twenty-second, and so on phrases in advertisements to provide large enough numbers for sufficient analysis.
17. It is worthwhile to emphasize that this means that each phrase is being measured as a percentage of all advertisements that have an Nth phrase. Of course, the number of phrases in an advertisement declines as the phrase number increases. But because I am measuring the percentage of eighteenth phrases that include a candidate-centered phrase, the decline in candidate-centered phrases is not aided by the decline in the number of observations at that point.
18. Feingold voted in favor of the Patient Protection and Affordable Care Act in March 2010 and then lost his reelection bid to the Senate later in the year.
19. Only two advertisements in the data set included mentioned the opponent's prepolitical biography or made the claim that their opponent lacked experience necessary to serve in Congress.
20. David Price (D-NC) "Student Loan Bill."

21. Randy Kuhl (R-NY 29th), "People First."
22. Geoff Davis (R-KY), "Made a Difference."
23. Jean Patterson (R-MO), "Father Knows Best." Jean Patterson (R-MO).
24. Patty Wetterling (D-MN), "Kennedy's Record."
25. Rick Renzi (R-AZ), "Babbitt Mining."
26. The dependent variable in the all candidate-centered appeals model was "1" if the advertisement or phrase included *any* candidate-centered appeal, "0" otherwise. The dependent variable in the candidate-centered appeals about the sponsor model was coded "1" if the advertisement or phrase included a candidate-centered appeal about the sponsoring candidate, "0" otherwise. The dependent variable in the candidate-centered appeals about the opponent model was coded "1" if the advertisement or phrase included a candidate-centered appeal about the opposing candidate, "0" otherwise.
27. *CQ* classifies races as "Safe Republican or Democrat," "Republican or Democrat Favored," "Lean Democrat or Republican," or "Toss-Up." *CQ* classifies every House and Senate race each election, allowing a consistent measure across all elections in my data set. Because the variable of interest is competitiveness, I folded the "Solid," "Favored," and "Lean" races together, regardless of party. The variable was coded "0" for solid races, "1" for favored, "2" for lean, and "3" for toss-up races.
28. This is measured by the percentage of the vote won in the state or district by George W. Bush in the previous (i.e., 2000) presidential election.

Chapter 5

1. Both ads were transcribed by the author from YouTube clips.
2. "Searchlight," Harry Reid (D-NV).
3. "Results for Iowa," Tom Latham (R-IA). "Social Security 2," David Wu (D-OR).
4. "Money for Education," Charles Taylor (R-NC). "Clout," William Jefferson (D-LA). "Go to Guy," John Sweeney (R-NY).
5. "Best New Congressman," Chris Van Hollen (D-MD).
6. "Proud," Jim Costa (D-CA).
7. "Opportunities," Cathy McMorris (R-WA).
8. "Long Term View 60," Don Barbieri (D-WA).
9. "Endorsements," Charles Schumer (D-NY).
10. I should note that phrases are mutually exclusive. Candidate-centered phrases can be either character-, position-, or competence-based. As a result, I cannot give analysis of the number of phrases that include two types of appeals.
11. "Family," Jim Bunning (R-KY).
12. "Veterans' Endorsement," Chris Chocola (R-IN).
13. "On the Job," Roy Blunt (R-MO).
14. It is worthwhile to remind readers that I limit the number of phrases that I analyzed to 20 phrases (the mean number of phrases in an advertisement

plus one standard deviation). There are not enough twenty-first, twenty-second, and so phrases in advertisements to provide large enough numbers for sufficient analysis.
15. To review, for the sponsoring candidate, there are codes for whether the ad mentioned the candidate's political record as an incumbent, in another political office, or in the private sector. I also coded whether the ad mentioned the candidate's prepolitical biography or made a general appeal about the candidate's experience. For the opponent, I coded whether the ad mentioned the opponent's record as incumbent, in other political office, or in the private sector.
16. Because the models include multiple phrases from the same advertisement, I calculated robust standard errors clustered on each advertisement.

Chapter 6

1. "Intro 60," Ken Salazar (D-CO).
2. "Dairy Queen," Ken Salazar (D-CO).
3. "Environmental Record," Ken Salazar (D-CO).
4. I can identify these "Personal Characteristics of Candidate(s)" issues because Sides included a list of all issue codes in the appendix to this article. The appendix includes the issues I listed above, but they are not tallied in the table in the body of the paper.
5. The Wisconsin Advertising Project does not code for candidate-centered appeals, so the findings in chapters 4 and 5 are based on my personal coding of advertisements from 2004. The Wisconsin Advertising Project does code for issues. Thus, I can expand my data set in this chapter to include three different election cycles. It is worth noting that the Wisconsin Advertising Project limits its coding to the first four issues discussed in each advertisement. It is worth noting that most advertisements include more than four issues (Sides 2005; Arbour n.d.).
6. There are a relatively few advertisements produced about constituent service. As a result, there are not enough degrees of freedom to have confidence in the results of such a model.
7. The competitiveness values come from the race ratings used by *CQ Weekly*. They employ a 4-point folded scale to determine who is likely to win a House or Senate seat. I assign a value of "0" to "Safe" races, "1" for "Likely" races, "2" for "Lean" races, and "3" for races rated as "No Clear Favorite."
8. This is measured by the percentage of the vote won in the state or district by the Republican presidential candidate in the previous election. So, for campaigns in 2000, I use Bob Dole's percentage from 1996. For 2002 and 2004, I use George W. Bush's result from the 2000 presidential election.
9. "Parents," Inez Tenenbaum (D-SC).
10. "First Hand Foundation 2," Jeanne Patterson (R-MO).
11. "Appreciate Home," Baron Hill (D-IN).

12. "Stillwater," Brad Carson (D-OK).
13. "Values," Rich Boucher (D-VA).
14. "Social Security," David Wu (D-OR).
15. "Newspapers Agree," George Voinovich (R-OH).
16. "Domestic Violence," Dave Reichert (R-WA).
17. "Babbitt Debt Record," Rick Renzi (R-AZ).
18. "Democrat Support," Steve Pearce (R-NM).
19. "Distorting Edwards," Chet Edwards (D-TX).
20. "Do the Right Thing," Robert Aderholt (R-AL).

Chapter 7

1. Transcript from "Georgia Democrat Shows His Family's Guns in New TV Ad" from TalkingPointMemo.com. Available online at http://talkingpointsmemo.com/livewire/georgia-democrat-shows-his-family-s-guns-in-new-tv-ad.
2. And I should note that, in reality, they did not. While national Democrats supported increased gun-control measures in the wake of the December 2012 shootings at Sandy Hook Elementary School in Newtown, Connecticut, Barrow remained opposed to these proposals. In fact, a gun safety group created a web ad that intercut scenes from Sandy Hook with the Barrow gun ad (Kiely 2013).
3. Kelley's party identification is in the campaign logo and not part of the text of the message itself. Kelley can be identified as a "Democrat for Congress," a "Republican for Congress," and, in the "No Party" condition, simply "for Congress." The logo appears on both the front and the back of the flier.
4. The text of the survey question is borrowed almost word for word from the National Election Study's thermometer rating question. It reads, "Now that you've read the flier from Sam Kelley's campaign, I'd like to get your feelings about him. Please rate Sam Kelley on a thermometer that runs from 0 to 100 degrees. A rating above 50 means that you feel favorable and warm toward the person. A rating below 50 means that you feel unfavorable and cool toward the person. A rating right at the 50 degree mark means that you don't feel particularly warm or cold. You may use any number from 0 to 100 to tell me how favorable or unfavorable your feelings are."
5. Respondents used a widget to rank the candidate's sincerity and effectiveness, which allowed them to see all 11 responses at the same time and place the widget at their preferred level. Under the 0 response was "Not Sincere/Effective at All," under the 10 response was "Extremely Sincere/Effective," and under the 5 response was "Neutral."
6. Thus, the "Doctor," "Politician," "Dr. Politician," and "Businessman" categories. By combining the four treatment groups together and comparing them to the control group, I could examine the effect of candidate-centered information itself on perceptions of the candidate.

7. The mean values and the N for each dependent variable in the experimental cell are included in Tables A7.2 through A7.4.
8. All analysis in this chapter includes one-tailed tests.
9. Among respondents in the University of Texas module of the CCES, 89.3 percent claim to have voted in the 2006 general election and 54.4 percent claim to be "very interested in politics."

Chapter 8

1. The campaign believed threats by the networks that they would not run the video. The Obama campaign ignored similar threats, and the networks aired an Obama video (Balz 2013).
2. Text of Kerry's convention speech is available online at http://www.washingtonpost.com/wp-dyn/articles/A25678-2004Jul29.html.

BIBLIOGRAPHY

Aberbach, Joel D., and Bert A. Rockman. 2002. "Conducting and Coding Elite Interviews." *PS: Political Science and Politics* 35(4): 673–76.
Abrejano, Marisa A. 2010. *Campaigning to the New American Electorate: Advertising to Latino Voters.* Palo Alto, CA: Stanford University Press.
Ailes, Roger, with Jon Kraushar. 1988. *You Are the Message: Secrets of Master Communicators.* Homewood, IL: Dow Jones-Irwin.
Alesina, Alberto, and Alex Cukierman. 1990. "The Politics of Ambiguity." *Quarterly Journal of Economics* 105(4): 829–50.
Alvarez, R. Michael. 1997. *Information and Elections.* Ann Arbor: University of Michigan Press.
Ansolabehere, Stephen, and Alan Gerber. 1994. "The Mismeasure of Campaign Spending: Evidence from the 1990 U.S. House Elections." *Journal of Politics* 56(4): 1106–18.
Ansolabehere, Stephen, James M. Snyder, and Charles Stewart. 2001. "Candidate Positioning in US House Elections." *American Journal of Political Science* 45(1): 136–59.
Aragones, Enriqueta, and Zvika Neeman. 2000. "Strategic Ambiguity in Electoral Competition." *Journal of Theoretical Politics* 12(2): 183–204.
Arbour, Brian K. 2013. "Candidate Background and Issue Agendas." *American Politics Research* 41(6): 1022–51.
Arbour, Brian K. n.d. "Issue Frame Ownership: The Partisan Roots of Campaign Rhetoric." *Political Communication.* Forthcoming.
Balz, Dan. 2013. *Collision 2012: Obama vs. Romney and the Future of Elections in America.* New York: Viking Adult.
Barbaro, Michael. 2013. "Luck and a Shrewd Strategy Fueled Ascension." *New York Times*, September 11, A1.
Bartels, Larry M. 1986. "Issue Voting under Uncertainty: An Empirical Test." *American Journal of Political Science* 30(4): 709–28.
Beniot, William L. 1999. *Seeing Spots: A Functional Analysis of Presidential Television Advertisements, 1952–1996.* Westport, CT: Praeger.
Benoit, William L. 2006. "Retrospective versus Prospective Statements and Outcome of Presidential Elections." *Journal of Communication* 56: 331–45.
Berelson, Bernard, Paul F. Lazarsfeld, and William N. McPhee. 1954. *Voting: A Study of Opinion Formation in a Presidential Campaign.* Chicago: University of Chicago Press.

Bierman, Noah. 2012. "Is 'Professor Warren' an Insult? Not to the Professor." Boston.com (the website of the *Boston Globe*), October 1. http://www.boston.com/politicalintelligence/2012/10/01/professor-warren-insult-not-the-professor/cCoycDHXkHfiwgSB16q6dO/story.html. (accessed March 23, 2014).
Canes-Wrone, Brandice, David W. Brady & John F. Cogan. 2002. "Out of Step, Out of Office: Electoral Accountability and House Members' Voting." *American Political Science Review.* 96(1): 127–140.
Brasher, Holly. 2003. "Capitalizing on Contention: Issue Agenda in U.S. Senate Campaigns." *Political Communication* 20: 453–71.
Budge, Ian, and Dennis J. Farlie. 1983. *Explaining and Predicting Elections: Issue Effects and Party Strategy in Twenty-Three Democracies*. London: Allen and Unwin.
Burden, Barry C. 2004. "Candidate Positioning in US Congressional Elections." *British Journal of Political Science* 34(2): 211–27.
Campanile, Carl, and Geoff Earle. 2008. "Joe D'oh Puts O in 'Crisis' Mode; Says World Would Test Young Prez." *New York Post*, October 21, 7.
The Institute of Politics: John F. Kennedy School of Government. 2009. *Campaign for President: The Managers Look at 2008.* New York: Rowman and Littlefield Publishers.
Campbell, Angus, Philip Converse, Warren Miller, and Donald Stokes. 1960. *The American Voter.* New York: Wiley.
Celock, John. 2013. "Chris Christie Unveils His First TV Ad of General Election." HuffingtonPost.com, September 12. http://www.huffingtonpost.com/2013/09/12/chris-christie-commercial_n_3913248.html (accessed December 22, 2013).
Coll, Steve. 2012. "The Truth in 'King of Bain.'" *The New Yorker*, January 19. http://www.newyorker.com/online/blogs/comment/2012/01/romney-king-of-bain.html (accessed November 23, 2013).
Cook, Charlie. 2012. "Romney's Anchor: Negative Impressions of Mitt Romney Are Preventing Him from Fully Capitalizing on the Sluggish Economy." *National Journal*, July 26. http://www.nationaljournal.com/columns/cook-report/negative-impressions-hold-romney-back-20120726 (accessed November 23, 2013).
Damore, David F. 2004. "The Dynamics of Issue Ownership in Presidential Campaigns." *Political Research Quarterly* 57(3): 391–97.
Damore, David F. 2005. "Issue Convergence in Presidential Campaigns." *Political Behavior* 27(1): 71–97.
Delli Carpini, Michael X., and Scott Keeter. 1996. *What Americans Know about Politics and Why It Matters*. New Haven, CT: Yale University Press.
Downs, Anthony. 1957. *An Economic Theory of Democracy*. New York: Harper and Row.
Druckman, James N. 2001. "On the Limits of Framing Effects: Who Can Frame." *Journal of Politics* 63(4): 1041–66.
Druckman, James N., Cari Lynn Hennessy, Martin J. Kifer, and Michael Parkin. 2010. "Issue Engagement on Congressional Candidate Web Sites, 2002–2006." *Social Science Computer Review* 28(1): 3–23.

Druckman, James N., Martin J. Kifer, and Michael Parkin. 2009. "Campaign Communication in US Congressional Elections." *American Political Science Review* 103(3): 343–66.
Dulio, David A., and Peter F. Trumbore. 2009. "Running on Iraq or Running from Iraq? Conditional Issue Ownership in the 2006 Midterm Elections." *Political Research Quarterly* 62(2): 230–43.
Ehrenhalt, Alan. 1991. *The United States of Ambition: Politicians, Power, and the Pursuit of Office*, 1st ed. New York: Times Books.
Enelow, James, and Melvin J. Hinich. 1981. "A New Approach to Voter Uncertainty in the Downsian Spatial Model." *American Journal of Political Science* 25(3): 483–95.
Faucheux, Ronald A. 2002. *Running for Office: The Strategies, Techniques, and Messages Modern Political Candidates Need to Win Elections*. New York: M. Evans and Co.
Fenno, Richard F., Jr. 1986. "Observation, Context, and Sequence in the Study of Politics." *American Political Science Review* 80(1) 3–15.
Fiorina, Morris. 1981. *Retrospective Voting in American National Elections*. New Haven, CT: Yale University Press.
Fishel, Jeff. 1985. *Presidents and Promises: From Campaign Pledge to Presidential Performance*. Washington, DC: Congressional Quarterly Press.
Franklin, Charles H. 1991. "Eschewing Obfuscation: Campaigns and the Perception of United States Senate Incumbents." *American Political Science Review* 85(4): 1193–214.
Freedlander, David. 2013. "Dante de Blasio's Killer Ad May Have Won NYC Primary for His Dad." The Daily Beast, September 14. http://www.thedailybeast.com/articles/2013/09/14/dante-de-blasio-s-killer-ad-may-have-won-nyc-primary-for-his-dad.html (accessed March 21, 2014).
Freedman, Paul, and Kenneth Goldstein. 2003. "New Evidence for New Arguments: Money and Advertising in the 1996 Senate Elections." *The Journal of Politics*. 62(4): 1087–1108.
Freedman, Paul, Michael Franz, and Kenneth Goldstein. 2004. "Campaign Advertising and Democratic Citizenship." *American Journal of Political Science* 48(4): 723–41.
Geer, John G. 2006. *In Defense of Negativity*. Chicago: University of Chicago Press.
Gill, Jeff. 2005. "An Entropy Measure of Uncertainty in Vote Choice." *Electoral Studies* 24(3): 371–92.
Glasgow, Garrett, and R. Michael Alvarez. 2000. "Uncertainty and Candidate Personality Traits." *American Politics Quarterly* 28(1): 26–49.
Goldstein, Kenneth, and Travis N. Ridout. 2004. "Measuring the Effect of Televised Political Advertising in the United States." *Annual Review of Political Science* 7(1): 205–27.
Goldstein, Kenneth, and Joel Rivlin. 2005. "Political Advertising in 2002." Combined File [data set]. Final Release. Madison, WI: The Wisconsin Advertising Project, The Department of Political Science at The University of Wisconsin–Madison.

Goldstein, Kenneth, and Paul Freedman. 2002. "Campaign Advertising and Voter Turnout: New Evidence for a Stimulation Effect." *Journal of Politics* 64(3): 721–40.

Grimes, William. 1992. "Big Screen Salute: Film Tribute to Clinton Focuses on Simple Values." *New York Times*, July 17, A11.

Gutman, Amy, and Dennis Thompson. 1996. *Democracy and Disagreement*. Cambridge, MA: Harvard University Press.

Haberman, Maggie. 2012. "New anti-Bain Ad: 'My Own Coffin.'" Politico.com, June 6. http://www.politico.com/blogs/burns-haberman/2012/06/new-antibain-ad-my-own-coffin-127072.html (accessed November 23, 2013).

Hayes, Danny. 2005. "Candidate Qualities through a Partisan Lens: A Theory of Trait Ownership." *American Journal of Political Science* 49(4): 908–23.,

Heilemann, John, and Mark Halperin. 2010. *Game Change: Obama and the Clintons, McCain and Palin, and the Race of a Lifetime*. New York: Harper Perennial

Herrnson, Paul S. 2011. *Congressional Elections: Campaigning at Home and in Washington*. 6th ed. Washington, DC: Congressional Quarterly Press.

Hibbing, John R., and Elizabeth Theiss-Morse. 2002. *Stealth Democracy: Americans' Beliefs about How Government Should Work*. New York: Cambridge University Press.

Hinich, Melvin J., and Michael C. Munger. 1997. *Analytical Politics*. New York: Cambridge University Press.

Hovland, Carl I., Irving L. Janis, and Harold H. Kelley. 1953. *Communications and Persuasion: Psychological Studies in Opinion Change*. New Haven, CT: Yale University Press.

Hovland, Carl I., and W. Weiss. 1951–52. "The Influence of Source Credibility on Communication Effectiveness." *Public Opinion Quarterly* 15(4): 635–50.

Ifill, Gwen. 1992. "The Party's Over: Democratic Team Opens by Appealing to Middle Class." *New York Times*, July 17, A1.

Impomeni, Mark. 2011. "Christie Wins on Pension, Health Benefit Reform." HumanEvents.com, June 22. http://www.humanevents.com/2011/06/22/christie-wins-on-pension-health-benefits-reform/ (accessed December 22, 2013).

Iyengar, Shanto, and Nicholas Valentino. 2000. "Who Says What? Source Credibility as a Mediator of Campaign Advertising." In *Elements of Reason: Cognition, Choice, and Bounds of Rationality*, edited by Arthur Lupia, Mathew D. McCubbins, and Samuel L. Popkin, 108–129. New York: Cambridge University Press.

Jackson David. 2008. "McCain Campaigns, Urges Public Service." *USA TODAY*, April 2, A9.

Jacobson, Gary C. 1978. "The Effects of Campaign Spending in Congressional Elections." *American Political Science Review* 72(2): 469–91.

Jacobson, Gary C. 1990. "The Effects of Campaign Spending in House Elections: New Evidence for Old Arguments." *American Journal of Political Science* 34(2): 334–62.

Jacobson, Gary C. 2013. "How the Economy and Partisanship Shaped the 2012 Presidential and Congressional Elections." *Political Science Quarterly* 128(1): 1–38.

Jacobson, Gary C. 2007. *The Politics of Congressional Elections*, 7th ed. New York: Longman.

Jacobson, Gary C., and Samuel Kernell. 1983. *Strategy and Choice in Congressional Elections*, 2nd ed. New Haven, CT: Yale University Press.

Jamieson, Kathleen Hall, Paul Waldman, and Susan Sherr. 2000. "Eliminate the Negative? Categories of Analysis for Political Advertisements." In *Crowded Airwaves: Campaign Advertising in Elections*, edited by James A. Thurber, Candice J. Nelson, and David A. Dulio, 34–65. Washington, DC: Brookings Institution.

Johnson, Dennis W. 2001. *No Place for Amateurs: How Political Consultants Are Reshaping American Democracy*. New York: Routledge.

Johnson, Luke. 2012. "Scott Brown Slams Elizabeth Warren's 'Elitist Attitude' after Speaking about Bipartisanship." HuffingtonPost.com, May 3. http://www.huffingtonpost.com/2012/05/03/scott-brown-elizabeth-warren_n_1474030.html. (Accessed March 26, 2014)

Kahn, Kim Fridkin, and Patrick J. Kenney. 1999. *The Spectacle of US Senate Campaigns*. Princeton, NJ: Princeton University Press.

Kahn, Kim Fridkin. 1993. "Incumbency and the News Media in U.S. Senate Elections: An Experimental Investigation." *Political Research Quarterly* 46(December): 715–40.

Kaplan, Noah, David K. Park, and Travis N. Ridout. 2006. "Dialogue in American Political Campaigns? An Examination of Issue Convergence in Candidate Television Advertising." *American Journal of Political Science* 50(3): 724–36.

Kerr-Dineen, Luke. 2012. "Conservative Southern Democrat John Barrow Hangs on in Hostile Territory." The Daily Beast, November 18. http://www.thedailybeast.com/articles/2012/11/18/conservative-southern-democrat-john-barrow-hangs-on-in-hostile-territory.html (accessed December 20, 2013).

Khimm, Suzy. 2012. "No, I Supported Dodd-Frank More!" WashingtonPost.com, June 27. http://www.washingtonpost.com/blogs/wonkblog/wp/2012/06/27/no-i-supported-dodd-frank-more/. (Accessed March 26, 2014).

Kiely, Eugene. 2013. "Anti-NRA Group's Shameless Editing Tricks." FactCheck.org, January 23. http://www.factcheck.org/2013/01/anti-nra-groups-shameless-editing-tricks/ (accessed December 20, 2013).

Kiewiet, Roderick D. 1983. *Macroeconomics and Macropolitics*. Chicago: University of Chicago Press.

King of Spades. 2013. "GA-12: The Makings of John Barrow's Win." DailyKos.com, August 7. http://www.dailykos.com/story/2013/08/07/1229653/-GA-12-The-Makings-of-John-Barrow-s-Win (accessed December 20, 2013).

Klein, Joe. 1992. "Clinton the Survivor." *Newsweek*, 120(3, July 20): 22–25.

Kormanik, Beth. 2008. "No Iraq Talk, but McCain Discusses Meaning of War." *Florida Times-Union*, April 4, A1.

Kranish, Michael. 2012. "Mitt Romney was hesitant to reveal himself." *Boston Globe* (BostonGlobe.com), December 23. http://www.bostonglobe.com/news/nation/2012/12/23/the-story-behind-mitt-romney-loss-presidential-campaign-president-obama/OeZRabbooIw0z7QYAOyFFP/story.html (accessed November 23, 2013).

Kroll, Andy. 2011. "GOP Smear Machine Targets Elizabeth Warren." MotherJones.com, August 31. http://www.motherjones.com/politics/2011/08/gop-smear-campaign-elizabeth-warren. (Accesssed March 24, 2014).

Krukones, Michael. 1984. *Promises and Performance: Presidential Campaigns as Policy Predictors*. New York: University Press of America.

Lazarsfeld, Paul F., Bernard Berelson, and Hazel Gaudet. 1948. *The People's Choice: How the Voter Makes Up His Mind in a Presidential Campaign*. New York: Columbia University Press.

Lipsitz, Keena. 2011. *Competitive Elections and the American Voter*. Philadelphia: University of Pennsylvania Press.

Lizza, Ryan. 2004. "The Ad War '04." NYMag.com (*New York* magazine). http://nymag.com/nymetro/news/politics/national/2004race/adwars/n_10182/index2.html (accessed December 20, 2013).

Lodge, Milton, and Ruth Hamill. 1986. "A Partisan Schema for Political Information Processing." *American Political Science Review* 80:505–20.

Lupia, Arthur, and Mathew D. McCubbins. 1998. *The Democratic Dilemma: Can Citizens Learn What They Need to Know?* New York: Cambridge University Press.

Malcolm, Andrew. 2008. "Now It's Joe Biden's Turn on the *SNL* Skewer." LATimes.com, October 26. http://latimesblogs.latimes.com/washington/2008/10/snl-biden.html (accessed March 18, 2011).

Matalin, Mary, and James Carville with Peter Knobler. 1994. *All's Fair: Love, War, and Running for President*. New York: Random House.

May, A. L. 1992. "For Clinton, Tonight's the Night Arkansas Governor to Get Nomination after Grueling Race." *Atlanta Journal-Constitution*, July 15, A1.

McCain, John. 2008. "Acceptance Speech; Republican National Convention." September 4, 2008, St. Paul, MN. Transcript downloaded August 18, 2009, from http://elections.nytimes.com/2008/president/conventions/videos/transcripts/20080904_MCCAIN_SPEECH.html.

McDermott, Monika L. 1999. "Shortcut Voting: Candidate Characteristics and Voter Inference." PhD diss., University of California, Los Angeles.

McDermott, Monika L. 2005. "Candidate Occupations and Voter Information Shortcuts." *Journal of Politics* 67(1): 201–19.

McGraw Katherine M., E. Hasecke, and K. Conger. 2003. "Ambivalence, Uncertainty, and Processes of Candidate Evaluation." *Political Psychology* 24(3): 421–48.

McGuire, William J. 1968. "Personality and Susceptibility to Social Influence." In *Handbook of Personality Theory and Research*, edited by Edward F. Borgatta and William W. Lambert, 1130–87. Chicago: Rand McNally.

Meirowitz, Adam. 2005. "Keeping the Other Candidate Guessing: Electoral Competition When Preferences Are Private Information." *Public Choice* 122(3–4): 299–318.

Miller, Zeke. 2012. "Massachusetts Republicans Cast Elizabeth Warren in 'The Elitist.'" Buzzfeed.com, February 29. http://www.buzzfeed.com/zekejmiller/massachusetts-republicans-cast-elizabeth-warren-in (accessed March 24, 2014).

Mondak, Jeffrey J. 1993. "Source Cues and Policy Approval." *American Journal of Political Science* 37(2): 186–212.

Mondak, Jeffrey J., Christopher J. Lewis, Jason C. Sides, Joohyun Kang, and J. Olyn Long. 2004. "Presidential Source Cues and Policy Appraisals, 1981–2000." *American Politics Research* 32(2): 219–35.

Norpoth, Helmut, and Bruce Buchanan. 1992. "Wanted: The Education President: Issue Trespassing by Political Candidates." *Public Opinion Quarterly* 56(1): 87–99.

Nowicki, Dan, and Bill Muller. 2007. "McCain Profile: Arizona, the Early Years." AZCentral.com (*Arizona Republic*), March 1. http://www.azcentral.com/news/election/mccain/articles/2007/03/01/2007030 1mccainbio-chapter5.html (accessed January 14, 2014).

O'Brien, Michael. 2012. "Brown Accuses Warren of Harboring 'Elitist Attitude.'" NBCNews.com (First Read), May 2. http://firstread.nbcnews.com/_news/2012/05/02/11507849-brown-accuses-warren-of-harboring-elitist-attitude?lite (accessed March 24, 2014).

O'Keefe, Ed. 2008. "McCain the 'Punk' Goes Back to School." ABCNews.com, April 1. http://abcnews.go.com/Politics/Vote2008/story?id=4565619andpage=1 (accessed June 18, 2011).

Obama, Barack. 2008. "Acceptance Speech: Democratic National Convention." August 28, 2008, Denver, CO. Transcript downloaded August 18, 2009, from http://www.nytimes.com/2008/08/28/us/politics/28text-obama.html?pagewanted=1and_r=1

Page, Benjamin I. 1976. "A Theory of Political Ambiguity." *American Political Science Review* 70(3): 742–52.

Page, Benjamin I. 1978. *Choices and Echoes in Presidential Elections: Rational Man and Electoral Democracy*. Chicago: University of Chicago Press.

Page, Richard E., Robert Y. Shapiro, and G. R. Dempsey. 1987. "What Moves Public Opinion." *American Journal of Political Science* 81(1): 23–43.

Petrocik, John R. 1996. "Issue Ownership in Presidential Elections, with a 1980 Case Study." *American Journal of Political Science* 40(3): 825–50.
Pietryka, Matthew T. 2012. "The Roles of District and National Opinion in 2010 Congressional Campaign Agendas." *American Politics Research* 40(5): 805–43.
Philpot, Tasha S. 2004. "A Party of a Different Color? Race, Campaign Communications, and Party Politics." *Political Behavior* 26(3): 249–70.
Plouffe, David. 2009. *The Audacity to Win: The Inside Story and Lessons of Barack Obama's Historic Victory*. New York: Viking.
Politifact.com. 2011. "Campaigns Volley over Biden's Warning." October 28. http://www.politifact.com/truth-o-meter/statements/2008/oct/28/barack-obama/campaigns-volley-over-bidens-warning/ (accessed March 18, 2011).
Popkin, Samuel L. 1994. *The Reasoning Voter: Communication and Persuasion in Presidential Campaigns*, revised ed. Chicago: The University of Chicago Press.
Pornpitakpan, Chanthika. 2004. "The Persuasiveness of Source Credibility: A Critical Review of Five Decades' Evidence." *Journal of Applied Social Psychology* 34(2): 243–81.
Portnoy, Jenna. 2013. "Christie's Latest Campaign Ad Touts Drug Treatment." NJ.com (*Newark Star-Ledger*), September 25. http://www.nj.com/politics/index.ssf/2013/09/christies_latest_campaign_ad_touts_drug_treatment.html (accessed December 22, 2013).
Portnoy, Jenna, and Salvador Rizzo. 2013. "Gov. Christie's Big Win Renews Questions about His Record." NJ.com (*Newark Star-Ledger*), November 14. http://www.nj.com/politics/index.ssf/2013/11/chris_christies_big_win_renews_questions_about_his_record.html (accessed December 22, 2013).
Prior, Markus. 2001. "Weighted Content Analysis of Political Advertisements." *Political Communication* 18(3): 335–45.
Rahn, Wendy M. 1993. "The Role of Partisan Stereotypes in Information Processing about Political Candidates." *American Journal of Political Science* 37(2): 472–96.
Romano, Lois. 2010. "Brown Kept on Truckin' Toward Win." WashingtonPost.com, January 20. http://articles.washingtonpost.com/2010-01-20/politics/36823592_1_america-s-sexiest-man-gail-huff-massachusetts-senate (accessed March 24, 2014).
Sapiro, Virginia, Katherine Cramer Walsh, Patricia Strach, and Valerie Hennings. 2011. "Gender, Context, and Television Advertising: A Comprehensive Analysis of 2000 and 2002 House Races." *Political Research Quarterly* 64(1): 107–19.
Sargent, Greg. 2012 "Elizabeth Warren Is No 'Elitist.'" WashingtonPost.com, April 26. http://www.washingtonpost.com/blogs/plum-line/post/elizabeth-warren-is-no-elitist/2012/04/23/gIQAUpCJcT_blog.html (accessed March 24, 2014).
Sellers, Patrick. 1998. "Strategy and Background in Congressional Campaigns." *American Political Science Review* 92(1): 159–71.

Shaw, Daron R. 1999. "The Effect of TV Ads and Campaign Appearances on Statewide Presidential Votes, 1988–96." *American Political Science Review* 93(2): 345–61.
Shaw, Daron R. 2006. *The Race to 270: The Electoral College and the Campaign Strategies of 2000 and 2004.* Chicago: University of Chicago Press.
Shear, Michael D. 2008. "McCain Talks about His Father." Washington-Post.com, March 31. http://voices.washingtonpost.com/44/2008/03/mccain-talks-about-his-father.html (accessed June 18, 2011).
Shepsle, Kenneth. 1972. "The Strategy of Ambiguity: Uncertainty and Electoral Competition." *American Political Science Review* 66(2): 555–68.
Sherman, Jake. 2012. "Rick Perry Dismisses Mitt Romney and New Hampshire Primary." Politico.com, January 11. http://www.politico.com/news/stories/0112/71306.html (accessed November 23, 2013).
Shyles, Leonard. 1984. "Defining 'Images' of Presidential Candidates from Televised Political Spot Advertisements." *Political Behavior* 6(2): 171–81.
Sides, John. 2006. "The Origins of Campaign Agendas." *British Journal of Political Science* 36: 407–36.
Sides, John. 2007. "The Consequences of Campaign Agendas." *American Politics Research* 35(4): 465–88.
Sides, John, and Andrew Karch. 2008. "Messages that Mobilize? Issue Publics and the Content of Campaign Advertising." *Journal of Politics* 70(2): 466–76.
Sigelman, Lee, and Emmett H. Buell, Jr. 2004. "Avoidance or Engagement? Issue Convergence in the U.S. Presidential Campaigns, 1960–2000." *American Journal of Political Science* 48(4): 650–61.
Silver, Nate. 2012. "As Swing Districts Dwindle, Can a Divided House Stand?" *New York Times* (NYTimes.com), December 27. http://fivethirtyeight.blogs.nytimes.com/2012/12/27/as-swing-districts-dwindle-can-a-divided-house-stand/ (accessed November 25, 2013).
Simon, Adam F. 2002. *The Winning Message: Candidate Behavior, Campaign Discourse, and Democracy.* New York: Cambridge University Press.
Slack, Donovan. 2012. "Axelrod: Romney's Failed to Define Himself to Voters." Politico.com, August 5. http://www.politico.com/blogs/politico-live/2012/08/axe-romney-failed-to-define-himself-to-voters-131112.html (accessed November 23, 2013).
Smith, Chris. 2013. "Bill de Blasio's Full-Spectrum Victory." *New York Magazine* (NYMag.com), September 11. http://nymag.com/daily/intelligencer/2013/09/bill-de-blasios-full-spectrum-victory.html?mid=facebook_nymag (accessed March 22, 2014).
Somnez, Felicia. 2012. "New Obama Ad Featuring Singing Romney Slams Candidate on Bain, Offshore Accounts." *Washington Post* (WashingtonPost.com), July 14. http://www.washingtonpost.com/blogs/the-fix/post/new-obama-ad-featuring-singing-romney-slams-candidate-on-bain-offshore-accounts/2012/07/14/gJQAVLZEkW_blog.html (accessed November 23, 2012).
Spiliotes, Constantine J., and Lynn Vavreck. 2002. "Campaign Advertising: Partisan Convergence or Divergence." *Journal of Politics* 64(1): 249–61.

Stein, Sam. 2008. "Obama on Grandmother and Campaign: 'Bittersweet.'" HuffingtonPost.com, November 3. http://www.huffingtonpost.com/2008/11/03/obama-on-grandmother-and_n_140698.html (accessed March 18, 2011).

Sternthal, Brian, Lynn W. Phillips, and Ruby Dholakia. 1978. "The Persuasive Effect of Source Credibility: A Situational Analysis." *Public Opinion Quarterly* 42(3): 285–314.

Stokes, Donald E. 1963. "Spatial Models of Party Competition." *American Political Science Review* 57(2): 368–77.

Strach, Patricia, and Virginia Sapiro. 2011. "Campaigning for Congress in the '9/11' Era: Considerations of Gender and Party in Response to an Exogenous Shock." *American Politics Research* 39(2): 264–90.

Sulkin, Tracy, and Jillian Evans. 2006. "Dynamics of Diffusion: Aggregate Patterns in Congressional Campaign Agendas." *American Politics Research* 34(4): 505–34.

Sulkin, Tracy, and Nathan Swigger. 2008. "Is There Truth in Advertising? Campaign Ad Images as Signals about Legislative Behavior." *Journal of Politics* 70(1): 232–44.

Sulkin, Tracy, Cortney M. Moriarty, and Veronica Hefner. 2007. "Congressional Candidates' Issue Agenda On- and Off-line." *Harvard International Journal of Press-Politics* 12(2): 63–79.

Sulkin, Tracy. 2009. "Campaign Appeals and Legislative Action." *Journal of Politics* 71(3): 1093–108.

Sullivan, Sean. 2012. "John Barrow's One-of-a-Kind Ad Campaign." WashingtonPost.com (The Fix), October 25. http://www.washingtonpost.com/blogs/the-fix/wp/2012/10/25/john-barrows-one-of-a-kind-ad-campaign/ (accessed December 20, 2013).

Sweet, Lynn. 2008. "Joe Biden at Seattle Fund Raiser Transcript, Says Obama Will Be Tested." SunTimes.com, October 21. http://blogs.suntimes.com/sweet/2008/10/joe_biden_seattle_fund_raiser.html (accessed March 18, 2011).

Tapper, Jake P. 2008. "New McCain TV Ad Uses Biden's 'Rhetorical Flourishes' against Obama." ABCNews.com. http://blogs.abcnews.com/politicalpunch/2008/10/new-mccain-tv-1.html (accessed March 18, 2011).

Trumbore, Peter F., and David A. Dulio. 2013. "Running on Foreign Policy? Examining the Role of Foreign Policy Issues in the 2000, 2002, and 2004 Congressional Campaigns." *Foreign Policy Analysis* 9(3): 267–86.

Vavreck, Lynn. 2001. "The Reasoning Voter Meets the Strategic Candidate: Signals and Specificity in Campaign Advertising, 1998." *American Politics Research* 29(5): 507–29.

Voteview. 2012. "2012 Elections Conference: Practitioner's Roundtable." Voteview.com, November 30. http://voteview.com/blog/?p=656 (accessed December 20, 2013).

West, Paul. 2012. "Defining Mitt Romney: Obama Has a Head Start." *Los Angeles Times* (LATimes.com), July 11. http://articles.latimes.com/2012/jul/11/nation/la-na-campaign-2012-analysis-20120711 (accessed November 23, 2013).

Williams, Juan. 1992. "Clinton's Reinvention Convention: Can the Candidate—and the Party—Get a Fresh Start?" *Washington Post*, July 12, C1.

Wright, Gerald C., and Michael B. Berkman. 1986. "Candidates and Policy in United States Senate Elections." *American Political Science Review* 80(2): 567–88.

Yglesias, Matthew. 2008. *Heads in the Sand: How the Republicans Screw Up Foreign Policy and Foreign Policy Screws Up the Democrats*. New York: Wiley.

Zaller, John R. 1992. *The Nature and Origins of Mass Opinion*. New York: Cambridge University Press.

Index

Aderholt, Robert, 138–9
advertisements. *See* campaigns, individual; television advertisements
Ailes, Roger, 172
ambiguity, 9, 29–30, 98–9, 165, 170
Anderson, Lee, 141
authenticity, 1, 18, 41–5, 55, 58, 163, 165
Axelrod, David, 159

Babbitt, Paul, 85, 137
background of candidates
    candidate-centered messages and, 65, 69, 71, 74–5, 80–2, 86–7, 90–1
    Clinton (Bill) campaign and, 1–2, 172
    credibility and, 23–6, 58–9, 161, 166
    Davis (Geoff) campaign and, 4
    defined, 65
    and effect on voters, 23–6, 144–57, 162, 165
    expertise and, 49
    issues and, 32, 53–6
    McCain (John) campaign and, 2–3, 21
    Obama (Barack) campaign and, 2, 21
    occupational, 26, 145, 156
    of opponents, 56, 58, 160
    personal issues and, 124–5, 135, 140
    political consultants on, 49–59, 163
    Salazar (Ken) campaign and, 3–4
    trustworthiness and, 46
    types of appeals and, 99–101, 104, 113–14, 119
    Warren (Elizabeth) campaign and, 62–3
    See also biography of candidates
Bain Capital, 160
Barbieri, Don, 104–5
Barrow, John, 141–2, 156–7
Benoit, William, 26, 69
Berelson, Bernard, 32
biography of candidates
    2008 presidential campaigns and, 2, 37–9
    availability to the electorate of, 49
    Boucher (Rich) campaign and, 134
    candidate-centered messages and, 65
    candidate status and, 128–9
    Carson (Brad) campaign and, 134
    character and, 97, 115
    Clinton (Bill) campaign and, 1–2
    credibility and, 23–6, 58–9, 80, 83–4, 100, 161, 166
    district demography and, 54–5
    Gibbons (John) campaign and, 135
    Hill (Baron) campaign and, 133
    implications of, 163–5, 168, 172–3
    issues and, 35, 53–5, 58
    Kerry (John) campaign and, 161

biography of candidates—*continued*
  McCain (John) campaign and, 28, 37–8, 57
  Patterson (Jeanne) campaign and, 84, 133
  personal issues and, 122–5, 128–40
  political consultants on, 49–56
  Romney (Mitt) campaign and, 160
  Salazar (Ken) campaign and, 122–4, 140
  Tenenbaum (Inez) campaign and, 130
  Warren (Elizabeth) campaign and, 61–3, 90–1
  Wu (David) campaign and, 135
  See also background of candidates; family of candidates; storytelling and stories
Bloomberg, Michael, 17–18
Blunt, Roy, 107–8
Booker, Cory, 93
Boucher, Rick, 134
Brown, Scott, 61–3
Bunning, Jim, 106–7
Buono, Barbara, 94
Bush, George H. W., 172
Bush, George W., 121, 123, 135, 161

campaigns, individual
  Aderholt, Robert, 138–9
  Barbieri, Don, 104–5
  Barrow, John, 141–2, 156–7
  Blunt, Roy, 107–8
  Boucher, Rich, 134
  Brown, Scott, 61–3
  Bunning, Jim, 106–7
  Carson, Brad, 134
  Chandler, Ben, 72
  Chocola, Chris, 107
  Christie, Chris, 93–5, 118
  Clinton, Bill, 1–2, 15, 127, 131–2, 172
  Coors, Pete, 121–3

Costa, Jim, 103
Davis, Geoff, 4, 83
de Blasio, Bill, 17–19
Edwards, Chet, 138
Feingold, Russ, 80
Gibbons, John, 135
Hill, Baron, 133
Kerry, John, 72, 161
Kuhl, Randy, 83
Latham, Tom, 99
McCain, John, 2–3, 20–1, 28, 32, 37–9, 57, 97
McMorris, Cathy, 104–5
Naples, Nancy, 136
Obama, Barack, 2, 21, 38, 93, 141–2, 159–60
Patterson, Jeanne, 84, 133
Pearce, Steve, 71–2, 137–8
Perry, Rick, 160
Price, David, 82–3
Quinn, Christine, 17–18
Reichert, Dave, 136–7
Reid, Harry, 97–8
Renzi, Rick, 85, 137
Romney, Mitt, 159–61
Salazar, Ken, 3–4, 72, 121–4, 140
Sargent, Greg, 62–3
Schumer, Charles, 71–2, 105
Tenenbaum, Inez, 130
Voinovich, George, 135–6
Walcher, Doug, 71–2
Warren, Elizabeth, 61–3, 90–1
Weiner, Anthony, 17
Wetterling, Patty, 84
Wu, David, 99, 135
Campaign Media Analysis Group (CMAG), 67–8
campaign promises, 2, 8, 22, 48, 168–70
campaign planning, 37–59
candidate-centered appeals
  candidate status and, 113–18
  competence-based, 96, 99–118, 123

Index

character-based, 96–8, 100–1, 103–4, 106–9, 111, 113–16, 118, 122–3
credibility and, 71, 76–9, 90–91, 96–8, 111, 113, 156, 161–2, 164
defined, 100
effect of, 141–57
and implications for campaigns, 164–7
and implications for democracy, 167–71
and opponents, 50, 56–8, 73–9, 84–91, 109, 111, 113–15, 135, 137, 160, 173
and placement within ad, 109–13
position-based, 95–6, 98–9, 101–2, 106–7, 109–19
types of, 93–119
See also background of candidates; biography of candidates; family of candidates; political record; private sector accomplishments
candidate status, 11–12, 83–91, 116–18, 128–9, 143
challenger, 29, 35, 83–91, 98, 100, 113, 116–19, 128–9, 165–6
open-seat, 83–7, 100, 103, 113, 116–18, 128–9
See also incumbency
Carson, Brad, 134
Carville, James, 1–2
certainty, 20, 29–30, 32, 96, 98–9, 103, 164–5, 167
challenger campaigns, 29, 35, 83–91, 98, 100, 113, 116–19, 128–9, 165–6. *See also* candidate status
Chandler, Ben, 72
character-based appeals, 96–8, 100–1, 103–4, 106–9, 111, 113–16, 118, 122–3
Chocola, Chris, 107
Choices and Echoes in Presidential Elections (Page), 30

Christie, Chris, 93–5, 118
Clinton, Bill, 1–2, 15, 127, 131–2, 172
Clinton, Hillary, 38
Clooney, Nick, 83
commonality, 22, 47–8, 143
competence-based appeals, 96, 99–118, 123
Cook, Charlie, 159
Coors, Pete, 121–3
Costa, Jim, 103
credibility
  authenticity and, 42–4
  candidate background and, 23–6, 58–9, 80, 83–4, 100, 161, 166
  candidate-centered appeals and, 71, 76–9, 90–91, 96–8, 111, 113, 156, 161–2, 164
  candidate status and, 98, 118–19
  character and, 106, 115
  Clinton (Bill) campaign and, 172
  Davis (Geoff) campaign and, 83
  development of, 6–7
  expertise and, 144
  Feingold (Russ) campaign and, 80
  Kerry (John) campaign and, 161
  McCain (John) campaign and, 39
  negative ads and, 73
  neutral sources and, 57
  partisanship and, 146
  Patterson (Jeanne) campaign and, 84
  personal issues and, 124, 135, 137, 139–40
  personal messages and, 26–33
  political consultants on, 39–43, 46–50, 53–8
  politicians and, 22–3
  Romney (Mitt) campaign and, 160
  source credibility, 20–2, 26, 33, 58, 143–4
  trust and, 144
  voter skepticism and, 40–2

credibility—*continued*
   Warren (Elizabeth) campaign
     and, 63
   See also source credibility

Davis, Geoff, 4, 83
Davis, Rick, 39
de Blasio, Bill, 17–19
del Cecato, John, 18–19
democracy, 167–71
demography, district, 48, 55, 58, 163–4, 166, 173
distrust, 23, 41–2. *See also* trust and trustworthiness
Downs, Anthony, 11, 22, 124, 163–4

Eastwood, Clint, 160
Edwards, Chet, 138
   experience
     and issues, 49, 144, 146
     McCain (John) campaign and, 21, 39
     of opponents, 58, 85
     and personal values, 14, 134–6, 142, 146
     political consultants on, 45, 48–9, 52, 55, 58
     private-sector, 6, 25, 27, 32, 65, 81–3, 85, 96, 100, 114–15, 136, 166
     and use of candidate-centered appeals, 86–90
     See also background of candidates; biography of candidates; incumbency
experience images, 26
expertise, 49, 58, 99–100, 143–4

Fauchaux, Ron, 78
family of candidates, 2–3, 18–19, 24, 38, 51, 62, 104–7, 122–3, 133, 141–2
Feingold, Russ, 19, 80
Franklin, Charles, 29

Gallagher, Tom, 74
Geer, John, 69, 73

Gibbons, John, 135
Gingrich, Newt, 160
Goldilocks approach, 161–2, 170
Goldstein, Kenneth, 5

Hibbing, John, 23
Hill, Baron, 133

incumbency, 35, 128–9, 144, 171
   biography and, 55
   character and, 28–9
   economy and, 9
   political belief and, 48–9
   types of appeals and, 31–2, 81–2, 86–9, 94, 100, 102, 108, 113–19, 128–9, 166
   voter skepticism and, 41
   wartime and, 9
   See also candidate status
issue ownership, 11, 124, 128, 156, 161, 163–4
issue positions, 29–31

Kennedy, John F., 61
Kennedy, Mark, 66, 84–5
Kennedy, Ted, 61
Kerry, John, 72, 161
Kuhl, Randy, 83

Latham, Tom, 99
Lautenberg, Frank, 93
Lazarsfeld, Paul, 32
likability, 42–4, 46, 53, 63, 139, 164
Lipsitz, Keena, 128
Liu, John, 17

Man from Hope (film), 1–2
McCain, John, 2–3, 20–1, 28, 32, 37–9, 57, 97
McMorris, Cathy, 104–5
McPhee, William, 32
median voter theorem, 11, 17, 124, 163–4
message-development process, 5, 8, 20, 34, 40, 51–2, 58, 64
Michels, Tim, 19

Index

Naples, Nancy, 136

Obama, Barack, 2, 21, 38, 93, 141–2, 159–60
occupational background, 26, 145, 156
open-seat campaigns, 83–7, 100, 103, 113, 116–18, 128–9. *See also* candidate status
opponents, candidate-centered appeals and, 50, 56–8, 73–9, 84–91, 109, 111, 113–15, 135, 137, 160, 173

Page, Benjamin, 30
partisanship, 93–5, 116, 146–7, 153, 155, 164–5
party labels, 150–6
passion, 42, 55, 163
Patterson, Jeanne, 84, 133
Pearce, Steve, 71–2, 137–8
Perry, Rick, 160
personal issues, 121–40
Petrocik, John, 11, 32–3, 124
political beliefs, 48–9
political consultants, 37–59
political record, 26–7, 34–5, 48, 55–6, 58, 81, 94, 124–6, 129–32, 135–7, 173
politicians, individual. *See* campaigns, individual
Popkin, Samuel, 23–5, 31, 44, 99
Pornpitakpan, Chanthika, 21
Porter, John, 73–4
position-based appeals, 95–6, 98–9, 101–2, 106–7, 109–19
Price, David, 82–3
Prior, Markus, 67
PrioritiesUSA, 160
private-sector experience, 6, 25, 27, 32, 65, 81–3, 85, 96, 100, 114–15, 136, 166

Quinn, Christine, 17–18

Reasoning Voter, The (Popkin), 23, 44
Reichert, Dave, 136–7

Reid, Harry, 97–8
Renzi, Rick, 85, 137
Ridout, Travis N., 5
Romney, Mitt, 159–61

Salazar, John, 72
Salazar, Ken, 3–4, 72, 121–4, 140
Sargent, Greg, 62–3
Schumer, Charles, 71–2, 105
Sellers, Patrick, 26, 32, 164
Sides, John, 124–5
skepticism, voter, 6, 19–23, 26–8, 40–4, 44–5, 49–50, 57–8, 96–7, 161–3, 168
source credibility, 20–2, 26, 33, 58, 143–4
stealth democracy, 23
Stokes, Donald, 31
stop-and-frisk program (NYC), 18
storytelling and stories, 1–7, 25, 27–8, 32, 38, 44–59, 122, 172. *See also* biography
Stutzman, Rob, 159

television advertisements, 25, 30, 64, 66–91, 156, 163. *See also* campaigns, individual
Tenenbaum, Inez, 130
Theiss-Morse, Elizabeth, 23
Thompson, Bill, 17
trust and trustworthiness, 5–7, 9–10, 21–5, 33, 41–4, 46–8, 58, 99, 143–4, 168–70

uncertainty. *See* certainty
United States Constitution, 10

valence issues, 31
Van Hollen, Chris, 101–3
Vietnam War, 2, 20, 28, 37, 39, 97, 161
virtuous experts, 7, 23
Voinovich, George, 135–6
voters
    effects of candidate-centered appeals on, 141–57

voters—*continued*
  median voter theorem, 11, 17, 124, 163–4
  and skepticism of politicians, 28, 40–4, 44–5, 49–50, 57–8, 96–7, 161–3, 168
Voting (Berelson, Lazarsfeld, and McPhee), 32

Walcher, Doug, 71–2
Warren, Elizabeth, 61–3, 90–1
Weiner, Anthony, 17
Wetterling, Patty, 84
Wisconsin Advertising Project, 65, 67–8, 77, 100, 124–5
Wu, David, 99, 135

Printed in the United States of America